Th...
DEVON
GARDEN

The Art of the DEVON GARDEN

Happy Birthday!

The depiction of plants and ornamental landscapes from the year 1200

Todd Gray

Todd Gray

THE MINT PRESS

dgt Devon Gardens Trust

Contents

Half title page Illustration:
'Seated gardener with a shovel',
William Egley, no date.

Title page illustration:
'Still life with rake' attributed to Peter
DeWint, early 1800s

'Clovelly' by Louisa Fortescue, 16 March 1857.

'Castle Hill', Louisa Fortescue, 1 May 1857.

'Exmouth &c from Mamhead House', Louisa Fortescue, October 1859.

To the memory of two founding members of the
Devon Gardens Trust:

Lady Margaret Fortescue
and **Mrs Mary Clarke**

Foreword

We are fortunate that Devon has such a rich and diverse garden history. Our gardens are as different as the parts of Devon in which they are located. This is in part due to the size of the county but also to the varying characters of our villages and towns as well as to our two cities, moors and coastlines.

Devon is known for having a great legacy in ancient records and these have been searched, notably through the work of the Devon Garden Trust, to help us understand the history of our garden landscapes. This book, however, is the first study to systematically grasp that history from its historic images. In these illustrations we have glimpses of gardens long vanished, private places are lain open to our eyes and access is given to some images that are now many thousands of miles from the places in which they were created.

Art enriches our lives as do our gardens. The linking of these two in one collection will give many hours of revelation and sustaining enjoyment. I warmly recommend this book.

Eleanor Arran

The Countess of Arran

Preface

This book was first sketched out in 1995 following the publication of *The Garden History of Devon* by the University of Exeter Press. The next five years were then taken up with some pressing projects: producing the four editions of the Picturesque writings of the Reverend John Swete, *Devon Country Houses and Gardens Engraved, Victorian Wild Flowers of Devon* and finally, the production of *The Lie of the Land*. After eight books on Devon gardens, most of which were associated with the Devon Gardens Trust, another seemed excessive and it seemed right to have a quiet period of private research. Other work then overtook this project's place.

A decade passed and the 25th anniversary of the Devon Gardens Trust resurrected the idea of this book. During these intervening years I tinkered with the project and it has been invariably improved by new discoveries and opportunities. It is a different book from the one I planned nearly two decades ago: research and publication have been transformed by the introduction of the computer, digital photography and electronic resources on the internet. Yet, despite all these advantages, it remains an incomplete book: invariably there are many other illustrations that could have been included but it is impossible to incorporate them all. Economic reasons alone makes this unfeasible.

A book of this type, with its extraordinary scope, has invariably incurred many debts. Recognition is given elsewhere to the copyright holders but it should also be acknowledged here that this book would not be possible without their permission to publish.

Individuals working, or often volunteering, in institutions have been generous with their time and expertise. This has included many in the United Kingdom as well as others in the United States, Australia and New Zealand. These individuals include those at the Bodleian Library, British Library, British

Museum, Christies, Cliff House Trust, Cornwall Record Office, Dartmouth Museum, Denver Art Museum, Devon & Exeter Institution, Devon Heritage Centre, Devon Partnership NHS Trust, Devon Rural Archive, English Heritage, Earle Vandekar of Knightsbridge, Exeter Cathedral Library & Archives, Exmouth Museum, Fitzwilliam Museum, Hampshire Record Office, Ilfracombe Museum, Library of the United States Congress, Lupton Trust, Metropolitan Museum of Modern Art, Museum of Barnstaple and North Devon, Museum of English Rural Life, National Gallery of Art (Washington), National Portrait Gallery, National Trust, North Devon Athenaeum, North Devon Record Office, Plymouth & West Devon Record Office, Plymouth Museum and Art Gallery, Public Catalogue Foundation, Royal Institute of British Architects, Salcombe Town Council, Somerset Record Office, Topsham Museum, Torquay Local Studies Library, Torquay Museum, Torre Abbey, University of Exeter Library, Victoria & Albert Museum, Western Morning News, Woburn Abbey and the Yale Center for British Art. I owe a particular debt to such private individuals as John Allan, Jane Bass, Dr Stuart Blaylock, Valerie Cann, Judith Cosford, Dr Jo Cox, Judith Farmer, Peter Hamilton-Leggett, Janet Henwood, Emeritus Professor Richard Hitchcock, Stephen Hobbs, Sue Jackson, Margaret Lewis, Elisabeth Maycock, Graham Parnell, Paul Pickering, Margaret Reed, Nigel Rendle, Margery Rowe, Charles Scott-Fox, Dr Richard Stephens, Richard Stone, Will Thompson and Keith Stevens. I am particularly grateful to Karen Sikorski and Karen McGovern for assistance given in a research trip to the Yale Center for British Art.

The production process has been made so much easier by the professionalism of Topics – The Creative Partnership and I am grateful to Delphine Jones for once again providing an exceptional cover.

I also owe a debt to the members of my Tuesday class who patiently endured a term of my sketching out an illustrated history of Devon's gardens. Finally, this book would not have happened without the encouragement, enthusiasm and support given by Dr Ian Varndell, Chairman of the Devon Gardens Trust. I am deeply grateful to him and hope this will be received as an appropriate way to celebrate the work of the Trust.

Taddyforde, Exeter
September 2013

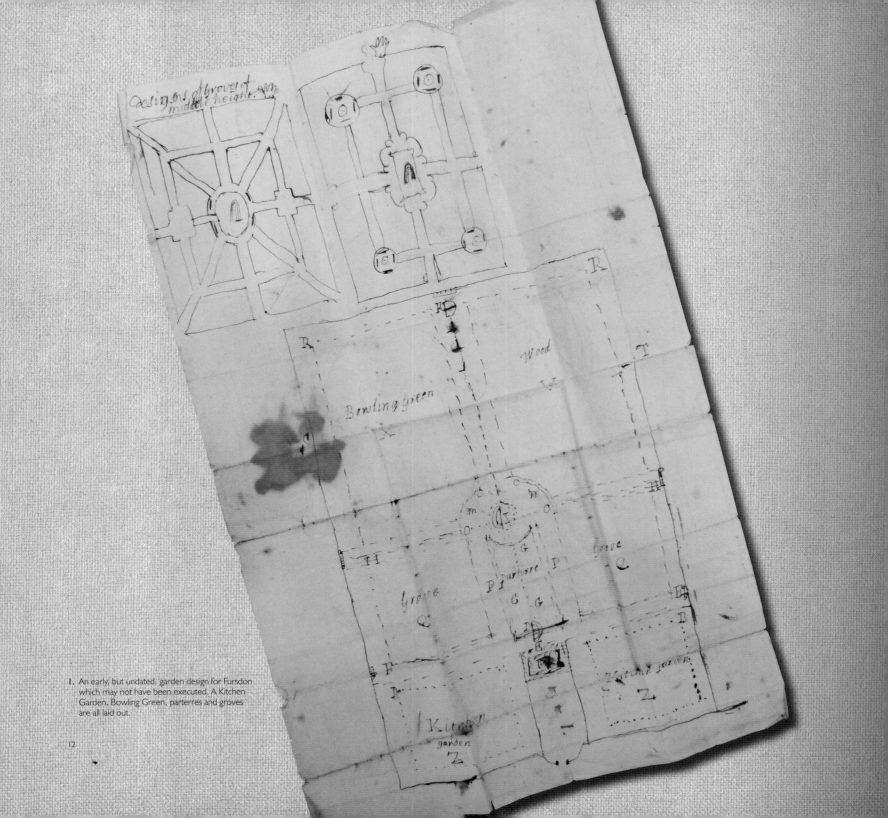

1. An early, but undated, garden design for Fursdon which may not have been executed. A Kitchen Garden, Bowling Green, parterres and groves are all laid out.

Introduction

The development of the art of gardening in Devon was accompanied by the changing depiction of these gardens in art. The historical portrayal of the county's gardens and their plants is surprising both in its variety and range. No doubt other parts of England have similar legacies but so far no similar study has been found for any other county.[1] Devon artists have created garden illustrations for more than eight centuries in such forms as pottery, fabric, plaster, glass, stone and wood as well as in paintings, sketches, photographs, prints and drawings. These are all explored in this collection as is one series of letters. The images appear through the kindness of archives, galleries, libraries, museums, private and public trusts and businesses, as well as individuals, in this country and in the United States.

Despite this collection standing at 677 images, it does not include all historical depictions of gardens in Devon. Only a few engravings have been included of the many hundreds that were made and there are undoubtedly many other images that have gone undetected in private or public ownership. An attempt has been made to include a wide variety of stimulating images and in formats that have not been previously discussed in the interpretation of garden history in Devon. These have been organised in 96 distinct sections.

The artwork in this collection, particularly with paintings, drawings and prints, provides insights into gardens that would otherwise be unknown. The topographical works in particular illuminate the history of many gardens which have little other substantive details and are thus extraordinarily important. The use of these images is crucial alongside fieldwork and documentary research.

The earliest depiction was created in about 1200 and the latest is from the early 1900s. The book is dominated by topographical views but there is a considerable amount of other media. The first two sections discuss illuminated manuscripts and provide insights into how plant motifs were used some eight hundred years ago. Medieval carvings in wood are also explored as well as plant designs in plasterwork. Similar examples in fabric include those found in medieval vestments, samplers, lace, a court dress and a bed cover. There are also two sections on earthenware which show sharp differences in their depictions of flowers.

The first ornamental garden landscape in this collection is an oil painting of 1673 but there are also several earlier prints which are of interest.

2. *'From Mr (Thomas) Luny's Garden'* at Teignmouth by Mary Luxmoore, c1830.

3. 'Teignmouth from Brookfield House, Mr Templers', c.1830. by Mary Luxmoore.

Altogether the work of more than 200 artists appear in this volume. Francis Danby, Annie Croker, Alexander Merivale and Reverend John Swete are the only ones to have painted their own gardens. Others, particularly Edmund Spoure and Edmund Prideaux, depicted the gardens of their relations. There is a broad range of artists including individuals with international reputations such as Francis Danby, Hendrik Danckerts, Nicholas Hilliard, Thomas Hudson, William Morris, Joshua Reynolds and J. M. W. Turner as well as many little known and even unidentified individuals. Some, such as John Gendall and Francis Towne, have found fame outside Devon but their work remains identified with this county. Some individuals created exceptional bodies of work: William of Devon was a master at his craft in illuminating manuscripts and the Abbot firm were leading artists in plasterwork.

Others were visitors to the South West, such as Miss Henrietta Matilda Crompton who came from Yorkshire to Devon in 1840. There is also Charles Napier Hemy who is remembered chiefly as a maritime artist but others were writers who also sketched such as William George Maton. An unknown Regency tourist of North East Devon has left behind a series of watercolours. A considerable number of images come from these travelling

artists. The Reverend John Swete, a local man, toured the county for over a decade in search of the Picturesque while Thomas Hewitt Williams, a landscape painter, published accounts of his own excursions such as *Picturesque excursions in Devonshire* (1801), *A tour to the north of Devon* (1802) and *Picturesque excursions in south Devon* (1804). Williams did not make his travels easy. He preferred to carry his equipment than use a horse and was known to walk twenty miles in a day.[2] In about 1830 Mary Luxmoore, another visitor to Devon, drew the view from the garden of Thomas Luny, the Teignmouth artist who lived at what is now known as Luny House. She was more interested in the coastal scenery than she was of his garden. Luxmoore also drew the view from the garden at Brookfield House in Teignmouth. This was the home of Henry Templer and again there are few garden features: only the walling is shown. At least one artist, a Chinese man by the name of Chowkura, does not appear to have visited Devon: he painted a view of Combe Royal whilst in Shanghai.

The majority of artists are male but there are some exceptions including not only the aforementioned Henrietta Matilda Crompton and Mary Luxmoore but also F. L. Oglander, Maria Pixell, Admonition Radcliffe and Christiana Philippa Maria Rolle. Most of them drew or painted but needle work in this collection was also created by a number of women. There are also examples from architects or from their workshops. This includes Edward Ashworth, William Burges, Humphry Repton, Anthony Salvin and George Wightwick.

Many of the images are seductive and all can be appreciated for an element of beauty. Many are also expressions of status, particularly the images of the great gardens. Each has been created by an individual who has given us what he or she wanted us to see. Few could claim to have achieved complete topographical accuracy. In 1792 two of the artists in this collection, Maryanne Burges and John Swete, met to discuss painting. Burges subsequently wrote that the other's depiction of the castle at Dartmouth *was by no means faithfully nor even characteristically drawn but the colouring & effect were delightful*.[3] What Reverend Swete's thoughts were of Miss Burges' watercolours is not recorded.

Few of the gardens are recognizable today from what was originally depicted. Gardens, as living entities, cannot remain unchanged and they are also vulnerable to the vagaries of fashion and changing taste. Even so, such landscapes as those at A La Ronde, Forde Abbey, Mount Edgcumbe and Great Fulford have the same outline features. Others, such as Heanton Satchville, Woodbine Cottage, Fordland and Silverton Park, were destroyed generations ago. Some have been bought or given to the National Trust and others have been converted into use as hotels (Bishopstowe, Boringdon Hall, Haldon House, Langdon Court). Several have been brought back into use as private residences (Combe Royal, Mamhead, Tawstock Court). Nine of the gardens which were depicted and are included in this collection remain in the care of the original families connected with the artwork: Castle Hill, Clovelly Court, Compton Castle, Great Fulford, Hartland Abbey, Mothecombe, Powderham Castle, Sand and Ugbrooke are all lived in by their descendants.

Three gardens in this collection are no longer in Devon. Forde Abbey, Mount Edgcumbe and Werrington were all formerly within the county borders but administrative changes have reassigned them to Dorset or Cornwall.

Some of the art depicts gardens that were available to the public, such as Mount Edgcumbe or Knowle in Sidmouth, but many images are of privileged spaces where the public gaze could seldom intrude. Many were meant to be seen; the purpose of some garden paintings was to emphasise the high status of the owner. Some of these images were in rooms freely accessible to visitors in order to accentuate the importance of the designed

landscape in which they have just travelled. The interior walls of Arlington Court, Saltram and Warleigh, for example, were used to show off the gardens and their owners. Others, such as the engravings, would have been seen by countless strangers in Devon and elsewhere. Prints of Regency Knowle, like those of other places, were purchased as mementos of visits in the same way as postcards were acquired by later generations.

There were different purposes for other images. Those in churches, in depicting the Garden of Eden or in the use of Gothic foliage, were instructive or created to glorify God. Others express beauty as a primary purpose: the needlework in its various forms used garden motifs to delight the eye. Plants were used in stained glass not only to project beauty but to instil a sense of wonder. Pottery was embellished with flowers and plants in order to transform them into even more desirable objects.

The images in this collection do not provide a narrative of the garden history of Devon but they tell aspects of that history. In many respects the county's garden history is like that of most of England. Little is known of the medieval period but it is clear that by the 1500s a typical garden would have been defined by most Devonians as a herb garden in which was planted a mixture of culinary, medicinal and ornamental plants. Early ornamental gardens were designed in regular outlines and in geometric plantings. The two earliest series of topographical views, by Edmund Spoure in the mid 1690s and Edmund Prideaux in the early 1700s, demonstrate how Devon

4. – 5. Winscott in Dowland, 1811, by John Mallett, showing an elementary garden.

conformed in this way to national taste. There is not enough evidence to gauge how Devonians were influenced by continental styles of gardening but there were strong trade links with not just the Low Countries but France, Spain and Portugal. By the early 1600s these had extended into Italy and many merchants served their apprenticeships as factors in these countries. It can only be conjectured how widely these men brought new ideas in garden design home with them. The garden at Mamhead is one where there is firm evidence of an Italian influence derived from the links of the Balle family with northern Italy.

Perhaps the main way in which local gardens differed from their counterparts elsewhere is in the use of exotic plants. The English Riviera is best known for this but gardens in Kingsbridge, Salcombe, Sidmouth and at Mamhead feature in this collection and deserve to be better known particularly those that planted citrus trees. The Veitch firm is the other local distinction: it became famous for sending out plant hunters across the world and then importing their plant discoveries. Other garden themes include views of the Picturesque, particularly those by the movement's chief advocate in Devon, the Reverend John Swete. The rise of the cottage orné is seen in images of Sidmouth, most notably at Knowle, but also with Woodbine

6. The opposite of the designed landscape as depicted in this watercolour with pen and ink entitled 'A View of the Valley of Stones Devon - with a scene in the Tempest Act 1' by an unknown artist and with no date given. In the 1850s an elderly man, by the name of Norman, created paths, shelters and seats for visitors at Castle Rock and planted garden flowers amongst the crags in order to transform the wilderness into a garden.[4]

Cottage in Torquay. There are many images of great houses with their parklands and also some of more ordinary cottage gardens such as one at Clovelly.

One of the most unusual gardens depicted is that of Heavitree House which was known as a Moorish Garden. Another curiosity was described at Woodbine Cottage. Here, in the gardener's moss house, scenes were created from pinecones. One of them was a farmyard scene with a fox intent upon taking a goose. A much-heralded event was the blooming of a Century Plant at Salcombe in 1842: three drawings were made of it. The Hobby Drive at Clovelly is also unusual. It is an interesting example of the creation of an ornamental landscape which took advantage of the natural topography. Similar to it is the development of Glen Lyn in Lynton. Both are very distinctive in their appeal. Knowle is another remarkable garden: the use of exotic animals in the garden, in the manner of a modern petting zoo, is striking but the garden itself was uncommon in the extent of its planting and embellishments. Another exceptional garden was that at Shute. The enthusiasm with which Sir Courtenay Pole planted fruit in the seventeenth century may only be unusual because it was so well documented but it is noteworthy all the same.

It is much easier to provide the historical framework for some gardens than for others. Those at Powderham Castle, Castle Hill and Endsleigh are supported by extensive family papers. Other sites such as Mount Edgcumbe, Glen Lyn and Saltram were featured in local guides. Visitor accounts survive for many notable gardens and horticultural specialists provided commentary on particular gardens such as Combe Royal. For others there is comparatively little supplementary detail. The vicarages at Ivybridge and Brampford Speke, for example, are bereft of relevant ancillary information or at least this author has failed to find them. Knightstone is another house for which there appears to be no garden accounts.

Relevant original accounts from such journals as The Gardener's Chronicle and The Gardener's Magazine have been reproduced at length not only to provide a historical background to the gardens but to also give a sense of how they were discussed at the time. Archaic spellings have been retained. Travel diaries, journals and letters have been used to provide additional personal perspectives of Devon's gardens. Many travel diaries of wealthy people, who had the leisure time to visit gardens, contain some references to enjoying ornamental landscapes. On the first day of March 1884 Mrs Oglander of the Isle of Wight stayed at Eggesford House with the Earl of Portsmouth and his family. She wrote to her husband:

'I got to Eggesford Station (after one change at a junction) about 5.13. Lord Portsmouth's carriage and a donkey cart came down to meet me, the lodge is close to the station, so we were not long getting here and Rosamond ran to the door to meet me and seemed so glad to see me.

She carried me off straight to my room and after a little talk she took me (having taken off my things) to her Mother's room to tea. Lady Portsmouth greeted me most warmly. She is certainly very charming, but, oh dear, it is a funny place and a funny family. They all speak in the same rather high key as little Rosamond. I can't describe it [at] all. I had a very cosy tea just with Lady Portsmouth and Rosamond and afterwards Rosamond took me to a tiny sitting room which her mother had fitted

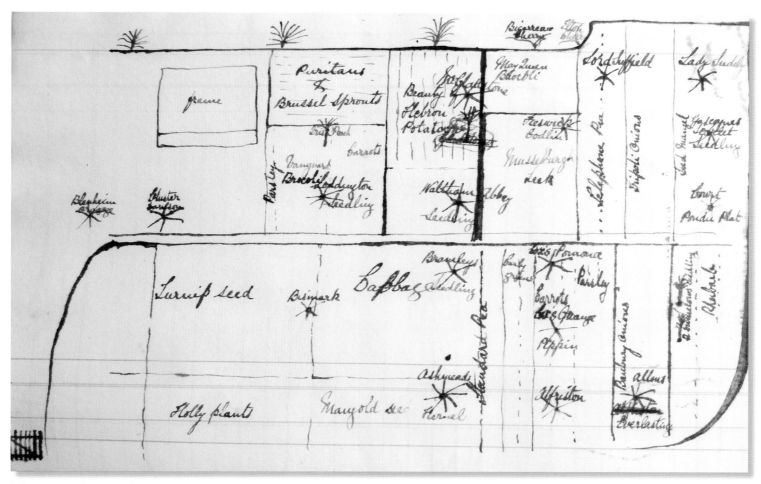

7. Functional plan of a garden at Cornworthy, late 1800s. No other illustrations are known to have survived for this garden.

up for her and we had a long talk - poor little thing, it is very sad to hear her speak so wearily and hopelessly at times and sorry now and then, and then she is so bright. She seems now to have a terrible horror of her husband - it appears his temper is something too terrible. I hope to have a talk with Lady Portsmouth. I wonder if I shall. I want you to tell me if that friend of Mr Powell's knew Mr Christie well and ever heard him swear? Will you answer this? She fetched me to go down to dinner and I was introduced to her father and several brothers and sisters and a pleasant Mrs Carleton (a cousin), a daughter of Lord Dorchester's, who is staying here. Lord Portsmouth is the funniest old thing. He was very anxious at dinner (which same was very badly cooked. Emily would have sent it up much better! perhaps it was a chance, some was good). He was in pain with a foot, which his hunter trod on today, so he went to bed early. Two of the party played the violin beautifully - accompanied by the Tutor. My room is so pretty and quaint. One of those old fashioned flowery papers, all the furniture black carved oak including the four post bed and hung with yellow damask. I must get into the four-poster now, my darling. It did seem so strange and independent travelling all this way without my darling. The journey was very pretty sometimes thro' miles of moor, and sometimes thro' little wooded gorges with clear streams dashing down them. Such delightful streams like Arola.'

Her letters are more informative of the household than of the gardens but in this letter she also made a passing mention to Glynn's Wood, a feature of the area.

'I was so glad of your letter, much interested in what you tell me about the Glynn ancestors here. It is very interesting how they crop up in the West Country. I had told Rosamond about what you said, as we were together when I read your letter and then it was time to get ready for church. I had told Lord Portsmouth last night that you were one of the Cornish Glynns and this morning, as soon as I got into the carriage (I drove to church with him and Mrs Carleton he told me that there is a portion of a wood towards Wembworthy called now `Glynns Wood' and then he told me a good deal that was interesting about the advowson

of the living. (He told me Admiral Glynn sold his share) of which he has got three out of five shares in the presentation. I am afraid I cannot remember all he told me, for I did not understand it (with Glynn name) of the 17th century. We went to Eggesford Church - so cold - very small with some curious monuments, mostly Donegal and some Portsmouth and Fellowes. We sat in a high square pew (left in spite of restoration) capable of holding at least 24 people, a stove outside it, steaming away, Lord Portsmouth much distressed because I did not sit by it, but it was enough to blow one's head off, and kept popping.'

8. Portrait of Nancy Fortescue by Thomas Hudson, c.1745, entitled 'Portrait of a Young Woman of the Fortescue Family of Devon'. It has the second title of 'Portrait of Nancy Fortescue, wearing a dark blue riding habit, with gold frogging and cap'.

9. Mezzotint by Thomas Watson after Joshua Reynolds of Lady Catherine Bampfylde, 1777.

10. Portrait by Joshua Reynolds of Lady Theresa Parker, 1773.

11. Portrait of Lady Ann de la Pole in the style of George Romney, 1793.

12. Engraving of Lady Acland by Samuel Cousins after Sir Thomas Laurence, 1826.

13. Mezzotint of Richard Edgcumbe by William Dickinson after Sir Joshua Reynolds, 1774.

It may be that she never walked in the woodland but she did enjoy The Walks at Eggesford the following day.

'I must not sit up long to write tonight, because of the cold, but my room had got much warmer since I first arrived in it. It really has been a beautiful day except for the cold wind. The sun was delicious. We were rather like a school at luncheon - 18 of us. Directly after Rosamond and I went out for a walk in what are called The Walks, thro' great plantations - some splendid Douglasses (I think they called them) two bigger than any in England, I should fancy. We did not go to Glynn Wood, but we are to go one day. When we came back from the walk, we sat in her tiny sitting room having tea there, which was very cosy - till dressing time.'[5]

Included in this collection are a number of Garden Portraits and the owners display themselves in the fullness of their pride of possession.[6] That for William 3rd Viscount Courtenay depicts him in an impressive garden. In the distance can be seen an elaborate fountain while the pillar against which he rests has his family crest's dolphin. Another in this collection is of Arthur Holdsworth, at Dartmouth in 1757, but he sits in an imaginary garden. A third painting is equally curious. This is a portrait of the three de la Pole children at Old Shute in 1793. It was at this time the family was building a new mansion above their ancient home. Half of the existing house was about to be pulled down. Curiously, this was the background chosen for the children's portrait. The painting shows the future of the family set against their past perhaps as an indicator of their ancient lineage or it may have been that New Shute was not yet in a finished state for a painting. However, a portrait of their mother was printed that same year. Lady Anne de la Pole is depicted standing at the south front of New Shute, in her new garden, with the sea in the distance. In contrast, her husband was represented in yet another painting inside their new home. Equally grand as Lady Anne is the depiction of Lady Theresa

14. Etching of Lady Edgcumbe by James Gillroy, 1791.

Parker at Saltram in 1773 or that of Lady Catherine Bampfylde at Poltimore in 1777. A major component of their Garden Portraits is the projection of their wealth, status and taste through their gardens. The portrait of Parker was painted by Sir Joshua Reynolds, a longstanding acquaintance of the family, and it was exhibited at the Royal Academy. Subsequent engravings of these portraits brought the images to a much wider audience than to those who only were able to visit these ladies in their homes.[7] Her daughter, also Lady Theresa, was later drawn by Henry Edridge and in comparison she is depicted with Saltram prominently featured in the background.

These portraits can be compared with two of John Tuckfield, one of Exeter's Georgian Members of Parliament. In the portrait which is now at the city's guildhall he is shown against a parkland background. The viewer would assume it represented his grounds at Little Fulford (later known as Shobrooke Park) near Crediton. In contrast, a second portrait has him holding the land grant he made with which the Royal Devon & Exeter Hospital was built. Tuckfield is depicted indoors. A background with a garden landscape would have been inappropriate given this was commissioned for the hospital.[8]

There are other owners of Devon gardens who have similar Garden Portraits. For example, in 1826 Lady Lydia Acland was depicted with her two sons in their garden at Killerton and the ten-year-old Richard Edgcumbe, second Earl Mount Edgcumbe, was painted by Sir Joshua Reynolds in his grounds. The least flattering depiction of a member of the Edgcumbe family is that of his mother, Lady Emma Edgcumbe, who was satirised as sitting atop Mount Edgcumbe in 1791.

In 1902 Frederick James Whishaw, a Russian-born writer who moved to South Devon, wrote of the joy he found in his Devon garden. He regarded himself as a utilitarian gardener, a man who knew nothing of growing flowers but who had become *'an acknowledged artist in potatoes'*. Many of his gardening experiences would resonate with succeeding Devon gardeners. He wrote of the annual Spring presence of his robin waiting for worms, of the joy of hearing a thrush sing and of his disappointment with previous owners

15. –16. Two portraits of what appears to be the same child, by an unknown artist and undated. On the backs there was noted 'Miss Orpen'. She may not have been from Devon although the portraits were framed in Exeter by Mr Worth of the Cathedral Close.

17. Watercolour after Francis Towne of Great Annery near Bideford, possibly early nineteenth century. The view provides little indication of the garden.

who had filled his soil with rubbish.[9] The thoughts that Whishaw expressed in words are also seen in what artists have depicted in plaster, glass, wood, stone, pottery and on paper and canvas. Many have a seductive quality although some have no pretentions to beauty. Each and every one, however, is a delight to the eye that also informs and thereby provides another means of understanding the garden history of Devon.

The following 96 sections are each centred on one principal image and supporting art have been included in order to help interpret the subject matter. Each section also opens with an image of art, generally the depiction of plants, which were made around the same time as the main illustration. Many of these artists have such international reputations, such as Constable, Cezanne, Monet, Manet, Pisarro, Degas, Renoir and van Gogh, that they are recognised just by their surnames.

omensis
propriat
do officio
te. Ikeay
nenda. A
tuo. Dor
me de th
ens est a
apitulo

Deus so iritur ad ordinale

Ecclesiastical illuminated manuscripts

1200 –1400

Perhaps the first plants to be recorded in Devon art are the illuminated manuscripts from the collections housed in Exeter Cathedral's archive and library. Many relate to John Grandison, bishop at Exeter from 1327 to 1369. Grandison is remembered as a great patron of the arts: he commissioned not just books but buildings, ivories, jewellery, metalwork and textiles.[10] Some of his private manuscripts are rich with floral imagery.

Eight examples from the cathedral's collection of books and manuscripts are illustrated here. One of the two earliest volumes in the library, that of the Exeter Book, the collection of Old English poetry, has decorated capital letters but none of them have foliage or flowers. The earliest example here shows six dragons, some with horns, either entwined around or making up a vine-like plant which forms a capital letter. This early thirteenth-century drawing has stylised foliage and it is interesting that a creature below, dragon-like but without wings, has a tail that ends with similar leaves. These hybrid creatures are more playful than menacing and the differently-coloured foliage was not necessarily intended to be representative of a particular plant.

The remaining images were made in the following century. These also show stylised plants. The designs are clearly inspired by plant forms but no such plants were ever grown in Devon. One manuscript, a copy of a fourteenth-century medical volume, has what appears to be a more accurate depiction of a vine as well as what would be commonly described by many modern commentators as a Tudor Rose. However, this image was made a full century before the Tudors came to the English throne. Each of these drawings demonstrates plants were used as inspiration in decorating the margins of manuscripts but not as accurate depictions of particular plants. They were devices to delight the eye. With them we can see how eight hundred years ago plants were used as a seductive agent in depicting beauty. The various creatures have a more elusive purpose, if any.[11]

1. **(Left)** This capital letters is both filled and surrounded by multi-coloured foliage and flowers. It appears within an Ordinal of the fourteenth century.

2. **(Right)** Red and blue unnatural ornamentation which appears to be inspired by foliage. This detail is from a book of ordinations and statutes relating to the cathedral of the fourteenth century.

   Inset: Head of a crozier with a serpent devouring a flower, early 1200s.

3. A rose set within a capital letter and surrounded by foliage. This appears in a copy of John de Gadesden's Rosa Medicinae, fourteenth century.

4. Illuminated capital letter B from Psalm 1 in a Psalter of the early thirteenth century. Two dragons are either consuming or disgorging other dragons and their bodies help to form the capital letter along with curling foliage.

24

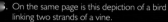

5. On the same page is this depiction of a bird linking two strands of a vine.

6. A geometric pattern further embellished by dual-coloured leaves and further decoration, possibly a nod towards flowers, of gold leaf, fourteenth century.

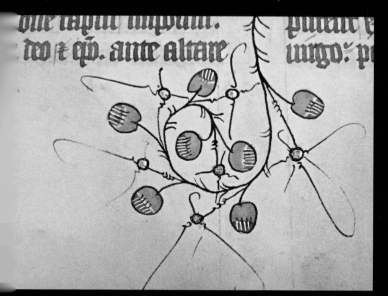

7. An abstract but striking elaboration from the same volume of lessons.

8. Detail from a Lectionary which belonged to Bishop Grandison in the fourteenth century.

9. Letters patent of Henry VI for Cowick Priory in which it is discharged for paying annual rent of twenty-four marks to the Crown and its possessions are confirmed, 1440.

Late medieval illuminated manuscripts

1440 –1549

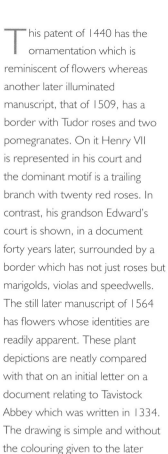

Later decoration, which occasionally can be discovered depicted on Devon's state documents, discarded the stylised plant designs of earlier centuries and instead aimed for accurate representations of actual plants.

10. Letter patent of Edward III regarding Tavistock Abbey, 1 May 1334, and the custody of the abbey during the vacancy of the abbot. The initial letter 'E' has the Virgin Mary and Child Jesus. Her hand is being held by the abbot. Delicate flowers decorate the capital letter and a vine leads from the end.

Inset: Tapestry of courtiers in a rose garden, c.1450.

This patent of 1440 has the ornamentation which is reminiscent of flowers whereas another later illuminated manuscript, that of 1509, has a border with Tudor roses and two pomegranates. On it Henry VII is represented in his court and the dominant motif is a trailing branch with twenty red roses. In contrast, his grandson Edward's court is shown, in a document forty years later, surrounded by a border which has not just roses but marigolds, violas and speedwells. The still later manuscript of 1564 has flowers whose identities are readily apparent. These plant depictions are neatly compared with that on an initial letter on a document relating to Tavistock Abbey which was written in 1334. The drawing is simple and without the colouring given to the later examples.

11. This Inspectimus for Bishop Hugh Oldham, includes his rebus, an owl, and depicts, within the capital letter 'H', the court of Henry VII, 1509.

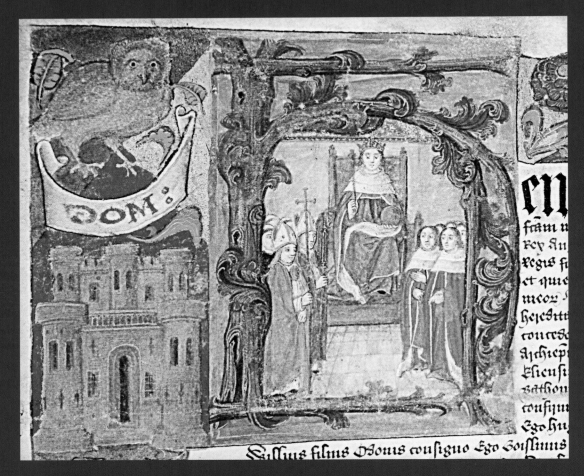

12. Detail from the *Inspectimus*, 1509.

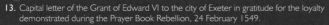

14. Detail of the floral border on the Ratification by William Hervye, Clarencieux King-of-Arms, of the arms of the City of Exeter, with the addition of a crest and supporters, 6 August 1564.

13. Capital letter of the Grant of Edward VI to the city of Exeter in gratitude for the loyalty demonstrated during the Prayer Book Rebellion, 24 February 1549.

16. Detail showing Temptation in, and Expulsion from, the Garden of Eden by William of Devon, 1265.

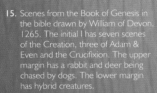

15. Scenes from the Book of Genesis in the bible drawn by William of Devon, 1265. The initial I has seven scenes of the Creation, three of Adam & Even and the Crucifixion. The upper margin has a rabbit and deer being chased by dogs. The lower margin has hybrid creatures.

The Garden of Eden
1265 – 1769

Perhaps it is not surprising that
the first representation of a garden to
be depicted in Devon art would be that
considered then as the world's first, the
Garden of Eden.

William of Devon, a scribe who is little remembered
within Devon,[12] illustrated this bible in 1265. It was a
monumental task and he acknowledged the effort by noting
in the closing page 'The end of the book: thanks be to the
Lord Jesus Christ, and the Blessed Virgin Mary, and all saints,
Amen. William of Devon wrote this book'. Now housed in
the British Library, the bible was written in Latin in Gothic
script on vellum and is sized 31cm by 19.4 cm. It is one of
a number of his works to survive. The decoration shows
a French influence on English design. Folio five comprises
Creation as well as the Crucifixion as part of marginal
decoration for the capital letter. Not surprisingly, the
Garden of Eden continued to be depicted in church art
with varying details of the garden's plants.

Inset: Embroidered cover to bible, c.1607, depicting the
Garden of Eden.

17. The Garden of Eden
as painted on a Devon
screen, c.1500.
In 1625 Francis Bacon
published his essay
'Of Gardens' and the
first line was *'God
Almighty first planted a
garden, and indeed it
is the purest of human
pleasures, it is the
greatest refreshment
to the spirits of man,
without which buildings
and palaces are but
gross handiworks'.*

31

19 – 20. Carving, in wood, at Bradfield House near Uffculme, c1600.

18. Wooden carving thought to be Adam with his shovel, from Paignton, early 1600s. Eve is depicted on another side with her apple.

22. Adam & Eve depicted, with navels, on the gravestone of Roger Vere, at St Peter's Church, Peter Tavy, of 1769.

21. Adam & Eve in a roundel on the Bluett family pew, c.1613, at All Saints' Church, Holcombe Rogus.

33

23. Detail of the cope at All Saints' Church in Malborough.

Late medieval vestments

at Barnstaple, Brixham, Culmstock, Malborough, Stoke Canon, Tedburn St Mary and Woodland

Devon's earliest depictions of flowers on cloth, which have survived, were not mere decoration but images to be venerated. Some, like those in our manuscripts, also relate to Devon's great patron of the arts, Bishop John Grandison.

A handful of ancient vestments, dating back to the late medieval period, can be seen in Devon today and most have representations of flowers. A vestment, the garment worn by an ecclesiastic during a service or ceremony, could take several forms. Copes resembled a long cloak or cape and were made of semi-circular pieces of cloth, chasubles took the form of a sleeveless mantle covering the body and shoulder, and an orphrey was a richly embroidered border or panel which was part of the vestment. These were part of what is now known as the *Opus Anglicanum*, or the English work.[13]

Unlike those of other flowers, these were images considered to be sacred and commanded a respect not accorded depictions of other plants. They formed part of the visual pageantry of the medieval church which was diminished at the Reformation. Many of these vestments were later reused to decorate communion tables.

The flowers were an elaborate floral design, usually embroidered in gold or crimson, and while some have been given the name of '*flower*',[14] like those on illuminated manuscripts, they were not designs

of flowers to be seen growing in the medieval period. The fleur-de-lys was associated both with the Virgin Mary, as was the lily, and with the Trinity.

Each of Devon's ancient vestments is on public view and most are held in a cabinet in the Anglican parish church. The Culmstock Cope, in All Saints' Church, was used as an altar cloth from 1828 to 1870 and then it afterwards decorated a wall in the chancel.[15] It features a row of fifteen saints, once part of an orphrey, while the Assumption of the Virgin forms the main scene. The background is decorated with fleurs-de-lys and pomegranates.[16]

That at Brixham features thirteen saints along the border, formerly orphreys as well, and in the centre there is the Virgin Mary and angels. It too was formerly an altar cloth which had begun life as several pre-Reformation copes. In 1830 a commentator thought it *'a curiously embroidered violet colour velvet cloth evidently part of the ancient furniture of the high altar. The border is adorned with figures of saints'*.[17] Woodland has a former altar cloth made from what might have beenan early sixteenth-century cope. The decoration comprises sprays of flowers.

24. Detail showing a spray from the Woodland vestment.

Inset: Sixteenth-century chasuble.

That at Malborough was rescued after being discovered protecting potatoes. It is thought to have been made from two copes reused in the late sixteenth century. It found another use as an altar frontal until a new communion altar was installed in about 1840. Village tradition is that one of the Victorian vicars hung it as a decoration at the vicarage. Questions were asked about its whereabouts in 1932 when it was found covering sacks of potatoes in a vicarage out building.[18] It is now displayed in its own cabinet.

The chasuble at Barnstaple was returned to the church presumably more than three hundred years after being taken into care by the family of a former churchwarden, John Peard, in 1910. Peard had been churchwarden in 1562 and the vestment is noted in an inventory completed two years earlier. The decoration includes Mary with the child Jesus, several angels and fleur-de-lys. The material is silk damask.[19]

25. Detail of the Barnstaple chasuble.

Another cope, that at Stoke Canon, was lost in a fire which destroyed the village in the 1840s.[20] Despite the loss, an earlier painting survives which shows floral decoration. Tedburn St Mary also had an ancient cope in 1866. Four other Devon chasubles can be seen at Ponta Delgada, St Michael's, and Angra do Heroismo, Terceira, in the Azores and they appear to have been owned by Bishop Grandison in the mid 1300s. In 1552 government commissioners removed vestments from the cathedral but a tradition in the Azores was that these came to them through relatives of John Fisher, the bishop of Rochester who was executed by Henry VIII in 1535. Yet another Grandison vestment, an orphrey, survives. This is in the collection of the Victoria & Albert Museum and is similar to one of those in the Azores. Floral decoration is not as prevalent as it is on those examples still in Devon.[21]

27. Watercolour entitled 'A cope St Mary's Stoke Canon' which has a note it was 'accidently burnt in 1846', 1845. The village was heavily damaged by the fire.

26. Detail of the spray on the vestment at All Saint's Church in Culmstock.

28. Detail of the cope at the Church of St Mary in Higher Brixham.

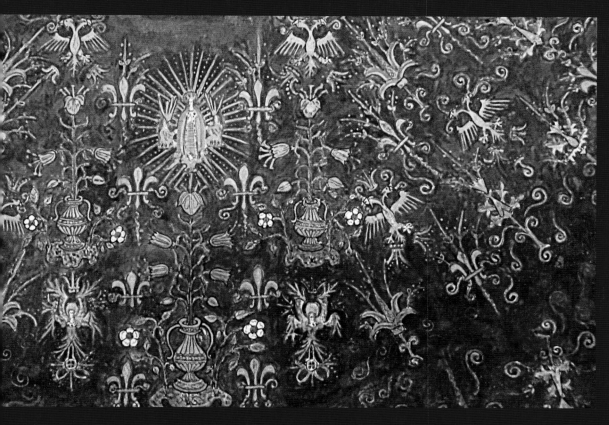

29. Detail from the Stoke Canon cope.

30. Detail from a watercolour entitled '*Ancient cope from the church of St Mary Tedburn Devon*', 1866.

31. The Grandison chasuble at the Victoria & Albert Museum is similar to one in the Azores and has some floral decoration.

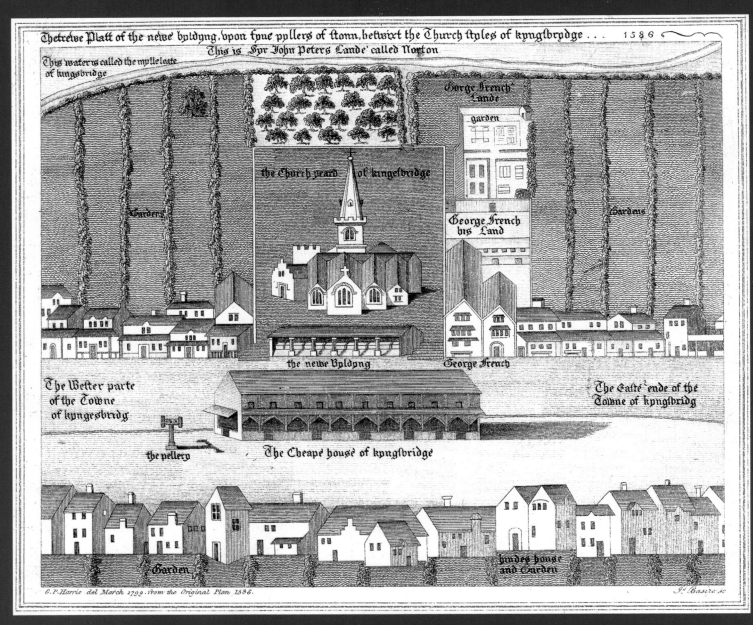

32. Engraving by J. Basire after G. P. Harris, 1586, of Kingsbridge showing burgage plots & ornamental garden.

Herb gardens
Kingsbridge
1586

Herb gardens were the most common garden in Elizabethan Devon. In 1615 the writer of *The Country House-Wife's Garden containing rules for herbs and seeds of common use, with their times and seasons when to set and sow them,* thought of herb gardens as the domain of women whereas men were more likely to be found in the orchard and agricultural fields.[22] Kingsbridge has the earliest printed representation of a herb garden in Devon.

Inset: *Flower print no. 11,* Nicholas Conchin after Balthasar Moncornet, 1645.

The Kingsbridge 'plot' illustrated here shows what was common throughout Devon towns: long burgage strips of land stretched behind houses situated in the main street. These are noted as gardens on the image. The perspective is inconsistent but it is clear that behind George French's house, to the right, there were gardens laid out in geometric patterns and that these were bordered by either walls or hedges. The artist drew the image as if it was early in the morning, with shadows stretching to the north, but the compass points are inaccurate: the northern end of Kingsbridge is noted as the east while the southern end is referred to as the west.

The chancellor at Exeter Cathedral had a herbarium in 1311,[23] near the treasurer's garden, but these strips of land shown in Kingsbridge were, by then, used in a similar manner to what would now be called cottage gardens but were then termed herb gardens. They held plants grown for medicinal, ornamental or culinary uses. Some were probably used for all three. Tithe records for the late 1500s and early 1600s provide details on which plants were likely to have been grown in Kingsbridge. These documents, in which a church representative disputed with a parishioner over the payment of this ecclesiastical tax, sometimes, such at Bovey Tracey in 1636, only referred to the plants as being *'pot herbs'* while another case at Mariansleigh of a similar date termed them *'herbs and roots for the pot'*. A woman living at Harpford in East Devon had *'so many herbs & roots of all sorts in her herb garden which*

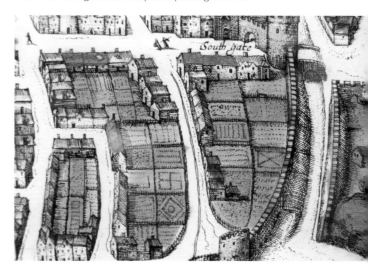

33. Detail of map of Exeter by John Hooker, late sixteenth century, showing garden plots.

she used in her pot for meat', by which she meant food in general and not just flesh. In contrast a parishioner of Bradworthy had a more detailed list: there were *'herbs & roots such as cabbages, leeks, onions, carrots, turnips and other herbs and roots'*.

A Modbury resident had an even lengthier description: the herbs, roots & fruits comprised onions, leeks, garlic, parsley, rosemary, cabbages, mulberries, strawberries, black currants, neaps (Swedes), radishes, carrots and turnips. The tithe records also show nuts, such as at Harberton one man was taxed on his filberts & walnuts while at Combe-in-Teignhead another was asked for a portion of his filberts, 'French nuts', walnuts and chestnuts. Fruit was also commonly grown such as the pears, wardens, peaches, cherries and plums at Broadhempston. These, as will be seen later in regards to Shute, were not exceptional.[24]

The most detailed list of all comes from the pen of John Hooker, Devon's first archivist and historian. This Elizabethan resident of Exeter noted in his unfinished history of the county that *'of herbs both of the garden and of the field'* there were in Devon the double red rose, double white rose, carnation, musk rose, civet, 'jolly flower', cowslip, primrose, daisy, (sweet) William, lily, 'convall' flower (lily of the valley), 'deluce' (iris) and Nonsuch pinks. There were also strawberry, gooseberry, mulberry, raspberry, rosemary, spike (French lavender), sage, thyme, 'pelomontetyne' (wild tyme), oregano, hyssop, parsley, lovage, fennel, carrots, coriander, anise, eyebright, cardens of all sorts, trefoil, sorrel, mugwort, betony, endive, scabious, lettuce, plantain, hart's tongue, dragon's vervain, chamomile, sea holm, wormwood, rue, violet, negotian, leek, onion, garlic, beans, peas, hops,

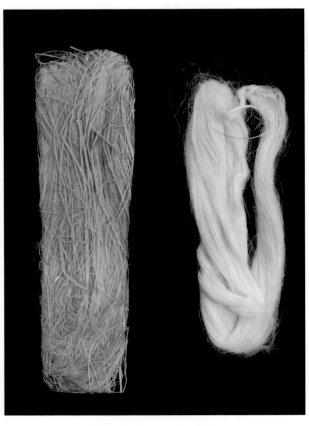

34. Sample of hemp and flax, 1803.

centaury, mints, parietaria and mallow 'besides an infinite number of others which to certify particularly it would be tedious to the reader and troublesome to the writer'.[25] Some of these plants were used to name local ships: in 1619 Dartmouth had the *Rose, Primrose* and *Mayflower* while in Plymouth there was the *Marigold*. West Teignmouth had the *Vineyard* and in Topsham there was the *Rosemary* as well as the *Violet*.[26]

Devonians engaged in another type of gardening which was probably not in these Kingsbridge gardens. In the early 1600s Tristram Risdon, one of our earliest historians, wrote of Combe Martin that it was *'a place noted for yielding the best hemp in all this county and that in great abundance'*.[27] A series of deeds for these hemp gardens survive for the early 1600s. They are noted as hemp gardens as well as hemp land and 'Hemp Hayes'.[28] Flax was also grown then and it continued to be practiced by later generations: in 1817 James Payne of Bovey Tracey called himself a flax dresser and by that date had been employed as one at Tormohun, St Mary Church and Drewsteignton.[29]

Roses would have been grown in many herb gardens. The earliest references to Devon's ornamental plants are to them: red roses appear as the annual rental fee for properties in such places as West Buckland in 1336, Buckland in the Moor in 1345, Axminster in 1380, Crediton in 1412, Honiton in 1419, Totnes in 1494 and Bridgetown in 1528.[30]

Of all the plants grown in Devon's herb gardens through the late medieval and early modern periods there is one which became nationally known. The Plymouth Strawberry was first in print in 1629. John Parkinson

35. The Plymouth strawberry.

wrote that it was found by John Tradescant, the Royal Gardener, *'in a woman's garden at Plymouth, whose daughter gathered it abroad and planted it there'*. He also noted *'this strawberry differs principally from the common sort in bearing a green flower, and its fruit being covered with prickles, which do not however wound the tongue; that its taste is not agreeable, but that it is pleasant to look upon, and that a handsome woman may very well, out of caprice, carry it in her hand instead of a flower'*.[31]

There are two plants which Tradescant does not appear to have noticed in Devon despite it being widely assumed that Devonians introduced them into England. Neither tobacco or potato plants are recorded by Tradescant in Devon nor are they noted amongst those grown in the herb gardens. Popular tradition has credited Sir Francis Drake, Sir Walter Raleigh or both with first bringing these plants into England from the Americas. If they were transported on the ships of either men at any point, the subsequent growing of them in Devon was not identified until generations later. Instead, local people had a variety of other plants growing in their Elizabethan gardens.

36. Miniature entitled *'Young man among the roses'* by Nicholas Hilliard, 1585-95, which is perhaps the most famous depiction of roses by a Devonian. Hilliard, a miniature painter, was born in about 1547, the son of an Exeter goldsmith. At the age of ten he fled Exeter with his family during the years of the reign of Queen Mary. These years brought him into contact with continental art which may have influenced him after his return to England on the accession of Queen Elizabeth.[32]

37. Aquatint by F. Jukes after W. Davey, 1791, entitled 'A south east view of the cathedral church of St Peter, Exeter taken from the terrace in the Bishop's garden'.

Bishop's Palace Garden
Exeter
c. 1590

The Bishop has had the largest garden in the city for as long as we have records for Exeter. His medieval palace was in itself one of the most impressive buildings and the most imposing domestic dwelling. It has changed dramatically with a pattern of rebuilding which was not experienced by the adjoining cathedral.

38. Detail of map of Exeter by John Hooker, late sixteenth century, showing garden plots

39. (Right) Detail from Juke's aquatint showing the bishop's gardener, 1791.

Inset: Flower print no.12, Nicholas Conchin after Balthasar Moncornet, 1645

This map by John Hooker, the city's chamberlain, was titled '*a platte of the churchyarde*' and made at some point in the late sixteenth century. He shows a large area, called the Palace Green, which appears to have been laid out to grass and planted with a few trees. Two centuries later an aquatint indicates succeeding bishops still had a largely open area but that it was now bordered with shrubs. This lack of a complex garden scheme is confirmed in an undated painting, probably made shortly afterwards,

40. Detail from an unattributed painting of the bishop's garden, possibly late eighteenth century.

which shows a wide open area. Although the bishops enjoyed the largest garden in the city it is also apparent that at the time these images were constructed the schemes were largely elementary in their designs. One exception was that the late Georgian bishops had a grotto at the bottom of the garden near the gatehouse.[33]

The palace garden has had patchy availability to the public with some generations having open access. During the episcopacy of some bishops, particularly that of Bishop Philpotts, it was unlikely that many local Exonians would have desired to spend time in his garden. Access to the gardens is now by personal invitation.

43

41.

41 – 43. Churchstanton bench ends with Gothic foliate designs, late fifteenth or early sixteenth century. The fruit of a vine is being consumed by four long-tailed birds while a curiously-faced animal, possibly a lion or even a sheep, sticks out his tongue at the viewer. Notice his floral tail. At the top of the vine two men have a sword fight. There is also a foliate border which is a feature of Devon's bench ends.

Bench end carvings

at Churchstanton, Marwood, Ottery St Mary
and Venn Ottery
15th & 16th centuries

42. Detail of carving at Churchstanton.

Inset: *A Fool Feeding Flowers to Swine*, early sixteenth century.

One of the earliest and least appreciated mediums for floral designs can be found in the county's ancient churches. These are examples of the workmanship of local craftsmen who were interpreting flowers in their carving of wood.

Gothic flower motifs run throughout a considerable number of Devon's ancient carved bench ends. In the 1400s and 1500s the county's churches were filled with sturdy, well-built benches which were highly decorated at their aisle end. Devon has a considerable portion of England's surviving church bench ends and the carvings are exceptional and, in many instances, unique to the West Country. It is also dominated by Gothic design and has a greater preponderance than the rest of England in the depiction of plants.

Medieval carvers used foliage and flowers as design components. Records show these men were local but they worked within a prevailing European design movement, the Gothic, which utilised plants most commonly in geometric

43. Churchstanton.

44. Churchstanton.

45. Ottery St Mary, a sacred emblem?

46. Marwood carving.

47.

48.

47. – 48. Venn Ottery carving of flowers. The secondary carving is particulary useful in adding to flower designs.

patterns. Carvings of stylised flowers can be found in great numbers at Ottery St Mary but also in other churches across Devon.

Some carvings may have been intended to have religious significance, such as a possible Tree of Life at Churchstanton, and it may be that some benches do not survive because at the Reformation they were considered devotional. Two benches have ends with carvings of plants in containers. These might have been considered sacred emblems.[34]

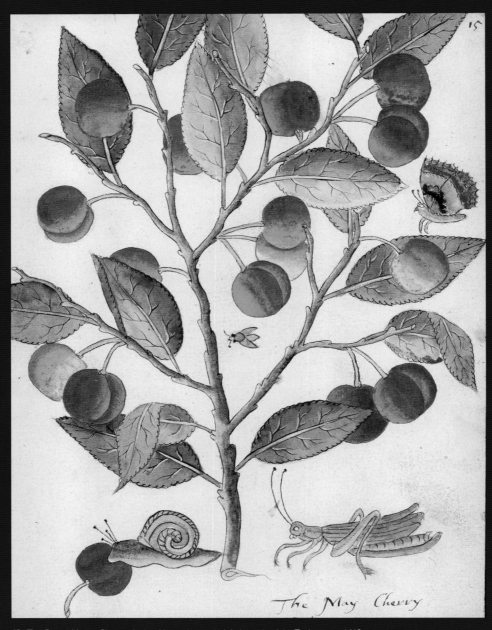

49. The Queen Mother Plum as depicted in a volume which belonged to John Tradescant, c.1612.

The Queen Mother Plum & Old Shute

1612

Had there been a Queen Mother in 1612 she would have been Mary Queen of Scots who would have reached the age of seventy had she not been executed twenty-five years earlier. She is unlikely to have been the inspiration behind the naming of this plum in about 1612. It comes from a collection of watercolours which had once belonged to John Tradescant the Elder, the Royal Gardener.

Inset: Gardener planting a tree, Jacques Callot, 1628.

This illustration is interesting in a Devon context because the Queen Mother Plum was recorded as having been planted at Shute near Colyton in 1660. The planter was Sir Courtenay Pole who was in the midst of transforming the landscape at what is now known as Shute Barton. During the 1660s and 1670s he planted many hundreds of fruit trees as well as a variety of other garden plants.

His interest in fruit appears to have transcended those in other plants. In December 1660 he recorded that he had purchased, from London, three young apricot trees as well as 3 Newington peaches, 3 Nutmeg peaches, 3 Roman peaches, 3 red nectarines, a green nectarine, a double blossom peach, 3 melocoton (a peach grafted onto a quince) and a fig tree. This was not the end of his fruit endeavours: that month he also had a Bergamot pear, a Grass plum, 2 Duke cherries, 2 May cherries, a Carnatian peach tree and 2 early apricots as well as his Queen Mother Plum tree.

Pole was a hands-on gardener and in his account book he noted in 1658 the trees that he grafted in the Great Orchard. He distinguished between the work he did and that of one Hurle. These grafts had come down to him from his father in London. There were 12 rows of trees in that orchard and the new varieties were the

50. The south side of Shute as it stood in 1781.

51. Sir Courtenay Pole as painted by an unknown artist, c.1670.

the Commonwealth and Pole wrote that he had reinvented himself as a nurseryman. He had been 'very choice and curious' in obtaining the best fruit trees. Nine years later Pole noted that the trees had cost him five pounds but that they had yet to yield him more than five shillings' worth of pears.[35]

Pole is mostly remembered for his work as a Member of Parliament. He introduced the unpopular Hearth Tax in 1662 and was subsequently lampooned as Sir Chimney Pole.[36] However important that tax was to national politics, he also deserves to be remembered for the fruit gardens at Shute. These were an extraordinary enterprise and perhaps were even a diversion for a man publicly ridiculed by his peers in Devon and in the House of Commons. The growing of this plum variety not only may have distracted him but provided a sanctuary of peace and calm far from the hurly burly of parliament.

52. John Tradescant the younger in an engraving by Wenceslaus Hollar, late 1600s.

Gillyflower, the Apple Dainty, the Old Wife (also called the Golden Rennet), the Spanish Pippin, the Codling and an apple he named the Bromley because, as he explained, *'I call it so because upon that bundle there was no name fixed on it as on the rest'*.

Pole acquired his fruit stock not just from London but from throughout Devon. In 1663 he proudly noted that a parcel of pear trees was from the vicar of Talaton. He had been expelled from his parish church during

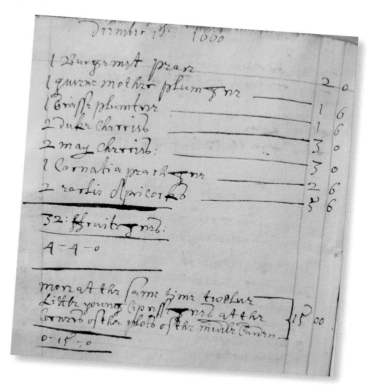

53. A page from Sir Courtenay's account book, 1660.

54. This early seventeenth-century sampler, by a member of the Chichester family, employs back, chain, cross, eyelet, faggot, rococo and faggot stitch with pulled work.

Embroidered sampler

Arlington
c.1612 to 1640

For centuries flowers have been used to inspire design in early embroidery work.

The sampler to the left was worked on by a member of the Chichester family of Arlington in North Devon sometime between 1620 and 1640. The initials MC may indicate it was the work of either Margaret or one of her two sisters who had both been named Mary. These initials can be seen in the top left corner. Needlework was an appropriate activity for a gentlewoman and a relevant description survives for another Devon woman at this time, for Lady Lucy Reynell of Forde House in Newton Abbot. She was remembered for making:

'coverings of tapestry and clothing of silk and purple; to look well to the ways of her household, and to clothe her family in scarlet; but especially reaching out her hand to the needy, in making all kind of garments for them. So that whensoever any came to visit her, they should find her like a princess in the midst of her maids of honour, triumphing on the throne of the affections of such as were about her.' [37]

The sampler was embroidered in silk with silver and silver-gilt metal thread. There are forty geometrical, floral, and heraldic motifs including the arms of the Chichesters. The floral motifs are stylised as are those done some two hundred years later by another Devon girl. Mary Herbert's early nineteenth-century sampler also has floral designs which would be impossible to identify.

55. Panel of stump work with birds, butterflies, plants and flowers, post 1660.

Inset: *A Vase with Flowers,* Jacob Vosmaer, c.1613.

Samplers were widely produced and many similar examples remain in the possession of their descendants. An earlier stump work panel, which has been sold at auction locally, also shows the use of floral motifs.

56. Detail of sampler worked by Mary Herbert of Exeter, 1830.

57. Cuffs and a collar made of East Devon lace of about 1620.

East Devon lace

c.1620

The floral motifs found in Devon's handmade lace are one of the most recognizable facets of Devon's industrial past.

58. Lace work by Miss Emma Radford, 1787.

Inset: *Bouquet of Flowers on a Ledge*, Ambrosius Bossschert, 1619.

Lace had been made in Devon on frames and with the use of bobbins since the middle of the sixteenth century. It had commonly been identified with Honiton and subsequently as being an East Devon industry but most recently the city of Exeter has been shown to have lace-making a generation earlier than any activity recorded before.[38] Young girls became the dominant workforce.[39]

The lace was made by hand, in cottages and not factories, with the motifs built from individual worked pieces. This style of lace lent itself to floral patterns. The invention of lace machines in the late eighteenth century led to a decline in the market for hand-made lace but this revived following the patronage of Queen Victoria in the 1830s. At first symmetrical design was followed in the continental style but increasingly Devon lace was less formal. Just as English gardens moved to less regimented lines, so too did Devon lace reflect the *jardin Anglais*.[40] Flowers continued to be popular in lace design through that century and into the last. As late as 1915 the Chudleigh Lace School, which had Lord & Lady Clifford as patrons, was supplying prickings of local ferns.[41]

59. Lace work by Lady Paulina Trevelyan, 1864.

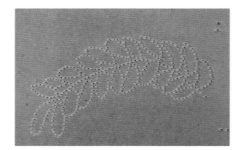

60. Pricking supplied by the Chudleigh Lace School of maidenhair fern for lacemaking, 1915.

61. Carved panel in the Muniments Room, Holcombe Rogus, early seventeenth century, with a representation of Adam and Eve in the Garden of Eden. It shows not only the tree of knowledge in fruit but Lucifer, as the snake, edging towards Eve. The writing on the banner, which is modestly placed, reads *'I have done evil in god's sight'*. Several letters are backward as are those in an accompanying panel on Sight.

62. The first panel in a series on husbandry which shows Sowing. The man's hand is filled with seed which he has taken from the seed-bag hanging from his neck. A ladder rests against one of two fruit trees.

63. Haymaking with a woman holding a rake with her right hand and to the left are piles of hay, possibly a stack or a rick. A pitchfork leans against the decorative arch. The woman holds with her left hand what appears to be a large jug. A divider separates the image from the decorative oak and other plants above.

64. Pruning or cutting down trees. A saw, mallet and chisel are in use.

65. Harvesting grain with a hand sickle.

66. The first of two panels connected with the senses, hearing music.

67. The second panel also features a woman looking into a mirror and reaching out to a tall flowering plant. The writing is carved almost backwards to read *'Seeing'*.

68. Crossed branches in which a bird perches. It may have been intended to represent a pigeon or dove.

Wooden panels
Holcombe Court
c. 1620

What is perhaps Devon's earliest series to depict husbandry was carved for an early seventeenth-century muniment room in one of the county's great houses.

Inset: *Sheet with Two Studies: A Tree and the Upper Part of a Head of Rembrandt Wearing a Velvet Cap,* Rembrandt van Rijn, c.1642.

69. A single plant in flower.

70. Three flowering plants, possibly intended to be carnations, with the central one rising illogically from a frame.

71. A hand, with a sleeve embellished with lace, holding a symmetrical plant which has two types of flowers.

72. A hand holding a cornucopia filled with fruit and flowers.

73. A lily, perhaps a symbol for the Virgin Mary.

The panels also include the garden of Eden, two of the senses (sight and sound), two depicting the coat of arms of James I, an angel guarding a fruiting tree, and a bird named as a pelican but most of the carvings have floral motifs. No two are alike. The Bluett family had lived in Holcombe Court since the 1400s and the new panelling was put in probably during the early seventeenth century.[42] The same carver was probably responsible for creating the family pew in the nearby parish church. It is not only stylistically similar but the carver used the same punch mark to create a matching design of three concentric circles. Interestingly, the parish church of St James at Curry Mallet in Somerset has similar carving. The connection would appear to be Lady Elizabeth Bluett who was born in the neighbouring parish of Orchard Portman.[43]

Some of the plants are identifiable and others are slightly fanciful.

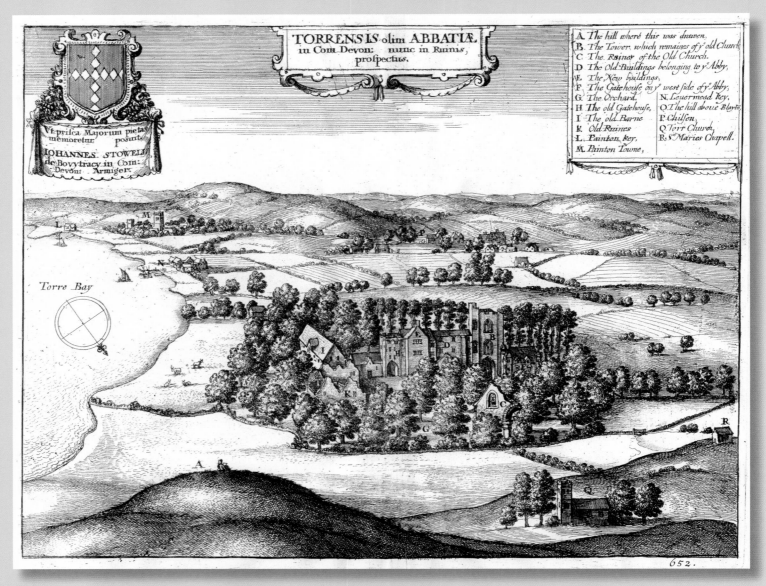

Inside the engraving:

TORRENSIS olim ABBATIÆ in Com Devon: nunc in Ruinis, prospectus.

Vt prisca Majorum pietas memoretur posuit IOHANNES STOWELL de Bovytracy in Com: Devon: Armiger:

A. The hill where this was drawn.
B. The Tower which remaines of y old Church.
C. The Ruines of the Old Church.
D. The Old Buildings belonging to y Abby.
E. The New buildings.
F. The Gatehouse on y west side of y Abby.
G. The Orchard.   N. Leuermead Key.
H. The old Gatehouse. O. The hill aboue Blayto.
I. The old Barne.   P. Chilfen.
K. Old Ruines.   Q. Torr Church.
L. Painton, key.   R. St Maries Chapell.
M. Painton Towne,

Torre Bay

652.

74. Engraving by W. Hollar entitled *'Torrensis olim abbatiae in com. Devon: nunc in ruinis, prospectus'* ('Prospect of Torre Abbey in the county of Devon, now in ruins'), 1662.

Torre Abbey

1662

This engraving, one of the earliest to show the Devon landscape, gives little indication of what the gardens might have looked like a century after the Dissolution of the Monasteries.

Like a number of other religious houses in Devon (see pages 77,86), Torre Abbey was acquired at the Reformation and then converted into use as a domestic building. It was the most imposing medieval building in Torbay and became the largest private home. Its closest rivals in size were the Bishop's Palace at Paignton and Compton Castle in Marldon.

Torre Abbey had been a prosperous religious house and would have had an extensive kitchen garden and most likely some form of ornamental planting. The engraving indicates that buildings had declined since they were given up in 1539. The abbey's fishpond is not shown nor is the garth, the grass plot or paved quadrangle which often featured in monastic life.

75. Watercolour by W. A. Glynn, 1810, entitled *'Torbay from Torre Abbey'*. By this date Torre Abbey was being visited by tourists.

Inset: *Flowers in a Delft jar*, Alexander Marshal, 1663.

76. Watercolour by John Swete entitled
'Gateway and barn at Torr Abbey',
December 1793. Swete's views show the
Abbey 130 years after Hollar's engraving.
By 1793 Torre Abbey was appreciated for
its picturesque character.

77. Watercolour by John Swete entitled
'Gateway at Torr Abbey',
December 1793.

78. Watercolour by John Swete entitled *'Tor Abbey'*, December 1793. Torquay was, at this time, being transformed into a fashionable resort.

79. Watercolour by John Swete entitled *'Arches at Torr Abbey'*, December 1793.

The engraving shows it was drawn sometime between 1653 and 1662 when the Cary family purchased the abbey.[44] The self-titled prospect notes that the abbey was then in ruins and in the top left hand corner John Stowell, the owner who hailed from Bovey Tracey, recorded below his coat of arms *'That the former piety of great men may be put into memory.'*[45] The artist himself is portrayed on the hillock above the bay whilst at work on the drawing. He took a certain amount of care in depicting the landscape: in the distance even the Bishop's Tower is shown alongside the parish church of Paignton. The engraving is transitional in that it shows the last vestiges in which the Torbay landscape was dominated by a religious house and before it would be transformed by holiday makers. It was not until the nineteenth century that Torbay would become known as the English Riviera and distinguished for its sub-tropical planting.

80.

81.

80. – 83. Four close-ups featuring vine, rose, cherry and plum designs.

Painted panelling
in 18 North Street, Exeter
c.1670

Painted decoration was once a feature of domestic dwellings in Exeter and across the county.

18 North Street, now known as The Conservatory, is a sixteenth-century building which was damaged by fire in 1995. That fire revealed the survival of some fifty wooden panels which have two decorative schemes. One of them features plant motifs: tulips, thistles, vines, roses and trees with cherries and plums were painted onto these boards. An analysis of the oak boards concluded that the panels were inserted in about 1600 and that the boards with plant designs were thought to date from the late seventeenth century.[46]

Inset: *A Bouquet of Flowers in a Crystal Vase,* Nicolaes van Veerendael, 1662.

82.

Tulips had, by 1670, become well-known throughout England, thistles were a common wildflower, roses had been grown in gardens for many generations, cherries and plums were commonly planted, and vines were familiar as a religious symbol as well as from travels abroad.

83.

84. Oil on canvas by Hendrik Danckerts, 1673. Mount Edgcumbe can be seen as a prominent feature in the landscape as seen from Plymouth. Danckerts depicts a line of vision from the house towards the Hamoaze. The sails of his ships are filled with wind blowing from various directions.

Mount Edgcumbe
1673

This panorama view of Plymouth in 1673 is the work of Hendrik Danckerts, a Dutchman who came to England just before the king's restoration in 1660. His works have been noted as being permeated by a sense of prosperity and well-being.[47]

85. This drawing by Edmund Prideaux entitled either *'Mount Edgcumbe'* or *'Mount Edgecumbe in Devon'*, c.1727.

Inset: A Hanging Bouquet of Flowers, Abraham Mignon, c.1670.

The painting shows the port dominated by the new citadel and surrounded by fields. It would be another two decades before the naval base would be built and attention refocused to the west of Plymouth where Mt Edgcumbe can be seen on the opposite side of the river Tamar.

86. – 87. These two drawings are by Edmund Prideaux and are entitled either *'Mount Edgcumbe'* or *'Mount Edgecumbe in Devon'*, c.1727.

Sir Richard Edgcumbe of Cotehele had begun building the house in 1547. Edgcumbe set his house within his newly-built deer park and it has been a prominent landmark for Plymouth ever since. Although the house is situated on the Cornish side of the Tamar, it was, until 1854, in the county of Devon.

Celia Fiennes visited some twenty years after Danckerts painted this view and thought the house could be renamed Mount Pleasant because of its tree-lined walk down to the waterside, walled terrace and two summerhouses.[48] The long walk is shown by Danckerts as is the Wilderness around it.

Some fifty years later, in about 1730, a Cornish gentleman, Edmund Prideaux, visited Mt Edgcumbe and drew three views of the house and grounds. One view in particular demonstrates a more formalised garden with three terraces and regimented planting.

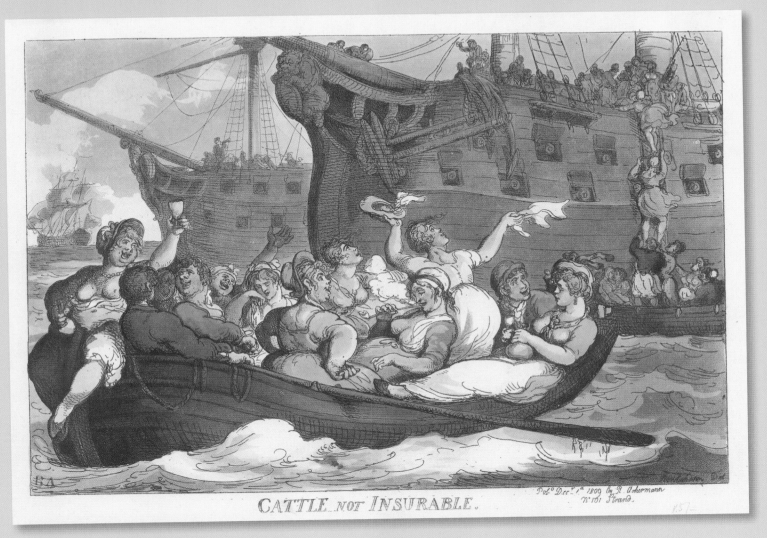

CATTLE NOT INSURABLE.

Pub.d Dec.r 1.t 1809 by R. Ackermann
N.o 101 Strand.

88. This watercolour by Rowlandson 'Cattle not insurable' of 1809 is a reminder that not all of the views of Plymouth would necessarily have been well-mannered.

One of the constant attractions of the ornamental landscape was the changing views of Plymouth. The passing commercial and naval ships provided a continually altering scene and this changed with the perspective of the viewer as one passed through the grounds. In 1785 a visitor from Hampshire commented in his diary that he and his party thought it *a delightful place, abounding with amazing prospects, & happening very luckily to be so fortunate as to meet with an exceeding fine day. We were entertained exceedingly with the noble views about Plymouth*.[49] His delight with the views was matched by countless other visitors.

89. View of the John Abbot ceilng in the Exeter Custom House, 1685.

John Abbot's plaster work
Exeter Custom House
1685

Sixteenth and seventeenth-century plaster work provided a new means of depicting local flowers and plants. Frithelstock's John Abbot embellished Exeter's Custom House with an elaborate plaster ceiling where flowers, fruit, snakes and masks were done in high relief.

90. Detail of flowers and fruit by John Abbot in the Exeter Custom House ceiling, 1685.

Inset: *Allergory on human life, Joris Van Son, c.1658-60.*

Similar work can be found in the Royal Hotel at East the Water across from Bideford. Abbot's plaster is both delicate and lively. He came from a long line of plasterers and a family book of designs shows a long interest in the use of flowers for decorative inspiration. One of these is an elaborate Garden of Eden. Other early plaster ceilings in Devon also used floral motifs but were often done in low relief. It is Abbot's work which is particularly pronounced in more careful depictions of garden flowers.

The plaster at Exeter's Custom House has been described as being, in comparison to the family's earlier work, a *'lighter and livelier style, with more delicate and refined wreaths in foliage, enlivened with fruit, cherubs, masks and even a few eels. The individual motifs include thistles, oak leaves, grapes and a number of exotic plants whose identification has not been resolved.'*[50]

91. Abbot's use of a mer-boy in the
Exeter Custom House ceiling, 1685.

92. Abbot's plaster at the Royal Hotel,
East the Water near Bideford.

93.

– **94.** Two designs
from the Abbot
family sketchbook.

94.

95. Edmund Spoure's drawing was entitled *'This is the draught of Bradfylde the Mansion house of Colonell Henry Walrond in county Devon'*. He had difficulty fitting the pond within a single sheet of paper and was forced to depict it at a sharp angle. The Spoures may have been connected to this house through the marriage of Ursula Specott, sister of Humphrey Specott of Launcells, to William Walrond. Bradfield continued in the possession of the Walronds until the early twentieth century. Spoure's view shows two statues in the front garden along with a pond and small island. The architectural details are broadly in line with the building as it is today. In contrast, a report on the garden in *The Gardening World* in 1899 noted impressive topiary with *'a large top, round or acorn shape'*, a flower garden enclosed by stonewalling, a Palm House and *'noble conifers'* in the pleasure grounds.[51]

Edmund Spoure's drawings
of Bradfield, Hooe, Marpool, Mount Wear House and Oakhay 1694

In 1694 Edmund Spoure, of Trebartha in the East Cornwall parish of North Hill, drew a number of Westcountry properties with which he had connections. He presented them to his daughter Mary and these six drawings of the five properties form the earliest group of images of Devon houses and their gardens.

Inset: *Study of a Plant with Red-Purple Flowers (Sebastiana africana purpurea)*, Maria Monninckx, 1695.

96. View entitled *'This is the Draught of the Barton house and Town of Hoe alias west How which also came to the Spoures by the Daughter and heir of Specott and is now possessed by Edmund Spoure Esquire'*. Edmund Spoure's interest in Hooe came in 1648 through his grandmother Elizabeth's marriage. She was the heir of the Speccott family. A map made during the Civil War, some fifty years earlier, shows a substantial house entitled *'The Barton House'*. An ornamental garden appears in Spoure's drawing as being on the north side of the house.

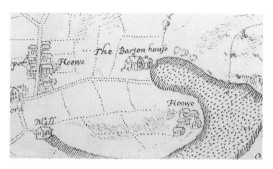

97. Detail of a Civil War map showing Hooe, 1645.

The Spoure family had resided in Somerset until about 1497 when Thomas Spoure married Anne Trebartha. Several generations later, in 1675, their descendant Edmund married Mary Rodd, the only daughter of James Rodd of Oakhay in Stoke Canon. Edmund Spoure died four years after completing the book. In 1694 he had travelled through Devon, including Exeter.[52] and it may have been on this visit that Spoure painted some of the properties.

These drawings were made only six years after the accession of William of Orange to the English throne. The new king was particularly interested in gardening and favoured the planting of evergreens. The depiction of the new garden at Oakhay may demonstrate the new fashion.[53]

98. View entitled *'This is the Draught of Exmouth the Mansion house of James Rodd Esq. Son of the aforesaid Bampfyld'*. This property most likely came into the possession of James Rodd through his wife or mother. Marpool Hall was demolished in 1951 and its grounds given to form what is now known as Phear Park.[54] Spoure's drawing shows what might have been a parterre along with some trees planted in a formal manner.

99. View entitled *'This is the Draught of the old Front of Oakhay, the Mansion house of Bampfylde Rodd Esquire in County Devon'*. Spoure provided his daughter with two views of Oakhay. Neither of them bears a resemblance to the house by that name today. Spoure's wife Mary had been raised in the house. Her father, James Rodd, had been living in Stoke Canon since at least 1641[55] and in 1669 was appointed Sheriff of the county.[56] The barton was, within a generation, sold to George Parker of Boringdon.[57] By 1763 at least it was known not only as Oakhay but also as Okey Place, and later it was called Oakey.[58] The first of the two drawings shows a line of trees outside of the front wall (in which is a door within a door) and the inner garden is formal.

100. View entitled *'This is the Draught of the new Front of Oakhay next to the garden Built by the aforesaid Bampfylde Rodd Esquire'*. The second drawing, of the modern house, looks like there were two sets of eight cypresses planted in a formal manner in the courtyard. A line of other trees surround the back of the house.

101. View entitled *'This is the Draught of Were the Mansion house of James Rodd Esquire, married Gertrude daughter of Sir William Bastard of Gereston, in County Devon'*. Mount Wear House, located at what is now known as 47 Countess Wear Road, was part of James' marriage settlement in 1679 with Gertrude, the daughter of Sir William Bastard of Gerston in West Alvington.[59] James Rodd was then living in Bedford House in Exeter and had moved to Mount Wear by, at least, 1690.[60] His family sold it in 1760 to the Spicer family.[61] The house was modern at the time of Spoure's visit and the garden is depicted as having what looks like a summerhouse to the west, a formal garden on the east and in the main courtyard there is a tree-lined path to the front door.

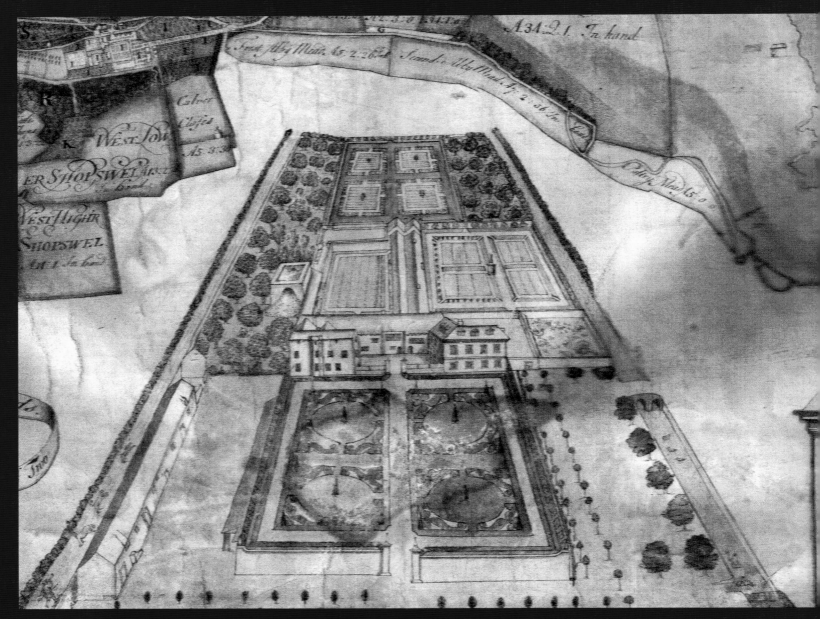

102. Detail from a map of Hartland Abbey by an unknown surveyor, c.1705. To the right of the house can be seen an aviary which includes at least two peackocks. In the distance groves were planted outside four formal plots boxed in with hedges. It is easy to overlook the huntsman with a horn and two hounds chasing a deer (left) and the anglers (right).

Hartland Abbey
c.1705

This map of about 1705 shows the most elaborate of the early geometric gardens in Devon to be depicted.

The taming of nature by the creation of strict order is shown with the gardens at Hartland Abbey. Four distinct compartments, all of the same design and in symmetry, were set within a high wall in the front of the house. A focal point is in each plot set amongst grass and parterres.

Behind can be seen a series of formal garden plots.

Hartland Abbey was one of the six religious houses in Devon to be converted to domestic use. Buckland Abbey, St Nicholas Priory, Forde Abbey, Torre Abbey and Exeter's Black Friars Monastery (later Bedford House) were also in use at this time as homes. A drawing made two generations later shows the continuation of the formal gardens.

103 – 104. Views of the east and south aspects of Hartland Abbey, 1767.

Inset: *Iranian textile fragment with flowers, birds and butterflies, seventeenth or eighteenth century.*

103.

104.

106. View of the house, in 1769, showing the front gardens. It is entitled *'An east prospect of abbey in Devonshire the seat of Paul Orchard Esquire Colonel of the Northern Battalion of Devon'.*

105. View of the west aspect of Hartland Abbey, 1767.

107. Copper plate engraving by T. Bonnor after E. Garvey entitled *'Hartland Abbey, the seat of Paul Orchard, Esquire'*, 1791. It shows the front aspect without the earlier formal gardens.

108. Langdon as painted by an unknown artist, c.1710.

109. Map of Langdon by Richard Davis in the Calmady Atlas, 1788. Sale particulars map, 1876.

110. Oil painting of Emily and Laura Anne Calmady of Langdon by Sir Thomas Lawrence, 1823. Lawrence said it was *'my best picture... one of the few I should wish hereafter to be known by'*.[62]

111. Detail from the tithe map of Wembury showing Langdon, 1839.

Langdon Court
Wembury
c.1710

This oil painting of Langdon is undated and unattributed but it presents a rare panorama of an early ornamental landscape in Devon.

The painting shows Wembury's church to the far left, a brick tower on the crest of a hill in the centre and Langdon itself on the right. The formal front garden is divided into four compartments laid to grass with several statues and enclosed with a wall. Three buildings in terraced formal gardens are depicted on what is the south side of the house. Other agricultural buildings are pictured around the house and there is a pond just below. Woodland surrounds Langdon and beyond are agricultural fields.

Langdon had been rebuilt a few years before this view was painted, in 1693, and the mansion house is set within three hills and a short distance of the sea. The Calmady family had resided there from 1564 until 1876 and were no doubt responsible for the view being painted.

Two generations later another visual device was created. An estate map drawn in 1789 shows the two projecting formal gardens still existed as did the small pond below the house but there were also considerable changes: the tithe barn and tower have been demolished. Three stretches of water have been added on the northern side: each is rectangular although one has a horseshoe end. The deer park has been divided and the warren turned to arable use. Along the northern side of one piece of water is a formal garden which possibly had been walled. Langdon Court is now a hotel.

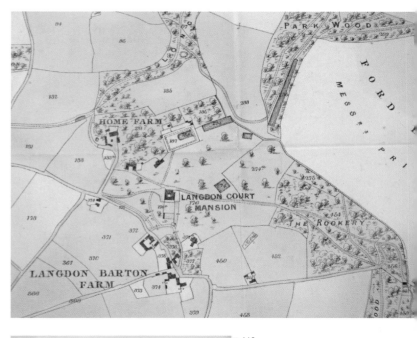

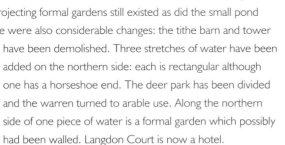

112. –114. Details from the sale catalogue of 1872 showing the estate's position near Plymouth, the grounds and the house.

Inset: A Vase of Flowers, Margareta Haverman, 1716.

112.

113.

114.

115. Portrait of Sir Edmund Prideaux, 1730, by William Aikman with Prideaux Place, Padstow, in the background. The portrait hangs in Blickling Hall, Norfolk.

Sir Edmund Prideaux's drawings

of Buckland Filleigh, Dunsland, Fallapit, Forde Abbey, Lyneham, Mothecombe, Poltimore, Portledge, Soldon, Thuborough and Wortham, 1716 & 1727 – 8

Devon's most important series of early drawings of houses with their gardens was made by an East Anglian gentleman during the reign of George I.

In the early 1700s a collection of 28 drawings were made of properties throughout Devon by Sir Edmund Prideaux, a gentleman who was raised in Norwich but who had family throughout Devon and Cornwall. Prideaux's family connections lay with a considerable number of the buildings particularly with his Cornish home at Place in Padstow. Many of the drawings are dated 1716 or 1727 to 1728, when he would have been 23 and 34 years old. It has been conjectured that the first visit took in Werrington, Dunsland, Thuborough, Solden, Portledge, Buckland Filleigh, Heanton Satchville, Wortham, Mothecombe and Lyneham. A second tour encompassed visits in September 1727 to Forde Abbey, Netherton, Poltimore, Mount Edgcumbe and Fallapit.[63]

Prideaux's drawings provide extraordinary insights into early Georgian garden design in Devon and show elements that would be standard throughout England: topiary and other shaped shrubs and trees, canals, parterres, statuary, wall plants, avenues and lawns were all depicted by Prideaux. Geometric patterns and a sense of symmetry dominate these landscapes. Clean lines are set within an ordered and obviously contrived or artificial form. There are key viewpoints throughout but these gardens were designed not merely to be seen whilst walking in them but also to be viewed from various positions, and heights, within their houses. The perception of the observer changed as the perspective altered. Prideaux's trees, sometimes seen in ranks and other times in avenues, are ill-defined in that it is not possible to identify which species were planted but those choices were likely to have been of considerable importance as a walnut, lime or evergreen would have made very different contributions to the landscape. He appears to have been careful in showing the topiary designs and the varying shapes. The drawings show considerable differences in these gardens which were all created within an understanding of what a fashionable garden was for the gentry.

116. Oil painting entitled *'South Prospect of Hampton Court'* by John Stevens, c.1705. No Devon landowner could compete with the grandness of this garden but many shared similar designs.

Inset: *Flowers in an Urn,* Jan van Huysum, c.1720.

117. Buckland Filleigh

A view from the south which Prideaux entitled *'Buckland Filleigh. William Fortescue Esquire and Buckland Filleigh formerly belonged to the family of Filly. Afterwards it came to Martin Fortescue, son in law to Lord Chancellor Fortescue who gave it to his second son William Fortescue from whom in the ninth descent is William Fortescue, 1728'*. This Fortescue house was damaged by fire in 1798 and was later extensively remodelled. Prideaux's family connection lay with the marriage of Honour Fortescue of Buckland Filleigh to Humphrey Prideaux of Soldon. The main entrance to the current house is now from the opposite side. Prideaux's view shows geometric planting which would appear at first sight to have been an orchard rather than ornamental trees. It may have been a grove.

118. Dunsland in Bradford. Watercolour by Edmund Prideaux entitled *'Dunsland William Bickford Esquire Devon'* 1716. Arscott Bickford married two Prideaux women, the second was Bridget daughter of Edmund Prideaux of Prideaux Place Fire also destroyed Dunsland in 1967, thirteen years after it was purchased by the National Trust and shortly after its restoration was completed. The Bickford family had acquired the house by the time Prideaux had drawn these views. The wooded setting continued but the gardens were greatly altered by subsequent generations. Nearly two hundred years after Prideaux's visit Dunsland was described as 'a garden in the wilderness'.[64] Even in 1716 the formality of the planting must have seemed at odds with the wild landscape around the house.

119. Watercolour by Edmund Prideaux entitled *'Dunsland in Devon William Bickford Esquire'*, 1716.

120. Fallapit in East Allington. Watercolour by Edmund Prideaux entitled *'Fallapitt near Kingsbridge in Devon Edmond Fortescue Esquire'*, dated 24 October 1727. This medieval home of the Fortescue family came to Humphrey Prideaux when he married Honour Fortescue in 1600. A stone path, courtyard laid to grass and wall plants dominate this plain garden.

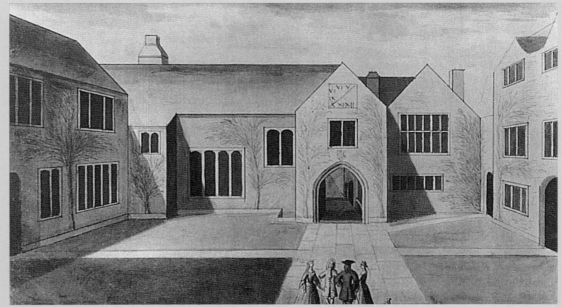

121. Forde Abbey, Thorncombe (now part of the country of Dorset). Watercolour by Edmund Prideaux entitled *'Ford in Devon'*, 1727. The abbey was purchased by Edmund Prideaux 110 years after it was dissolved at the Reformation. He made particular alterations to the interior of the building. In 1702 Prideaux's granddaughter Margaret inherited and the abbey passed into the Gwyn family. It may have been at this time that the gardens depicted by Prideaux were created. Elements of that design have survived. Nearly three generations after the Gwyn family acquired the abbey it was described as a magnificent building 'striking beyond exception'.[65] Prideaux shows this was then one of Devon's most highly-designed gardens. It had not only an impressive topiary garden laid out with parterres but vistas with extensive planting, wide avenues with shaped trees, clipped hedges, wall plants and a canal with a cascade. Forde Abbey must have been one of the most impressive gardens in Devon.

122. Watercolour by Edmund Prideaux entitled *'Ford from the North'*, 1727.

123. Watercolour by Edmund Prideaux entitled *'Ford in Devon late Edmond Prideaux now Francis Gwyn Esquire'*, 2 September 1727.

124. Watercolour by Edmund Prideaux entitled *'Long Walk & Garden at Ford'*, 1727.

125. Watercolour by Edmund Prideaux entitled *'Garden and Park at Ford'*, 1727.

126. Watercolour by Edmund Prideaux entitled *'Cascade & Wilderness at Ford'*, 1727.

127. Watercolour by Edmund Prideaux entitled *'Ford South front'*, 1727.

128. Watercolour by Edmund Prideaux entitled *'Ford'* and inscribed *'Arches in Devon'*, 1727.

129. Lyneham at Yealmpton. Watercolour by Edmund Prideaux entitled *'Lynam Courtney Crocker Esquire in Devon'*, 1716. The house had recently been rebuilt by the Crocker family when Prideaux painted this watercolour. He shows an impressive avenue to the house. On each side is a section filled with what could have been fruit trees or possibly a grove. Evergreens have been shaped and clipped whilst four urns form another focal point on the approach to the house.

130. Mothecombe at Holbeton. Watercolour by Edmund Prideaux entitled *'Wembury John Pollexfen Esquire Devon'*, 1716. The house in Prideaux's drawing was, like Lyneham, built on or near the site of an earlier building by John Pollexfen in the early 1700s. Also, like Lyneham, there are urns. There is statuary in the garden as well as what could be a gravel path which separates the plots laid to grass and the oval plot at the centre. The garden is bordered by what may have been an evergreen hedge or a stone wall.

131. Netherton in Farway. Watercolour by Edmund Prideaux entitled *'Netherton Sir John Prideaux'*, 1727. Edmund Prideaux, an Elizabethan member of the family who was raised at Soldon, purchased Netherton and rebuilt it. The date 1607 is on the West Front.[66] Netherton had the most extraordinary topiary of all these gardens: Prideaux shows the taller plants had two distinct designs. A similar shape can be seen in one of the drawings for Poltimore. The grass plots and wide paths accentuate the starkness, and what must have been startling shapes of these clipped plants which punctuate the garden. A second view shows a much more standard approach to the house.

132. Watercolour by Edmund Prideaux entitled *'Netherton Sir Edmond Prideaux baronet, and Netherton in the parish of Farway in the county of Devon built by Sir Edmond Prideaux, baronet, in the time of King James the 1st was parcel of the possessions of the abbot of Canonsleigh. It was purchased by Sir Bernard Drake after the Dissolution, who sold it to Sir Edmond Prideaux, second son of Roger Prideaux of Soldon in the county of Devon, esquire. Edmond Prideaux, the present possessor of Netherton, is the fifth in descent from the first baronet'*, 5 September 1727.

133. Poltimore, perhaps 1727. Watercolour by Edmund Prideaux entitled *'Poltimore Sir R Bampfylde'*. By the time that Prideaux visited the house it had been lived in by the Bampfylde family for nearly two centuries. Sir Copplestone Bampfylde built a south entrance range in the early eighteenth century, as shown in the drawings.[67] The grounds show a canal and high clipped trees but the main interest lies with the three sections of parterres accented by topiary and a statue. Along the edge lies planting of what could have been specimen plants.

134. Watercolour by Edmund Prideaux entitled *'Poltimore in Devon Sir Copleston Bampfyld'*.

135. Watercolour by Edmund Prideaux entitled *'Poltimore Sir Copleston Bampfyld'*.

136. Portledge in Alwington, perhaps 1716. Watercolour by Edmund Prideaux entitled *'Portledge in Devon Richard Coffin Esquire'*. The family connection to Portledge lay with Anne Prideaux of Place in Padstow who married Richard Coffin of Portledge in 1673.[68] The perspective allows a clearer impression of the extensive planting. The garden is divided into four squares with the central feature being one clipped plant. Each square has rectangular strips of grass which enclose a circular area of shaped planting which are formed around what might have been more grass. Within that area are fleurs-de-lys. There are two distinct shapes to the plants which alternate throughout the garden.

137. Watercolour by Edmund Prideaux entitled *'Portledge in Devon Richard Coffin'.*

138. Soldon near Holsworthy, perhaps 1716.
Watercolour by Edmund Prideaux entitled *'Soldon in Devon John Prideaux Esquire'. Soldon was owned by the Prideaux family since the mid sixteenth century.*[69] *The house is shown having a bare entrance garden with two grass plots and a line of trees to the side. It is enhanced by parterres to the side which look far more complicated than the main garden.*

139. Thuborough in Sutcombe, perhaps 1716. Watercolour by Edmund Prideaux entitled *'Garden and Park at Ford'*, 1727. Thuborough had been in the Prideaux family since the fifteenth century.[70] The watercolour shows stark symmetry with the garden laid out into two sections. The outer garden has geometric planting of what could have been clipped trees, or possibly a fruit orchard, whilst the inner garden is divided into two grass plots by a wide path. Minimal planting of a handful of shaped trees or shrubs complete the garden. A seat in the corner provides the only visual distraction.

140. Wortham near Lifton, perhaps 1716. Watercolour by Edmund Prideaux entitled *'Wortham in Cornwall Devon'*. This was a late medieval home of the Dinham family who married with the Prideaux family. Wortham has the plainest of all of the gardens depicted by Prideaux with an open courtyard ornamented by very restrained wall planting. Now owned by the Landmark Trust.

142.

143.

141. – 144. Details of a linen bed cover which belonged to the Parminter family, c. 1725-50.

141.

144.

Parminter family bed cover
c.1725-1750

Floral motifs were a favourite design for bed covers in the early eighteenth century. This example, made of linen and embroidered with silks, once belonged to the Parminter family in the early 1700s and is now housed at A La Ronde.

The second example is a shawl, more than a century later, which could be one which was designed for W. L. Gill of Colyton and which appeared at the Great Exhibition in 1851. It is a combination of machine-made net with applied flower sprigs worked in coloured silk bobbin lace.

Inset: Panel With Design of Fruit Trees produced at Spitafields, c.1720.

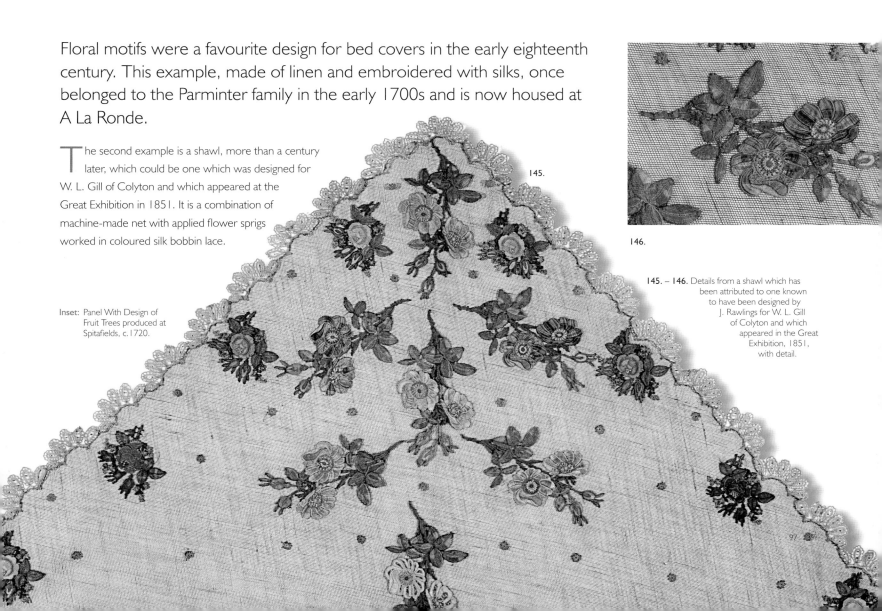

145.

146.

145. – 146. Details from a shawl which has been attributed to one known to have been designed by J. Rawlings for W. L. Gill of Colyton and which appeared in the Great Exhibition, 1851, with detail.

97

147. Copper line engraving of the east view of Powderham Castle by Samuel & Nathaniel Buck, 1734. Along the front of the house alternately high and low conifers have been planted. On either side of the door are two pots with plants.

Powderham Castle
1734

Powderham Castle has been in the ownership of one family for nearly seven hundred years. The Courtenays vacated their home on three occasions but retained possession, and have largely been resident in it, over the course of these centuries.

Inset: *Still Life with Fruit*, Jan van Huysum, early 1700s.

The building was captured in print by the Buck brothers who were initially known for their engravings of ruins in the 1720s but came to draw and engrave gentlemen's seats.[71] Powderham Castle was one of their chosen great houses.

This view was engraved following the period in which the Courtenay family had abandoned their castle for nearby Forde House: destruction at Powderham Castle during the Civil War had made their Newton Abbot property

148. Copper line engraving of the south-east view of Powderham Castle, 1745, by Samuel & Nathaniel Buck.

a more attractive option in the 1640s. They remained there for some time and did not lease Forde House until 1762 but by then they had been repairing and renovating the castle and its grounds for many years.[72] The Courtenays had been unlucky in their forays into national politics: the head of the family was executed for treason in 1538, his son was entangled in later accusations and a successor failed to welcome the new king, William III, when he stayed at Forde House in 1688. By 1735, when this view was engraved, they had managed a period of stability.

The engraving shows an elemental formal garden. Cypresses line the inner courtyard as do other plants in pots. Paths and grass plots form three segmented areas. Outside the walls lie several terraces and rows of similar planting. Estate accounts show that in 1720 144 garden pots were purchased and in 1727 and 1728 there were at least eleven men and five women employed in the garden. The latter may have been weeding. Some work may not have involved ornamental plants but could have been agricultural, including the planting of cherry and apple trees. There are also references to 'firs' but subsequent entries indicate these were most likely furze, the local name for gorse, rather than to any conifers.[73]

Eleven years later, in 1745, a view from the river Exe was engraved. This shows formal planting as well as two substantial ornamental buildings along the river. Another building on the far right may be a boathouse. Estate accounts note that in 1738 an Octagon at the 'water side' and a Bowling Green House were being built. The Octagon appears to have been brick-built, stuccoed and had a platform with gates in front. The windows had shutters. A total of 12,500 bricks were purchased and these may have been used for the two buildings.[74]

149. Portrait of Edward Courtenay by T. Chambers, c.1724 – 1789. Courtenay was one of the family who became embroiled in national politics and had fifteen years' incarceration in the Tower of London.

Jos. Highmore pinx.ᵗ

Rich.ᵈ Houston sculp

*Long, Ancient Structures and enobled Domes,
The Work of Ages past, neglected lay,
Till you, O BUCKS! by Emulation fired,
Snatched from th'inexorable Jaws of Time
The Mouldering Ruins of each lofty Pile.
To future Ages fhall your Fame be known:
And your great Works immortalize your Names,
While others, by Misfortune, fcarce furvive:
You, Phoenix like, by your own RUINS live.*

Samuel Buck.

London, Printed for Rob.ᵗ Sayer, N.º 53, Fleet Street.

Nathaniel Buck.

Published as the Act directs 10 April 1774.

150. Portraits of Samuel and Nathaniel Buck by Richard Houston after Joseph Highmore, 1774. Below the portrait was written '*In 1730 he (Samuel Buck) was issuing his series of engraving of abbeys etc. from The Golden Buck in Warwick Street, near Golden Square, St James's after 1738 the prints were dated from No 1 Garden Court, Middle Temple. He, assisted by his brother Nathaniel, drew & engraved many hundreds of views of ruins of noted abbeys, castles & views of seats & cities*'. His celebrated work is '*Buck's Antiquities or Venerable Remains of above 400 Castle's etc. with near 100 views of cities*' 1774, to which this double portrait plate was prefixed... The Golden Buck was the sign of the publisher Robert Sayer at No. 53 Fleet St from 1762. He (Nathaniel) assisted his brother Samuel but died many years previous to the issue of the later publications.

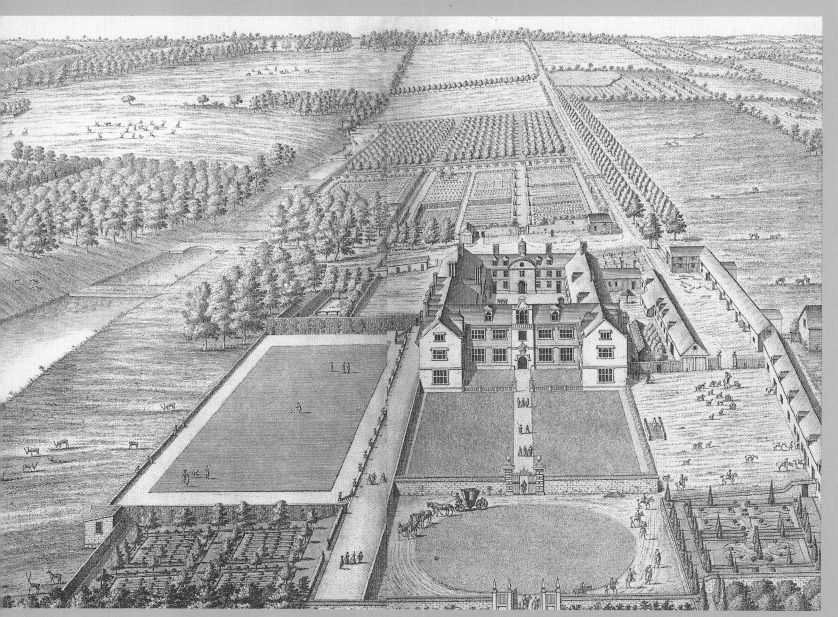

151. Engraving entitled 'Heanton Hall and Park in Devonshire, the Seat of the Right Honorable Robert Lord Walpole Ld. Lieutenant of the County of Devon and Knight of the Most Honorable Order of the Bath' by William Henry Toms, 1739.

Heanton Satchville

Petrockstowe
1739

A house and garden
which has truly
been lost.

This engraving depicts a considerable building with an elaborate ornamental landscape. Extensive kitchen gardens and plantations appear behind the house but to the left, on what would have been the west, is a long rectangular stretch of water set within an extensive deer park. There are outbuildings in the distance which may be the keeper's cottage. On that side, to the front of the house, is a bowling green while on the house's eastern side is a pack of hounds with a number of riders. Here there is also a formal garden: within stone or brick walls are two main beds with at least two types of geometric planting. The parterres have two distinct designs. Fifteen years earlier Edmund Prideaux drew the house and gardens. One of his two views shows a formal garden where the bowling green was depicted in the 1739 engraving. The house that was drawn by Prideaux, and in this engraving, was destroyed by fire in 1796 and shortly afterwards Reverend Swete saw the ruins. He noted it as:

> 'a vast pile built at different periods having a date of 1639 engraved in a tablet of moorstone which is certainly from the architecture not the oldest but simply ascertaining the time in which the portal over which it has been placed was erected - from the figure of the house, which wears the form of the letter E in its front the period of erection is possibly determined... on the southern side of the house is a most noble terrace of considerable width and in length 130 paces which, with the bowling green and the walks around are kept in most excellent order, and are the finest of the kind that I have ever met with. On the parapet walls, the mullions and the flat pavement, all of which are moorstone, I observed that a white moss had so encroached as nearly to hide the superficies... All that is seen from the terrace of any note are the adjoining oak trees which are generally of great height and wonderful magnitude, particularly a clump of 5 or 6 close to the house.'[75]

Inset: *The Gallant Gardener*, Jacques de Favanne after Antoine Watteau, eighteenth century.

152.

152. – 153. Two drawings by Prideaux entitled 'Heanton Lord Walpole' and 'Heanton Satchville formerly belonging to the family afterwards it came to the Killigrews in the time of Edward 3rd Nicholas Yoe married Elizabeth the daughter and heiress of Killigrew. Afterwards Henry Rolle son of John Rolle of Stevenstone married Margaret the daughter and heiress of Samuel Rolle of Heanton married to Robert Lord Walpole', 1724.

In 1843 John Claudius Loudon visited Heanton Satchville a century after the view was engraved and noted:

'*This is a place of great extent, and capable of very great improvement. The house is situated on an immense bank, with another immense bank facing it, about a mile distant, with a broad valley between, the whole or any part which might be covered with water at very little expense, it might be laid down in meadow or covered with wood for pleasure. This broad valley joins a narrow one with lofty banks covered with natural wood, the whole or any part of which might also be flooded. Every natural feature here is on a large scale, and the arts required are chiefly draining and planting, both of which, as far as they have been carried, evince good judgment. The masses of trees in the park were projected by Mr Gilpin, and are judiciously placed. Various recent improvements have been devised by His Lordship and his intelligent gardener Mr Cato; and we had the honour of staking out an approach above a mile in length. The house is not large, but it is well arranged, and, as far as a stranger can judge in a day or two, it cannot be better placed. In a shrubbery walk there is a living arbour, formed by Mr Cato, of ash trees, in the manner recommended in our Volume for 1841, page 312, which has succeeded admirably. The kitchen-garden and nursery grounds here, as well as the pleasure-ground, are kept in excellent order.'* [76]

This was Heanton Satchville but it was a different building which had been given the name of the ancient house which was consumed by fire. The Clintons had purchased Innis House in nearby Huish and renamed it.[77] Their home engraved in 1739 has been all but forgotten.

153.

154. Oil painting of Raleigh House in Pilton entitled *'View of Barnstaple from Fort Hill, Devon'*, c.1740. Pilton can be seen to the left, and Barnstaple to the right with Raleigh House in between.

Raleigh House
Pilton
1740

Two Georgian views of Raleigh House near Barnstaple show it as a prominent feature in the landscape.

155. Oil painting entitled *'Barnstaple from Sticklepath'*, c.1740, which also shows Raleigh House in the distance.

Shortly after these paintings were made Dean Milles wrote it was *'a very handsome seat belonging to John Bassett, Esq., called Rawleigh. It was built by Sir Nicholas Hooper, is a square building with three good fronts, having windows in front. The Rooms are lofty… upon the whole one of the best in this country… now disparked. It commands a near view of a pretty country and the town of Barnstaple and of the river Taw'*. The older house, which was situated nearby, was described as being in ruins.[78] Raleigh is now converted into multi-occupational use.

156. Raleigh as shown in Benjamin Donn's map of 1765.

Inset: *Still life of flowers and fruit in a garden,* Franz Werner von Tamm, 1700 – 1710.

157. Oil painting by John Wootton entitled *'Castle Hill, Devonshire, the seat of Hugh Fortescue, Lord Clinton'*, 1735 to 1740.

Castle Hill

near South Molton
1735 –1740

This view of Castle Hill is easier to reconcile with what can be seen today than with many other early ornamental landscapes in Devon.

158. Copper line engraving entitled 'North Prospect of Castle Hill, in Devonshire, the seat of the Right Honorable Hugh Earl of Clinton', 1749. The high status of the owners is indicated by the arrival of a coach with the Fortescue coat of arms on its sides.

Inset: *Parrots and Fruit with Other Birds and a Squirrel*, Tobias Stranover, 1710 – 1724.

Castle Hill has retained the outline of its Georgian scheme. Few others remain in Devon and while Mount Edgcumbe and Bicton are also particularly significant it is Castle Hill which is the most remarkable for its extent. The basic structure has remained in that the house nestles under a hill which has a castle at its crest, terraces descend to a stretch of water, an open line leads the eye from the house to the triumphal arch across the valley and the estate is dotted with ornamental buildings.'

Hugh, first Lord Fortescue, rebuilt the house in the 1720s and the outline of the garden followed shortly thereafter. His successors were also keen to embellish the landscape. Water was particularly important to the design. It has changed shape in three hundred years. In the 1720s it took a cruciform form which was then in fashion as a formal geometric shape. A generation later Matthew, second Lord Fortescue, altered it along the lines he had discussed with his predecessor. The pool became less formal and the shape came to be serpentine. Symmetry was replaced by natural contours and a port was built with nearby trees 'shredded' so that their branches gave the appearance of the masts of ships. A schooner was built. Ornamental buildings have included not just the castle but Satyr's Temple, Sybil's Cave, the Chinese Temple, Temple of Venus, Sunrise Temple, Sunset Temple, Spa Bath House, the Hermitage and even the estate forge was renamed Vulcan's Temple. Pyramids, a crenellated limekiln, an octagonal menagerie and a sham village, with a church tower attached to one of the cottages, have also ornamented the landscape. The engraving shows five terraces, a stretch of water, an obelisk and formal planting of trees.

The parish church, which stood near the house, was demolished and a new building was erected half a mile distant in 1732. It had a new purpose in acting as an eye-catcher. The two landmark architectural features were the castle and the triumphal arch. The castle differs from that depicted in Wootton's painting. A bowling green lay below the castle. The eye-catcher, which consists of one principal arch with smaller ones on either side, is situated nearly a mile across the valley from the house.[79]

Castle Hill is also notable as remaining the family home of the Fortescue descendants.

159. Pen and Ink sketch by Louisa S. A. Fortescue, 1855.

160. Oil painting, composed of sixteen pieces of canvas, by Thomas Hudson entitled *'The Radcliffe Family'*, c.1742. Hudson may not have painted it in its entirety.

The Radcliffe family of Warleigh House in Tamerton Foliot

c.1732

This family portrait shows a proud and prosperous couple surrounded by their children and all placed in front of their imposing home.
Not all is as it seems.

The painting depicts the family of Walter Radcliffe in front of Warleigh, their newly purchased home at Tamerton Foliot near Plymouth. Radcliffe, who was raised at Franklin House near Exeter, was then aged about fifty and his wife, Admonition Bastard, was nearly ten years younger. The couple had married in 1721,[80] and some twenty years later moved into their new home. Warleigh was sold to them by John Bampfylde, a relation of Mrs Radcliffe. The painting may have celebrated their new purchase which was a much grander house than that from which he came. However, the building bears no relation to Warleigh and is as fictitious as the background to the portrait of Arthur Holdsworth at Dartmouth (see page 129).

161. Watercolour entitled 'Warleigh seat of Radcliffe Esquire' by John Swete, 12 September 1792.

Inset: *Lysimachia*, Elizabeth Blackwell, 1737.

162. Detail of steel line engraving entitled *'Warlegh House, Devonshire, the seat of Walter Radcliffe Esquire'*, by W. Le Petit after T. Allom, 1831.

In the portrait Walter Radcliffe stands with his family around him. He is wearing one glove. Identifying the children is difficult because it is undated and only nine of the twelve children are depicted. It has been assumed that Thomas Hudson painted the family in about 1742 but it is more likely to have been the following year or possibly 1744. There were too many boys and too few girls in 1742 for this painting to be accurate.

The couple's first four children were Ann Grace, Jane, Joanna and Mary and they can be clearly identified to the left and far right of the picture. The daughter playing with her dog, on the far left, may be one of two girls,

Admonition or Martha, for whom no birth or baptism records have survived but must have been born in the early 1730s. The remaining four figures are more difficult to identify. In March 1743 a son was born, Pollexfen, and the eldest, Jaspar, died eight months later. This would date the painting to either by February 1743 or after June 1744. If the earlier date, then the boy with the drum was Jasper but if the painting was done in 1744 then it was the next brother, Walter. The remaining sons, John and William, would be the siblings attired in long dresses. The baby whom Mrs Radcliffe is holding could be either of the younger sons.[81]

The most commented upon Georgian feature of the gardens were the myrtles growing in front of the house. Mrs Bastard wrote to a friend that *'four myrtle trees grew in the open air, in the recesses of Warleigh House, from twenty-seven to thirty feet in height, the branches spreading nearly from the roots. One was a foot and a half in circumference at the base, and*

proportionately large to the top. The other three were nearly as high and one of them was two feet in circumference near the root. Two of the four were of the broad-leaved kind, one small leaved, and the other double-blossomed, the flowers of which might be gathered from the windows. They were cut down in 1782, from the apprehension of their causing the walls of the house to be damp'. The family had tea caddies made from the wood which when cut down weighed 452 pounds. Mr Radcliffe thought they were the largest myrtles in England.[82] Mrs Bray, to whom Mrs Bastard sent this description, wrote a novel at this time entitled *Warleigh*.

In 1832 a visitor noted the family portrait was at the house and commented upon the grounds. He wrote the:

> *'large and ancient mansion, appears, both from old records, and from its internal structure, to have been erected prior to the Elizabethan age. The south front bears the form of the letter E; and the entrance-hall, from its lofty and imposing aspect, has the character of a baronial one. At the upper end is a family-piece of eleven figures, executed by Hudson. The grounds, which possess great natural beauty, including extensive woods, are bounded on one side by the river Tavy, and on the other by Tamerton Lake. On the left, the higher points command a view of the Hamoaze, with a large portion of the navy of Britain, now (January, 1832) peaceably moored in that fine haven; the churches of St. Budeaux and Landulph, and the junction of the Taw and Tamar rivers, with a long undulating line of the varied banks of the latter, bounded by the heights of Hengeston-down, in Cornwall; and, on the right, the Tavy, with equal beauty, is traced beyond Marystow, the distant landscape affording a glance of Buckland Abbey, and being terminated by the Dartmoor hills.'*[83]

Before the Radcliffe family came to Warleigh the gardener, in 1728, was John Grills who was paid forty pounds a year, had a share in the garden produce and was given housing at the estate.[84] Nearly a hundred years later a vegetable grown in that garden became a curious episode in the history of the house. In 1822 a turnip was pulled from the ground at Warleigh and it was claimed in the local press that it resembled the right-hand of a man. Moreover, it looked like that *'of a very fat man, puffed where the fingers join, the wrist commencing with the green part'*.[85] The interpretation of the Warleigh Turnip needed as much imagination as that of the garden depicted by Thomas Hudson several generations earlier.

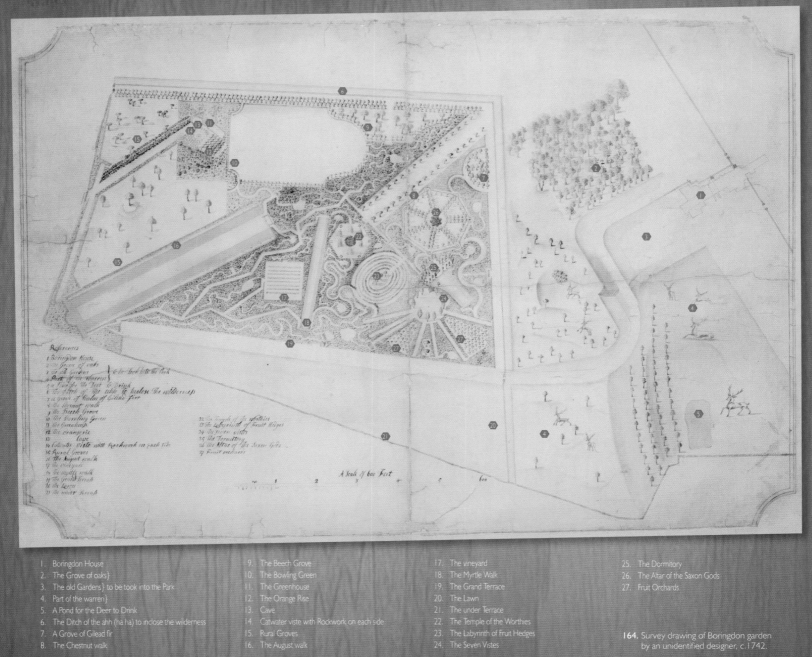

1. Boringdon House
2. The Grove of oaks}
3. The old Gardens} to be took into the Park
4. Part of the warren}
5. A Pond for the Deer to Drink
6. The Ditch of the ahh (ha ha) to inclose the wilderness
7. A Grove of Gilead fir
8. The Chestnut walk
9. The Beech Grove
10. The Bowling Green
11. The Greenhouse
12. The Orange Rise
13. Cave
14. Catwater viste with Rockwork on each side
15. Rural Groves
16. The August walk
17. The vineyard
18. The Myrtle Walk
19. The Grand Terrace
20. The Lawn
21. The under Terrace
22. The Temple of the Worthies
23. The Labyrinth of Fruit Hedges
24. The Seven Vistes
25. The Dormitory
26. The Altar of the Saxon Gods
27. Fruit Orchards

164. Survey drawing of Boringdon garden by an unidentified designer, c.1742.

Boringdon Hall

Plympton St Mary
c.1742

Boringdon has been eclipsed by its near neighbour, Saltram, as has its gardens. However, in the first half of the eighteenth century the intended design for the garden would have overshadowed what was subsequently created at Saltram.

The Parker family lived at Boringdon from 1583 until they moved to Saltram in the mid 1700s. Several hundred years of residence in that much grander house has effectively obscured their time at their earlier seat. This was heightened by Boringdon's architecture becoming old-fashioned and it was later derided for being the home of a farmer. Even so it was a grand building and the Georgian landscaping plan would have created one of Devon's most remarkable gardens.

In 1793 the travelling Reverend John Swete wrote:

'Lady Catherine, the mother of the late Lord Boringdon, by rebuilding the old mansion had intentions of reinstating it in the honour it once possessed of being the place of the family's residence. How much to the credit of her taste I will not say, let those who have traversed the beautiful grounds of Saltram decide'.[86]

165. Joseph Mallord William Turner's oil painting entitled '*The Plym Estuary from Boringdon Park*', 1813. His view of the Laira does not include sight of Saltram House *(on the left)* and looks out from what would have been the proposed garden at Boringdon.

Inset: The Sense of Smell, Philippe Mercier, 1740s.

166. Copper line engraving by W. Woolnoth after J. R. Thompson and Samuel Prout of Boringdon entitled *'Boringdon House, Devonshire, the ancient seat of the Parker family, and now belonging to Lord Boringdon'*, 1809.

Lady Catherine's father-in-law, George Parker, died in 1743[87] and she along with her husband John moved to Saltram that year. Most likely they abandoned what had been a very ambitious plan for the grounds of Boringdon. Swete had no detailed knowledge of Lady Catherine's scheme for her former home. He also wrote on his visit that:

'in former days everything was substantial, snug and sheltered but taste and elegance were unknown. So that, if I cannot congratulate the present times on their superiority over the past in the points of policy, morality or religion, in the most unqualified manner I am able to do it on their gardening. The environs of almost every gentleman's seat is now a garden laid out by the bewitching hand of nature and if there are any to be found who admire the tonsil works of other days, and on that account had rather have been a contemporary of King William, I can only shrug up my shoulders & exclaim Let ancient times delight other folk, I congratulate myself that I was not born till now.[88]

Lady Catherine hired a man who had an awareness of national trends but whose identity is now not known. It has been suggested that he was from the provinces and not a leading designer.[89] His plan was not only ambitious but would have involved a considerable outlay.

The Hall itself is only lightly depicted on the right hand side of the scheme. The plan retained the existing deer park and would have subsumed *'the old garden'* on the west side of the house and a rabbit warren to the

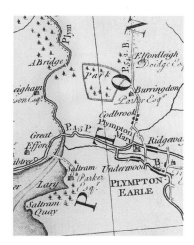

167. Detail from Benjamin Donn's map of 1765 showing the situation of Boringdon in relation to Saltram.

168. Detail from the tithe map of Plympton St Mary showing the grounds of Boringdon, 1841.

southwest. An extensive and nearly rectangular block of designed landscaping, some 450 feet from the house, would have been carved out of what were agricultural fields. This space was between 900 and 1,000 feet at its longest and about 700 feet from top to bottom. A ha-ha (termed in the plan an 'ahh') separated it from an extension of the deer park on the east and extended itself along the northern edge of the plan. Along the south side of the scheme were two terraces. The Grand Terrace, nearly 1,000 feet long, was immediately alongside the plan and further out was the Under Terrace. A lawn was planned for the furthest southwest end of the new scheme.

The rectangle had more than 20 features. The plan made use of the potential for views. Near the house, in the southeast corner, lay *'The Seven Vistes'*. Seven lines of view radiated from a circle. Two fruit orchards were to be planted within the gaps and it appears two ancient trees were retained. Serpentine walks linked the Seven Vistas as they did with all the other features. Another outlook was created for looking towards the Laira: the Catwater Vista was planned in the northwest corner. Interestingly, it is nearly from one of these vantage points that J. M. W. Turner painted a century later.

There were two other walks in which to promenade. The Chestnut Walk lay on the north east corner and the August Walk on the south west. A Myrtle Walk was planned for what was nearly the centre of the scheme. Plantings of trees were included throughout such as the set of Rural Groves on the northwest, the Beech Grove on the north and the Grove of Gilead Firs to the east. A vineyard was also planned for the central and southern part of the scheme.

There are two curious areas on the plan. In the northwest corner the Catwater Vista had *'rock work'* on each side and led to a cave. Near it would have been a greenhouse and alongside both was the Orange Rise. The plan shows concentric circles alongside and it may be that the Orange Rise was a low hillock on which Citrus Trees in pots would be moved to in warmer months from the greenhouse.

The southeast corner has the most curious collection of features. A building was drawn and noted as the Dormitory, presumably a type of summerhouse. Near to it would have been the Labyrinth of Fruit Hedges, a maze with espalier fruit trees and three trees at the top. Further along was planned the Temple of the Worthies, a hexagonal space for what appears to have been statues along the edge, six topiary plants in an inner ring and a building or pool at the centre. Most intriguing of all is the Altar of the Saxon Gods. At its centre lay a seven-sided structure with seven tree-lined avenues radiating outwards and at each end point there was what appears what would have been statues, perhaps for each figure for whom our seven days are named.

Today there are remains of terraced gardens to the north and west of the house, evidence of the deer park as depicted on the garden plan, a pond and a triumphal arch which was built in the 1780s.[90] Boringdon is now a hotel.

Mantua of Isabella Courtenay
c. 1744

This dress is a stunning example of the Georgian use of floral motifs.

This grand mantua is associated with Isabella Courtenay of Powderham Castle. She married Reverend John Andrew at Exeter Cathedral in May 1744 and was then 28 years old.[91] The dress is made of white ribbed silk which has Rococo embroidery with botanically-accurate flowers. It was necessary for the wearer to go sideways through doors. The petticoat was shaped to have side hoops which were five feet at their widest.

Isabella Courtenay was the sister of William de jure 8th Earl of Devon. Her husband was appointed rector at Powderham and died fifty-five years after their marriage.[92] In effect, she moved from the castle to the rectory. The couple were part of ALPS, a club which met at the time of the full moon and dined on venison from the Powderham estate.[93] The couple had seven children and Mrs Andrew died in 1825.[94] Presumably her family kept the dress until it was acquired by the Victoria & Albert Museum nearly one hundred and fifty years later following her death.

169. A Court dress consisting of a white silk mantua robe and petticoat embroidered with polychrome silks and silver threads.

Inset: *The Flower-Garden Display'd*, James Smith, 1734.

170. Portrait by Thomas Hudson of a woman thought to be Isabella Courtenay, c.1740.

171. Detail of the plan of Sharpham's formal gardens as drawn by William Doidge, surveyor, 1749.

Sharpham

Ashprington
1749

The Exe, Tamar and Dart rivers were exploited in the eighteenth century by wealthy men seeking views for their new country houses such as Sharpham.

In 1770 Captain Philemon Pownall rebuilt an existing house from the proceeds of privateering. This map, dated 21 years earlier, shows this earlier building that was partly demolished. It was not a grand building: part of it appears to have been thatched.

Sharpham's position on the river Dart made it a landmark to passing river traffic; one visitor from Hampshire rowed by and thought that from there it appeared *'to great advantage'*.[95] The map shows the immediate landscape was dominated by orchards and confirms the only ornamental garden was that

Inset: *The Servant Justified,* Nicolas Lancret, c.1740.

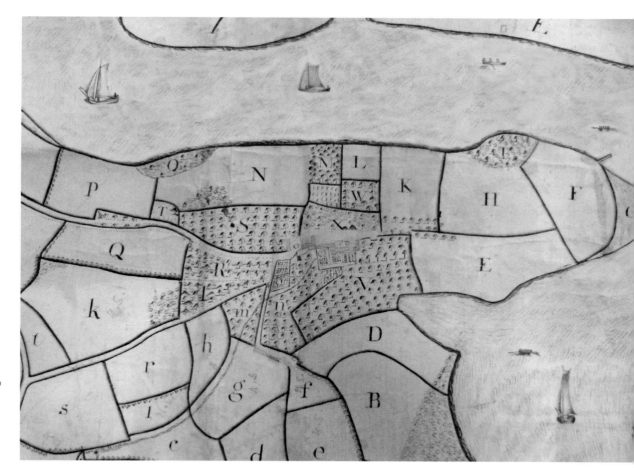

172. Sharpham and the curve of the River Dart as shown on the 1749 map.

immediately in front of the house. Three separate areas, possibly on two levels and set within high walls that also divided them, were laid out with four sections of parterres, geometric planting and grass plats.

Nearly a hundred years later, in 1842, John Claudius Loudon recorded the state of Sharpham. He wrote:

> *'Notwithstanding the wretched state in which this place was, we noticed in a flower-garden near the house very large plants of Clianthus puniceus and fuchsias; Bouvardia triphylla, 4 feet high, and forming a large bush; rosemary, 6 feet and 8 feet high, forming most beautiful bushes; large magnolias of different kinds; and a bed of broad-leaved myrtles pegged down, so as to cover the entire bed with their white flowers. Among the trees and shrubs, along the walk before mentioned, were, a straight erect arbor vitae, upwards of 30 feet high, with a clear trunk 1 feet in diameter; immense rhododendrons, azaleas, and laurustinus; and a black spruce, 50 feet high, feathered to the ground, its lowest branches rooted in the soil, and their points forming a circle of young trees ranged round their parent.'* [96]

This was a very different garden from that on the map of 1749. Sharpham is now owned by the Sharpham Trust, an educational charity.

173. *'View of Totnes'* by William Havell, c.1830. One of the attractions of Sharpham has been the view of the river Dart as well as that from its grounds upriver towards Totnes: in 1842 John Claudius Loudon, the botanist and designer, was a great admirer of this drive. He suggested that by widening it would become one of the *'loveliest drives in the world'*. [97]

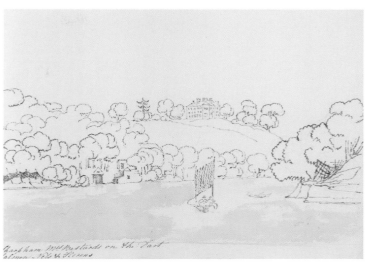

174. View entitled *'Sharpham, Mrs Bastards on the Dart, salmon nets and herons'* by Henrietta Matilda Crompton, 1840.

175. Photograph of Sharpham from the river Dart, c.1890-1900.

Outwell 28.th February 1755

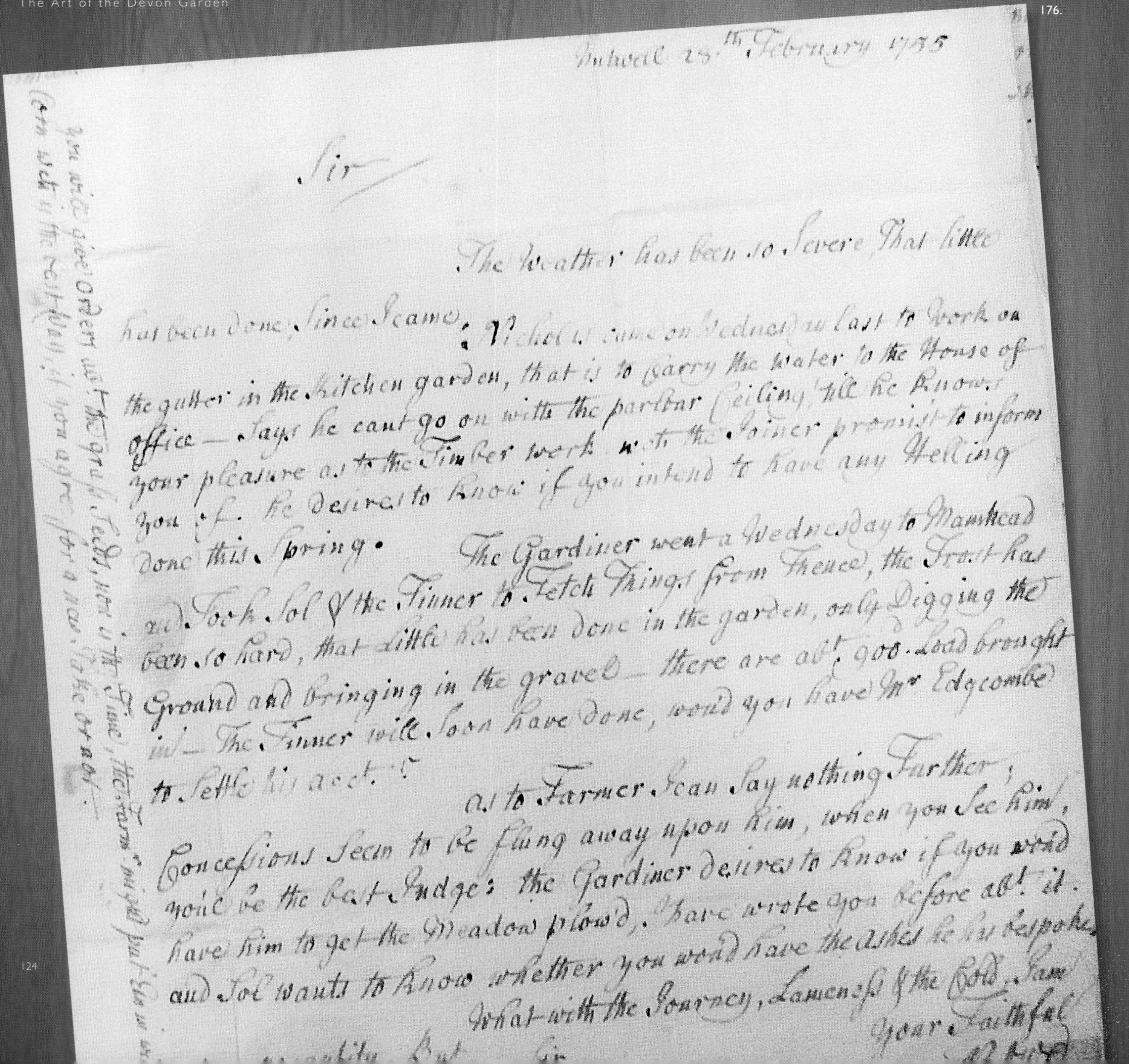

Sir

The weather has been so Severe, That little has been done, since I came. Nichols came on Wednesday last to work on the gutter in the kitchen garden, that is to carry the water to the House of office — says he cant go on with the parlour Ceiling, till he knows your pleasure as to the Timber work. w.th the Joiner promist to inform you of. He desires to know if you intend to have any Welling done this Spring.

The Gardiner went a Wednesday to Mamhead and Took Sol & the Tinner to Fetch Things from Thence, the Frost has been so hard, that little has been done in the garden, only Digging the Ground and bringing in the gravel — there are ab.t 900 Load brought in — The Tinner will soon have done, wou'd you have Mr Edgcombe to Settle his acc.t

As to Farmer, I can say nothing Further; Concessions seem to be flung away upon him, when you see him, you'l be the best Judge: the Gardiner desires to know if you wou'd have him to get the Meadow plow'd, I have wrote you before ab.t it. and Sol wants to know whether you wou'd have the ashes he has bespoke.

What with the Journey, Lameness & the Cold, I am

Your faithful

The letters of Nicholas Rowe at Nutwell Court near Lympstone

1749 – 1767

177.

178.

Devon's most informative series of garden letters written by an estate manager to his employer are those of Nicholas Rowe to Sir Francis Henry Drake. This Georgian correspondence comprises nearly three hundred letters and provides a unique view of the day-to-day events in a garden.

The Drake family acquired Nutwell Court through the Pollexen family. Sir Francis Henry Drake came into his inheritance at the age of 18, in 1741, and used Nutwell as his main seat while his mother lived in the dower house, Buckland Abbey. Its position near Exeter may have been more convenient to Drake who was an absent owner. He lived mainly in London where he found employment as clerk comptroller of the Board of Green Cloth in 1753 and then eighteen years later as Master of the Household in the court of King George III.[98]

Even so, he greatly valued his garden and the privacy that it gave him. In 1793 one learned vicar, who resided across the river Exe, wrote that Drake *was pleased to confine himself within the narrow circuit of his own grounds; averse from social communication and particularly inaccessible to men of talents and literature*'. Drake's successor was equally known for his privacy. One visitor commented, in 1795, that no Spanish Don was more jealous of other men eyeing his wife than Lord Heathfield was of visitors to his garden. A generation later another owner corrected the text of an intended book on Devon by deleting that his garden was open to the public. He wrote that it *never has been the case*'.[99]

176. Letter of Nicholas Rowe to Sir Francis Henry Drake, 25 February 1755.

177.–182. Six watercolours by John Swete of Nutwell, 1793.

Inset: *Ornamental Design with Fruit and Flowers*, Alexis Peyrotte, mid 1700s.

179.

180.

181.

182.

183. Sketch by Admonition Radcliffe of the new house at Nutwell, 1830s. Admonition Peter Radcliffe was the daughter of the vicar of Tamerton Foliot and would have been in her forties when she made this drawing.

Nutwell, located on the eastern bank of the river Exe between Topsham and Lympstone, was more convenient for Drake as a residence than Buckland Abbey. Even so, it needed considerable repair and the letters are full of the details of restoration and rebuilding. Drake's heir destroyed the house and rebuilt it in the shape that it has today.

Rowe's letters reveal that he knew little about gardens and that his employer was highly enthusiastic about them. Rowe had been born in 1692 and was thus aged 57 when the surviving correspondence on Nutwell's garden began. Drake was only 27. The correspondence suggests a mutual respect between the two men and it may be that Rowe had known Drake's father, who had died when his son was aged 16, and was taking a paternal role.

The letters demonstrate Rowe's lack of knowledge in gardening. He informed his employer of various events such as the rabbits eating the flowers, the birds ravaging the cherries, the wasps that consumed the figs and plums and even worms that devoured the roots of trees. He thought the rats were like an Egyptian plague. Drake chronicled the planting of cedars (1754), laurels and evergreen oaks (1755), black poplars (1758), barberries (1759), orange trees (1760), Weymouth pines (1761), a white fig (1762), myrtle (1763), Scotch pines (1765) and phillyrea (1766). Through his letters it is learned that there were grape vines, a cistus, plane trees, a raspberry tree, a strawberry tree, weeping willow and cypresses. Rowe's letters also show how in 1755 the gardens at Mamhead were plundered for plants when the house was sold to Wilmot Vaughan, first Earl of Lisburne.

In November 1754 Rowe informed Drake:

'The gardener has laid the walk next the upper wall & is forward in that against the new wall, he has planted several pears, but can't find Number IX as directed by the paper you left him. But the label lay in the passage window, so presume you forgot it.'

The care with which Rowe informed his employer of garden developments and the keen interest obviously taken by Drake in his garden also demonstrate a familiarity between them. The letters are informative about mid Georgian gardens but they also show the practicalities of getting work done. Rowe died in 1785 and Drake followed him only nine years later.[100] Nutwell is a private residence.

185. Detail from Benjamin Donn's map showing the position of Mount Galpin in relation to Dartmouth, 1765.

184. Oil painting by Arthur Devis of Arthur Holdsworth entitled *'Arthur Holdsworth Conversing with Thomas Taylor and Captain Stancombe by the River Dart, 1757'*

186. Oil painting by Arthur Devis entitled *'Robert and Elizabeth Gwillym and their family, of Atherton Hall, Herefordshire'*, 1745-7. Another portrait painting by Devis in which a conversation is taking place.

Arthur Holdsworth

Dartmouth
1757

This painting is misleading if the viewer is intent upon discovering details about the sitter's garden. This type of portrait, known as a conversation piece, is also known for being deceptive about the landscape.

This portrait of Arthur Holdsworth indicates the type of garden that he or the artist, Arthur Devis, wanted to project. The artist's construction has little to do with topographic reality and only one of his other paintings was accurate in this respect.[101] Holdsworth had two homes: one situated on the northern side of Dartmouth below what was then Mount Boone and the other in the parish of Stokenham. If Holdsworth had wanted to view the castle from his Dartmouth home, which was named Mount Galpin, the river would have been on the opposite side to that painted. His other home, Widdicombe, lies some ten miles from the castle. This is not only too far from which to see the castle but it is situated in a different direction. The artist has most likely included the castle because Holdsworth was its governor and the prominent ship is an indicator of the family's long interest in fishing and trade. The background is meant to signify Holdsworth's status as is the aspirational garden in which he sits. Arthur Devis, born in Lancashire, was in his mid forties when he painted Holdsworth. Many of his 300 surviving paintings are of members of the established classes. He drew his clientele from the gentry and the professions.[102]

The painting is entitled *Arthur Holdsworth Conversing with Thomas Taylor and Captain Stancombe by the River Dart* and is dated 1757. This would have made Holdsworth 24 years old at the time. Taylor was his brother-in-law and presumably Stancombe, who is pointing towards the ship and castle, was one of his captains. The artist might have taken his inspiration from the garden at Widdicombe. The house had been recently rebuilt and the garden may have been redesigned. It follows a fashionable ideal for an aspirational member to the gentry. The tower is in some ways similar to that of Stokenham's ancient church. Devis may be attempting to suggest that Holdsworth, even at a distance from the castle, was au fait with any developments at the castle, but the composition would have puzzled many viewers. What the composition successfully conveys is the status of the main seated figure and the depicted garden plays a subtle part in that impression.

Inset: *Flowers in a Silver Caster, Fruit in the Foreground,* Jacques André Portail, eighteenth century.

187. Oil painting by Arthur Devis entitled *'Members of the Maynard Family in the Park at Waltons',* c.1755/1762.

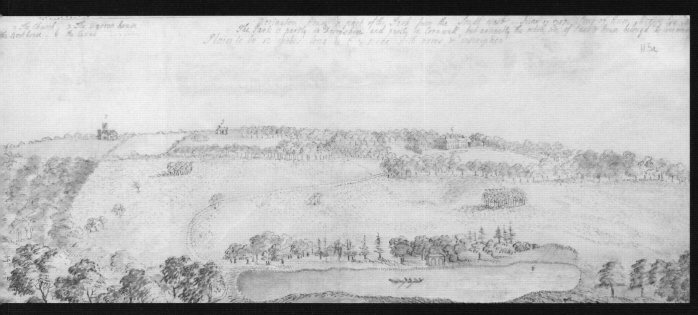

Drawing by William
Borlase, 1757. Borlase
inscribed on his drawing
'Werrington House and
part of the park from the
southwest, June 17 1757.
Seat of Hum: Morice
Esquire. The Park is partly
in Devonshire and partly in
Cornwall, but anciently the
whole site of Park & House
belonged to Cornwall'.

189. Detail showing lake, boat and ornamental building.

190. Drawing by Edmund Prideaux, 1716, entitled `Werrington Sir Nicholas Morice baronet in the county
of Devon', 1716. Harris noted that Elizabeth Prideaux married Sir William Morice.

Werrington Park

1757

Werrington is one of the two Devon gardens to be associated with an ancient curse.

Reverend William Borlase, a Cornishman, is best known as an antiquary and naturalist but he was also a draughtsman. In the 1750s he recorded, in a small book, a number of views of houses in Cornwall. He was then 61 years old and intent upon writing a topographical history of the county but abandoned the project in 1757, at the time this view was created.[103]

Like Mount Edgcumbe and Forde Abbey, this house and garden were formerly part of the county of Devon. Borlase noted an amphitheatre which lay on the far west and a building later recorded as the Temple of the Sun. The church, which had only recently been moved, was noted and by it the warren house. Borlase also pointed out the canal and its boathouse. Prideaux's drawing, 41 years earlier, has fewer details of the landscape and shows the church in its original position.

In 1750, in between when these images were drawn, a visitor to Werrington noted there was, among the features, a folly in the shape of a ruined castle, the Temple of the Sun in a woodland, a terrace, Triumphal Arch and hermitage. The moving of the church and bodies from their graves gave rise to a local legend that the family was cursed. It was later said that *'parishioners watched with outraged feelings the carts removing their dead'*.[104] The former graveyard was then used by the family to extend their garden. The house remains in private ownership.

192. Detail of map by Mathew Blackamoore of Tracey showing the front garden, 1763. A sheet of water lies outside eight distinct compartments with the two nearest the house particularly highly designed. The walls are lined with trained plants.

Tracey House

Awliscombe
1763

The gardens depicted at Tracey were, by 1763, of an outdated style which was then giving way to the naturalistic movement with which English gardens have become associated.

193. Lithograph entitled 'Tracey House, the seat of H. B. Lott, Esquire M. P.', by Featherstone after T. Earle, c.1830.

The year that this map was drawn was also the year in which Tracey's most illustrious occupant was born. Mary Anne Burges would become a linguist, successful author and noted botanist. She is also the first Devon woman to be credited in print as being intelligent. According to one Georgian

Inset: *A rose-eyed nightingale,* George Edwards, eighteenth-century.

194. Blackamoore's map shows the formal garden as well as the kitchen garden and several orchards. In the early 1800s the garden was developed with an extensive series of woodland walks with specimen trees, a rustic summerhouse and a yew circle.

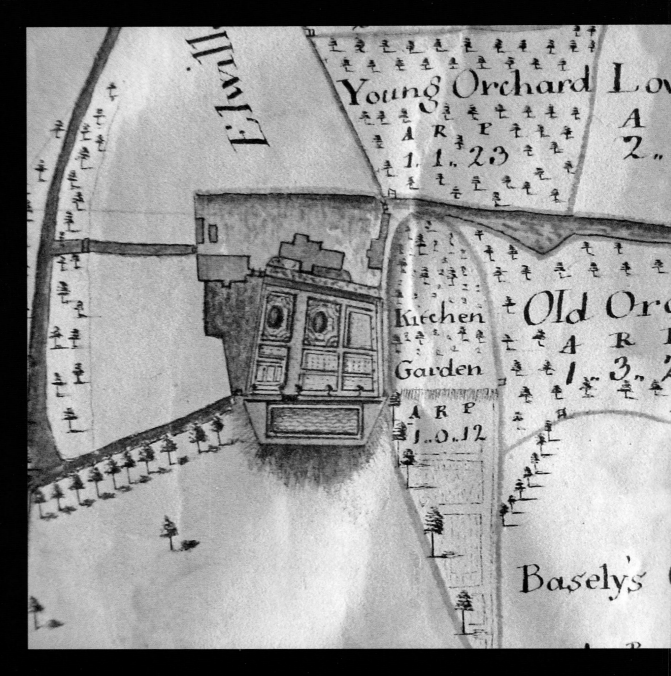

writer, Reverend Richard Polwhele, her 'classical taste and knowledge of botany and ornithology are accompanied with all the diffidence of an ingenious mind'. In 1792 he met her at Oxton, the home of John Swete who was Polwhele's neighbour, fellow cleric, onetime friend and eventual rival. Burges noted that 'Mr Polwhele was there and took notes of some discourse I held relative to cowslips'. Perhaps her female successor in local botany was Agnes Ibbetson, who lived in Exeter and who experimented with green manure in 1817.[107]

A collection of her letters reveals her interest in watercolours and in plants. In one letter of 1792 she wrote:

'I went this morning with Mr & Mrs Martin to see a collection of flowers painted in a new style. The impression of the plant, with all its fibres, is first taken off (it appeared to me in the way I have formerly seen with two Balls of Leather) & it is afterwards painted from life. Very little shading is requisite to produce an effect much superior to what is to be met with in most painted flowers & the natural habit of the plant is preserved in the utmost perfection. If I can get him to tell me exactly how it is done, I will transmit it to you; as you may perhaps like to try it. He then carried me to Ford's [nursery] Garden & showed me all the curious plants, &, as he is a great Botanist, I gained much information.' [108]

That same year she visited John White Abbot, the Exeter artist.

'I was extremely gratified by being carried to Mr Abbot's & seeing all his Pictures, which I admired full as much as you had given the reason to expect. Besides these, he has done a most beautiful & voluminous collection of views of the lakes of Scotland & Westmoreland & the country he passed thro in going there.' [109]

Burges leased Tracey in 1786. On one occasion she was visited at home by a Turkish admiral who expressed astonishment that an English lady would live alone without the protection of a male relative.[110]

By 1763 Tracey's gardens were becoming old-fashioned. The formal gardens were giving way elsewhere to less geometric patterns. Two generations later, in 1840, the grounds were laid out in a far simpler way: the tithe map shows two drives converged just before the house and the area in front of the house has been sectioned off to provide a square shape for the house and ornamental garden. By the late nineteenth century a more complicated garden had evolved with walks through the neighbouring woodland.

Tracey House was demolished in 2003 and the site remains in private ownership.

195. Oil painting of the Amphitheatre by William Tomkins, 1770. Boringdon Hall is in the distance.

The Amphitheatre
Saltram
1770

Amphitheatres were a Georgian feature found in several Devon gardens but this one is the only one to survive. William Tomkins is known as a painter of landscapes and was in his late thirties when he made this view.

It is one of seven paintings of his in the collection at Saltram, the former home of the Parker family.[111] Tomkins' view of the Amphitheatre was made not long after this ornamental feature was created along the Laira. It no longer has a roof nor the urns on the parapet but is seen each day by thousands of passengers who travel into Plymouth on the main approach road from Exeter. Tomkins shows how in 1770 it acted as Saltram's entry point for those coming by boat. The grounds were being developed then by Nathaniel Richmond, the landscape designer who had worked with Capability Brown. The statue of a gladiator is thought to have been stolen in the early 1800s.[112]

Twenty years after Tomkins painted the Amphitheatre it was visited on 17 May 1790 by Reverend John Swete. He was more interested in the limekilns which appear in the distance of Tomkins' painting but he noted that the Amphitheatre was a woodland theatre. Swete annotated his watercolour.

'The lime kilns on the Plymouth road opposite Saltram Woods are several of them in a ruinous state, and thus dilapidated and chequered with ivy, have the appearance of fortified towers fallen to decay. The situation is peculiarly beautiful. From the one taken, is seen the arcade building, all of moorstone, exhibiting itself in the center of a theatre of firs and other trees — walks lead from hence on the left towards the house, on the right thro a stretch of woods on the cliff, to a promontory which thrusting itself into an arm of the sea terminates the grounds of Lord Boringdon — in the range are seen several edifices — an ice house, a grotto, Baths and a battery. The lawn very fine, skirted by green sward walks within a pale fence where is a gothic temple of no striking beauty, and a large Green House. The House itself hath a handsome front and is very well situated. The only room of any consequence (is) the Saloon which is exceeded in elegance & expence by few in the kingdom. The pictures in several rooms admirable — excellent portraits by Sir Joshua Reynolds, a native of Plympton just

196. Drawing entitled *'Gladiator at Saltram'* by William Brockedon, 1800.

Inset: *Basket of fruit with parrot*, A. M. Randall, 1777.

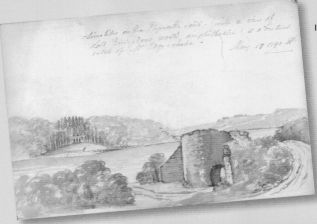

197. Pen and wash by John Swete with inscription *'Lime kilns on the Plymouth road with a view of Lord Boringdon's woods Amphitheatre & a distant catch of Mount Edgcumbe',* 17 May 1790. The road is still known as Plymouth Road.

198. Untitled watercolour by William Payne, no date given. The view is towards the south with Saltram on the left and the Amphitheatre also shown. Payne was born in 1760 and although a Londoner he knew the area well from 1783. That year he began a six-year project of surveying Plymouth's defences and during this time he married in the port. Payne became a popular drawing master particularly among members of the aristocracy.[113]

199. Drawing entitled *'Saltram, Lord Boringdon's House at Plymouth'*, no date, by Richard Cooper the Younger.

by, Van Dyke, Titian, Loutherbourg, Canaletto etc. magnificent Pier Glasses in Saloon, beautiful inlaid tables of square pieces polished foreign marbles, chimney pieces, painted ceilings &c – approach to the house there a lodge & fine wooded hollow – near lodge fine Gardens hot houses etc.'

Swete came to Saltram a year after it had hosted George III and his household. Fanny Burney, the well-known writer who was with the party, noted of the Laira, which borders the northern edge of the grounds, that `the sea at times fills up a part of the domain almost close to the house and then its prospect is complete'. Burney thought the woodland was enchanting.[114] Twenty years later, in 1810, Joseph Farington visited Saltram and noted 'at *high water the appearance must be fine, but at low water much shore of a bad colour and naked effect cannot be pleasing*'.[115]

The royal visit of 1789 is the most famous single event to take place at Saltram. One of those present assessed the garden as being:

'about a mile from the house, extensive and replete with every fruit and vegetable, both native and exotic. The Greenhouse, if possible, commands a still more extensive prospect – on the left of it is a neat domestic chapel. In short, there is nothing in nature more beautiful, nothing in art more elegant and curious.' [116]

That same year another visitor acknowledged that the grounds at Saltram would be more highly thought of had it not been for 'so great a rival (Mount Edgcumbe) just opposite'.[117]

201. Candlestick figure made of Plymouth porcelain, 1770. She carries flowers in one hand and a basket in the other. The trunk of a tree, covered with flowers, forms a background, 1770.

202. A statue made of Plymouth porcelain to resemble a Native American woman, 1770. She is meant to signify America, is partly wearing cotton fabric decorated with flowers and has a floral headdress. The animal at her feet is puzzling.

200. Vase made of Plymouth porcelain, 1770. It has been painted with a bouquet and detached sprays of flowers around which is a butterfly and ladybird.

203. A candlestick figure of a gardener.

204. Figure group of two boys feeding a goat.

Plymouth porcelain
1770

Plymouth Porcelain is not as well known as other Devon pottery for one very good reason.

The production of porcelain in Devon can barely be discussed in terms of years: experiments were undertaken at Bovey Tracey in 1766 and then at Plymouth where the factory opened for production in 1769. The following year operations had moved to Bristol. This brief period witnessed the first attempts at recreating Chinese porcelain in the South West and the few objects that can be identified from these years show how local china clay and china stone were used to produce hard paste porcelain, otherwise called true porcelain, of a high quality.

This endeavour was the first in England and it would not be attempted again until the twentieth century. The impetus behind the idea was William Cookworthy, a successful Quaker pharmacist who lived in Plymouth.

Many of the designs incorporate floral motifs. These were Rococo designs, slightly old-fashioned by then, and probably dependent upon French design. One Monsieur Soqui, who may have originated from Sevres, appears to have been working at the factory.[118] The delicacy of the porcelain, and of its designs, stands in stark contrast to the pottery being produced at this time in north Devon.

Inset: *The Music Lesson,* Joseph Willems at Chelsea. 1765.

205. Another candlestick figure which has also been painted with enamels and gilded.

Whiteway
near Chudleigh
1771

These two paintings are unusual in that they provide not only a view of a substantial house but also one of the view from it.

William Tomkins' paintings of Saltram are supplemented by these two of Whiteway near Chudleigh, a second Parker house. The house was rebuilt by the first Lord Boringdon shortly before Tomkins painted these views. His treatment is similar to that at Saltram, as well as with other views of Mount Edgcumbe and Tapeley Park. The house sits within impressive grounds and the viewer is assured of the status of the occupants.

Whiteway was the home of Lord Boringdon's younger brother and it continued in the possession of the Parker family. During the late 1800s they, like the Courtenay family at Powderham Castle, rented their main home and moved into a smaller residence.[119]

Ordnance survey maps show that by the late 1800s there was a formal garden in front of the house and the drive was much as it had been in the late eighteenth century. A century after Tomkins painted Whiteway the census recorded that there was only one gardener by the name of William Campbell, a forty-six year old Scot.

206. Painting by William Tomkins entitled *'Whiteway, Devonshire'*, c.1771.

207. Painting by William Tomkins entitled *'View from Whiteway towards Dartmoor'*, c.1771.

   Inset: *Brucea Antidysenterica,* Frederick P. Nodder, 1777.

208. Watercolour by John Swete entitled *'Whiteway, seat of the Yardes'*, 10 July 1795. Swete was particularly interested in Whiteway because his mother had been born there. He noted that the house had a commanding position but ignored whatever garden may have been in the front courtyard.

209. Drawing by Mathew Blackamore, Exeter, entitled '*A view of the house of Robert Orme, near Topsham in Devon*', May 1773.

The Retreat

Topsham
1773

210. Watercolour by John Swete entitled *'South east view of the Retreat'*, 1796.

211. Swete's second watercolour, also of 1796, is entitled *'Retreat seat of Sir Alexander Hamilton'*.

The formal garden at the Retreat, a former sugar house, must have had a striking effect from the river Exe.

This view was drawn in 1773 and shows geometric planting on the side of the house with the river in the background.[120] By 1794, when Reverend Swete visited, the gardens had changed. He noted the Retreat as *'this, now a most excellent house, was about thirty years ago a sugar house – with the materials Mr Orme received for himself a mansion, which by the addition of an attic storey has received vast improvements from the hand of the present possessor'*. He noted gardens, a greenhouse and that the *'greater part of the beautiful shrubberies have been raised by him'*.[121]

The Retreat began in 1684 when a Plymouth sugar manufacturer purchased the land and erected the building to refine sugar. Nearly a hundred years later, in 1769, it was acquired by Robert Orme of nearby Clyst St George. He rebuilt it as a domestic building.

Orme employed Mathew Blackamore, an Exeter surveyor and artist, to draw the new house. Blackamore kept a drawing school opposite the Guildhall in High Street where he not only taught architectural drawing but also garden design. He also worked at Tracey in 1763.

The building to the right of the house could have belonged to the earlier sugar refinery and may have been the pavilion with hot and cold baths which was noted in 1773. The Retreat is now in multiple ownership.[122]

Inset: *The Flower Garden,* Matthew Darly, 1777.

212. North Devon harvest jug
by John Phillips, 1780.

North Devon pottery
1780

Clay deposits at Fremington have been used to create pottery in North Devon since the late Medieval period and the results contrasted greatly with the porcelain which was for a short while being produced in Plymouth.

Potters decorated either by applying liquid (or slip) clay to dip pots or trail patterns on them, known as slip trailing, or by scratching designs which is termed sgrafitto.[123] This harvest jug was made by John Phillips and, like many, incorporated floral motifs. It has on the opposite side the motto:

> When I was in my native Place, I was a lump of Clay, and Diged was out of the Earth and Brought from thence a Way, but now I am a Jugg became, by Potters Art and Skiel, and now your Servant am Become, and carry alle I will. Made by Jo(hn) PH(illips) Pott. 1780.

Potters were occasionally inspired by local plants but the designs were less sophisticated than those used for Plymouth's porcelain. The North Devon pottery came from an older English tradition rather than the new porcelain, made at the same time, which was following China in production and a new Georgian manner in design. The North Devon floral designs were also more accurate in depicting local plants.

Inset: *Mid-Day Rest, harvest,*
William Frederick Witherington, c.1840.

214–215. This jug by T. Jones, 1792, features Ceres, *'goddess of the harvest'* and the motto *'Harvest is come, all busy now, in making of the Barley mow, If you the Barley now neglect, you cannot then Good Ale Expect'.*

213. A slightly earlier jug with a compass, birds and flowers, 1764.

213.

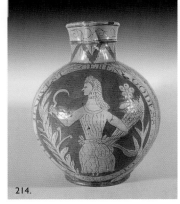

214.

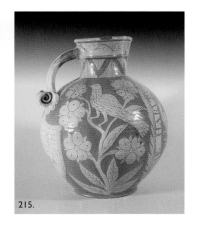

215.

216. Watercolour by an unknown artist entitled *'A colored view of Great Fulford House, the seat of Baldwin Fulford, Esq., in the parish of Dunsford'*, 1780.

217. Detail of Reverend John Swete's watercolour of Great Fulford, 6 September 1792.

Great Fulford
1780

Great Fulford had already been home to the Fulford family for generations when this watercolour was made.

218. Graphite and ink on paper entitled *'Great Fulford'* by Francis Towne, 8 August 1776.

Inset: *Vase of Flowers and Conch Shell,* Anne Vallayer-Coster, 1780.

It was singled out by Professor Hoskins in his landmark history of Devon: he wrote:

> *'it is the only house of this kind in Devon which still remains in the hands of the original family who have occupied this site since at least the latter part of the 12th century and who take their name from it'.* [124]

John Fulford had the lake created in the 1760s. [125] Thirteen years later Reverend Polwhele noted the house had gardens, fishponds and a park.
He wrote:

> *'The approach to the house from the lodge is about a mile, through the park. The house stands on a rising ground near a sheet of water. It consists of a quadrangle. The entrance is through a gateway, in which is a door leading into a small but neat chapel. There are two good eating-rooms, and a very handsome drawing room, 42 feet in length, and of proportionable height and breadth, containing several good paintings. There are a great number of convenient bedchambers. Great Fulford house, as Westcote and Prince describe it, is a large and stately pile, standing pleasantly on a gentle ascent, in an open but somewhat coarse country. It suffered much in the grand rebellion; when it was garrisoned on behalf of Charles the 1st. It was, however, completely repaired at the expense of Colonel Francis Fulford'.* [126]

A few years later, in 1819, another writer added somewhat to Polwhele's description by noting:

> *'It stands on a rising ground, near an extensive sheet of water: its form is quadrangular; and it has a large entrance gateway… The park, which abounds with trees, and has received considerable improvement from the present proprietor, affords many delightful views'.* [127]

The tithe map of 1838 shows the sheet of water, a complicated series of drives and walkways leading around and to the house, and planting behind.

219. Oil painting entitled *'Haldon Hall near Exeter'* by Francis Towne, 1780.

Haldon House
near Exeter
1780

Haldon was once one of the great houses of Devon and its landscape was filled with acres of woodland.

Haldon was built in the early 1700s for Sir George Chudleigh and at the time that Francis Towne painted this view it was the home of Robert Palk. Eight years later he built the now familiar landmark (Haldon Belvedere) that commemorates his friend General Stringer. The house is perched just below the Haldon Ridge and looks out towards Exeter.

The development of the house was sketched out by Reverend Polwhele in 1793:

'In point of architecture, Haldon-house merits attention. About 70 years since, Sir George Chudleigh began to build Haldon House: it is one of the best modern houses in Devonshire, executed after the model of Buckingham-house in St. James's park. Sir George Chudleigh died before the building was completed. At his decease, Haldon House consisted of four regular fronts, six rooms on a floor, with suitable offices in separate wings. Haldon House was built of brick, which Sir Robert Palk covered with Rawlinson's patent stucco: this gives it the appearance of a free-stone structure. There were formerly slopes and steps that led up to the hall door; so that the offices below were underground. All this ascent Sir Robert Palk removed, and laid open the offices; by which the house appears one story higher than before. The great front is eastward. Two geometrical staircases, one at the north, the other at the south end, were lately erected. The gardens on the south side of the house were removed to some little distance by Sir Robert and their place is now occupied by lawn, with suitable plantations. The improvements round the house are happily planned: and the rapid and vigorous growth of the many thousand trees, which have been recently planted, excites our surprise, from the high and open situations where they flourish. Sir Robert Palk has, by act of parliament, enclosed some hundreds of acres from Haldon, for the purposes of extending his plantations.'[128]

In 1898 it was said that the original building had 365 windows, one for each day of the year.[129] The main house was demolished in 1920. Part of the remainder now forms the Lord Haldon Hotel.

Inset: *A flower piece,* Benjamin Green, 1779.

220. Drawing by Thomas Allom for a steel line engraving by W. Le Petit, 1831.

221. The old house at Oxton in 1781, as painted by Reverend Swete.

222. Reverend Swete's new home as depicted in a watercolour by himself entitled *'East view of Oxton House'*, August 1789.

223. Oxton's stretch of water as painted by Swete, 1795.

224. Oxton as situated below Haldon Hills by John Swete, 1795.

225. The ruined entrance gate by John Swete, 1795.

226. The quarry and entrance to the hermit's cave, 1795.

Oxton
near Kenn
1781

This series of watercolours demonstrate the leisure time the artist enjoyed after he changed his surname from Tripe to Swete in order to inherit a fortune from his childless aunt.

The wealth also allowed Reverend John Tripe to demolish his home, Oxton, and redesign the landscape. He estimated that he spent £6,000 in his endeavours. Swete was then nearly thirty years old. A few years later he married and the couple had twelve children, all but two of whom were girls. Swete's wealth partly came from sugar plantations in Jamaica and Antigua where he noted he had *'slaves, negroes and piccaninnies'*.

Oxton is situated below Haldon Hill with views down to the Exe Estuary. Just as William Gilpin was the father of the national Picturesque Movement, Swete was its greatest proponent in Devon. The grounds were laid out in its terms. He removed the terrace with its topiary work and created a lawn with open views of the landscape. It became a Picturesque Paradise.

A lake was formed in the valley and near to it was built a gate to suggest an ancient structure. Unfortunately the workmen built it too perfectly and it had to be taken down to achieve the correct ruined effect. A rock face was cut to give the appearance of a quarry and a hermit's cave was carved out of its side. It had a bed of stone with a pillow of the same material. A summerhouse was built above Oxton and nearby was the Shed, a thatched structure in which to take in the views.

Swete was well-read and studied the work of not just Gilpin but Capability Brown and William Kent. He was all but forgotten by the generation following his death in 1821. Two generations later interest revived in his written work and watercolours.[130] Oxton is now divided into multi-ownership.

227. The summerhouse by John Swete, 1795.

228. The thatched *'Shed'* by John Swete, 1795.

Inset: *Study of Three Flowers,* Johann Christian August Birnbaum, 1781.

229. Watercolour entitled *'Mamhead'*, by Miss F. L. Oglander, 1787. The Obelisk is seen to the right.

Mamhead

1787

In 1785, two years before this view was painted, a Hampshire visitor recorded in his travel journal that Mamhead was a *'very noble place seeing so many fine views around it, rather a poor House'.*[131] By that date the prospects from it were impressive as was the landscape but the house had become unimposing.

Mamhead has one of the most remarkable recorded histories, and visual records, of a house and garden in Devon. It was noted by the Normans, more than 900 years ago, in the Exeter Domesday Book. The name is a conglomeration of the words teat and head and refers to the shape of this prominent hill.[132]

The Balle family were lords of the manor from the sixteenth century and it was Sir Peter Balle, a lawyer and Attorney General to Queen Henrietta Maria, who rebuilt it in the mid 1600s. He *'was allured by the beauties of the situation which he could not resist'*. A later writer commented that his political ambitions were unsuccessful at the Restoration and thus he could not afford to develop the estate to the extent he had wished.[133]

In the late 1600s his son Robert was resident in northern Italy as a merchant in the firm of Death & Skinner. He was described there as *'known to be a turbulent sort of man, that never speaks well of any one behind their backs, but fawns to their faces'.*[134] Once he returned to England Balle became a Member of Parliament and set up home at Mamhead. He was one of 15 surviving children. Balle landscaped the grounds with the Italian plants he had become interested in. One Georgian writer commented that he *'fell into the old error of torturing nature and deforming the face of it, by raising gardens with terraces, and making ponds and fountains on the sides of hills'*. The formal gardens were accompanied by extensive plantations.[135] This was presumably the terrace described in 1750 as rising behind the house up along the hill.[136]

His nephew Thomas, also a member of Parliament, built the stone obelisk which stands at some one hundred feet and continued to embellish *'the boldly-swelling grounds at Mamhead with*

230. The earlier house at Mamhead as depicted by William Glynn in his watercolour entitled *'Mamhead'*, 1810.

231. Watercolour of the south face of the house by Anthony Salvin, c.1832.

232. Watercolour of the stables by Anthony Salvin, c.1832.

plantations; and is said to have brought, for this purpose from the Continent, a great quantity of cork, wainscot, oak, Spanish chestnut, acacia, cedar, and other exotic trees'. At some point it appears to have been known as *'Balle's Folly, so strong was the opinion, that trees would not bear such exposure'* but these plantations have defined the grounds.[137] Another Georgian writer credited the Balle family with planting the first acorns of the Quercus ilex in England[138] while the writer of an early eighteenth-century gardening book attributed Thomas Balle, a *'curious and learned gentleman'*, with great knowledge in transplanting *'forest trees'*.[139] Balle employed William Lucombe, the founder of the nursery which was at St Thomas near Exeter.[140]

Thomas Balle was the last of his family to live at Mamhead and was noted by one visitor as a *'humourist'*. He described him in unflattering terms as a *'mule of such a stubborn temper that he does no one thing that any person would or would have him do'*. Mamhead was grudgingly described as a good house but it was claimed that the rooms with filled with broken furniture and the floors were *'strewn with turds of dogs'*.[141]

Mamhead was subsequently purchased by Sir Robert Newman, yet another member of Parliament, who rebuilt the house on a new site and redesigned the gardens. Anthony Salvin, then twenty-six, was chosen in 1826 as the architect.[142] The new building received enthusiastic praise for its Tudor style. One writer thought that it embraced *'almost all the beautiful peculiarities remarkable in the domestic architecture of that period'*. He went on to describe:

> *'the whole exterior of the mansion, nearly eight hundred feet in circumference, is of Bath stone, very skilfully wrought, the tall chimney stacks and gables, highly ornamented, present a variety of different forms in succession, which are relieved by two square and two octagonal towers rising with extremely good effect. There are four fronts to this edifice, uniform in general design but considerably varied in detail, a mode of construction hitherto un-attempted by modern architects, but much practiced in the earlier periods. The whole building being raised on a broad terrace, gives it all the dignity required in a mansion of importance'.*

He added that along the southern front was a flower garden and an elegant conservatory stood at the end of the building.[143] A generation later, in 1858, a visitor was overwhelmed by the grandeur of a single bed in the terrace. It stood between 50 and 60 feet in diameter, was raised slightly in the centre, and was planted only with scarlet geraniums.[144]

The first census taken after Mamhead was rebuilt, in 1841, listed Newman's household as standing at 25 persons. Sixteen of them were servants. John Claudius Loudon visited the following year and made a curious comment on the interior of Mamhead. He described it as being in general admirable but thought the representations of plants in the ceiling, although accurate and beautiful in itself, were in bad taste.[145] Loudon was more enthusiastic about what had been achieved in the grounds. He wrote:

233. Undated graphite, watercolour and ink entitled *'View of Mamhead, Devonshire'* attributed to John Preston Neale, c.1832.

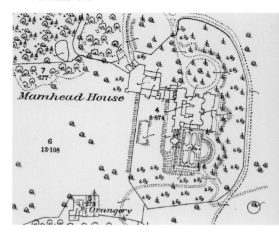

234. Pencil and ink sketch by Henrietta Matilda Crompton inscribed `View from the library window at Mamhead of Exmouth the woods of Powderham. Sir Robert Newman built a beautiful house on the splendid property belonging to Lord Lisbourne. Mr Salvin the Architect. Poured with rain', 1840.

235. Detail from Ordnance Survey map of Mamhead, 1890.

'The conservatory at Mamhead is much too small for the situation; but, considering the house as a villa, it is, perhaps, not altogether out of proportion. Part of the roof is opaque, which we were surprised at; because that part is completely concealed by the parapet, and the light would have been of essential importance to the plants. There are upper and lower terraces; but the latter is not, in our opinion, sufficiently separated from the park by architectural parapets and other forms to justify the introduction of flowers on it. The fortification-like character is also, we think, too conspicuous in some parts, and the lines of slope and surface of glacis are, in others, disproportionately large for the height of the house. There is a flower-garden in a sunk panel, very judiciously designed and laid out; but it is planted with shrubs and other articles growing to the height of 3 or 4 feet, which prevent the shapes of the beds from being seen in a birds-eye view, so as to form a whole. Instead of this, the beds should have been planted with articles which do not rise above the height of 6 or 8 inches; or with roses having their shoots pegged down on green moss, so as not much to exceed that height. As an appendage to such a house, this garden ought to have been in much higher keeping: but perfect high keeping, in Devonshire we have only seen at Luscombe and at Endsleigh. The terrace walks at Mamhead are not yet united with the pleasure-ground, which, indeed, remains to be formed; and a finer situation for forming a pleasure-ground walk very rarely occurs. We took the dimensions of two or three immense Lucombe oaks and cork trees, which we need not here repeat, because they are much the same as those given of the same trees in our Arboretum as measured in 1837. The dimensions now taken were, for want of time, not made with sufficient accuracy to be useful in showing the increase of the trees since that period. The kitchen-garden is at a distance from the house, very unfavourably situated in a hollow; but, notwithstanding this, we have seldom seen walls more beautifully covered with fruit trees, especially with peaches and nectarines; the borders are not cropped.' [146]

The grounds at Mamhead remain in part, nine centuries after being recorded. The house and grounds are in private ownership.

236. Watercolour entitled *'From the Belvedere at Powderham'* by Miss F. L. Oglander, 1787. Exmouth can be seen in the distance.

237. Painting by unknown artist, c.1850, of the Powderham Belvedere.

The Belvederes
1787

Devon has two belvederes, each triangular, which were built fifteen years and only six miles apart. Each was constructed as ornaments for large estates and both have served as local landmarks for more than two hundred years.

That at Powderham was built in the early 1770s by William, second Viscount Courtenay. In 1793 Reverend Polwhele wrote approvingly of it. He noted:

'To enjoy a full and uninterrupted view of this beautiful scene, and of the diversified country around it, some building was necessary to be erected on one of the most commanding heights. And the late Lord Courtenay, whose taste deserves every commendation, made choice of a hill that is, indeed, happily calculated to answer this purpose. Here, under his inspection, the Belvedere was built; the form of which is triangular, with a hexagonal tower at each corner. From Lawrence-castle at Haldon, and from the obelisk at Mamhead, we have a greater extent of prospect: but, for a command of objects, the Belvidere is, perhaps, the first spot in the western counties. The views from the Belvedere are a complete garden - its parts discriminated with the most brilliant distinctness, yet flowing into one beautiful whole.'

Polwhele was so enamoured of the Belvedere that he wrote at length about the views from each of the three windows.[147] In about 1800 the author of *A guide in a tour to the watering places, and their environs, on the south-east coast of Devon* was equally fulsome when he noted that it commanded *'a prospect of the lovely interchange of wooded heights and descending vales.'*[148]

Its companion, Haldon Belvedere, also known as Lawrence Tower, was built in 1788 by Sir Robert Palk near his country seat of Haldon. Its purpose was to further the memory of Major General Stringer Lawrence and a statue of him survives in the tower. This three-sided tower was constructed after that erected at Powderham Castle. Whilst the former has been rescued and restored, the latter was gutted by several fires in the twentieth century.

The Powderham Belvedere remains in private ownership and the Haldon Belvedere is owned by the Devon Historic Buildings Trust.

239. Pen and wash by Mary Luxmoore entitled 'View from the Belvedere at Powderham', c.1830.

238. Lithograph by L. W. Martens entitled 'Belvedere at Powderham Park', 10 September 1829.

Inset: Flowers by a Stone Vase, Peter Faes, 1786.

240. Watercolour by Swete entitled *'West Teignmouth'* which shows Bitton to the left, no date given. Swete visited Bitton in 1795 and noted then that the house, which belonged to Mackworth Praed, was a *'most agreeable spot'* and was highly picturesque. He regarded it as so closely positioned near the Teign River that it required a wall to prevent flooding. Swete recorded no details of the gardens.[149]

John Swete's Picturesque Sketches of Devon

Bitton, Buckland Filleigh, Cleave, Escot and Exminster
1789–1800

In 1789 Reverend John Swete began touring Devon in search of the Picturesque. He recorded his thoughts in twenty volumes which he illustrated with his own watercolours.

Each of these, except some which were destroyed during bombing at Newton Abbot in the second world war, were given to the Devon Heritage Centre. Swete finished his tours, which brought him to every corner of the county, in 1800. Amongst the details which he noted were descriptions of the grounds of large country houses. Of some he wrote very little about the gardens.

Swete was visited by Joseph Farington, the diarist, twenty years after his Picturesque tours were finished. Bishop Fisher had recommended Swete to Farington as an authority on the Picturesque. Swete showed him one of the volumes and Farington was impressed with what he saw and how he was treated (*'his appearance was prepossessing, being handsome, and his address agreeable'*). Mary Anne Burges visited him at Oxton, nearly twenty years earlier in 1792, and wrote to a friend *'I saw them all and I need not add I was very highly gratified. I like his style very much indeed.'*[150]

The Tour of Doctor Syntax, in search of the picturesque was published in the early 1800s as a satire on travelling vicars such as Swete who sought the picturesque scenery of England and provides another way of viewing Swete's work.[151]

241. Watercolour entitled *'Buckland Filleigh'*, no date given. Swete visited in 1796 and was taken through the adjoining woodlands by the Fortescue family, the owners, who showed him three pleasure buildings. These he described as being rustic temples with seats inside. The three buildings and seats were composed of 'trunks, limbs and roots of trees'.[152]

Inset: *Dr Syntax sketching the lake,* Thomas Rowlandson, 1812.

242. Watercolour entitled *'Cleve, seat of Thomas Northmore, esquire'*, 1796. Swete criticized the grounds of Cleave, near Exeter, for not being picturesque enough. He felt the gardens and outbuildings should be hidden from view, the lawn smoothed and the entrance changed from a straight line to a winding one. Swete did however approve of the view of Exeter from beyond the shrubbery.[153]

243. Watercolour entitled *'Escot'*, December 1794. Swete approached the house between an avenue of ancient oaks and then came to the pool of water of which he disapproved. Its oval shape was too formal for Swete. In his opinion Capability Brown would have altered the dams and expanded the extent of the pond. Swete recounted that a yacht had been kept on the pond and that at the start and end of the working day shots were fired from cannon on board. He also paid attention to the two marquees set upon the lawn and noted that Sir George Yonge, whose family had built Escot in 1685, had advertised his house for sale. Swete added that Escot was purchased shortly afterwards by the Kennaways.[154]

244. Watercolour entitled *'Gateway of the vicar's house at Exminster'*, 3 November 1794. Swete approved of the ruins which he noted were older than the vicarage. He described the house as surrounded by shrubs amongst which were exceptional Arbutus. Swete's greatest praise was for the ruins and included in his watercolour is a gardener with a roller.[155]

245. Watercolour entitled *'Cottage of — Lardner'*, 3 November 1794. Swete wrote that as he was leaving Exminster his attention was arrested for a few minutes by the `singular simplicity and added elegance' of a thatched cottage which belonged to Mr Lardner. He criticized the size of the upper windows and of the two wings but approved of the overall design. Swete noted that the grounds comprised of a field in front of the house with the sides lined with shrubs.[156]

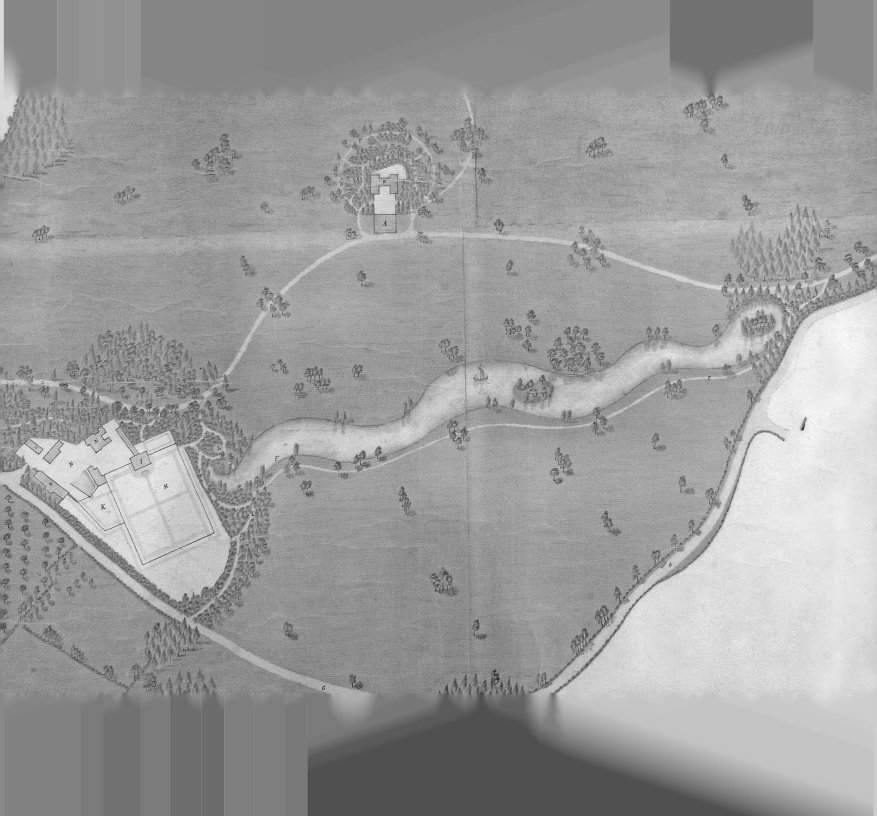

Bridwell

near Uffculme
1789

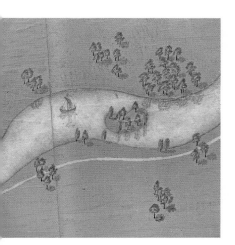

Bridwell is a neat example of the type of house and garden that was considered good taste for a late Georgian gentleman.

Bridwell was built for Richard Hall Clarke in the late 1770s and the grounds were improved at the time of this map. The surveyor, Thomas Gray, shows the serpentine lake which remains today as well as the two lakes and the kitchen garden near the work buildings. The tithe map of 1838 likewise details the lake stretched out in front of the house but the surveyor made no attempt to depict trees in the parish although they were undoubtedly there.

Clarke built his new house partly with stone from an ancient chapel he pulled down.[157] He also constructed a monument, composed of a lump of stalagmites, and a chapel, which was later used as a museum, shortly after this map was drawn.[158] The house is today in private ownership.

247. Detail of Gray's map showing the sheet of water and the varying shadows of the trees.

Inset: *Studies of the blossoms, fruits and trunk of an English oak (Quercus robur),* Ludwig Pfleger, 1788.

248. Copper line engraving entitled *'Bridwell, the seat of Richard Hall Clarke, esquire'* by and after T. Bonnor, 1793.

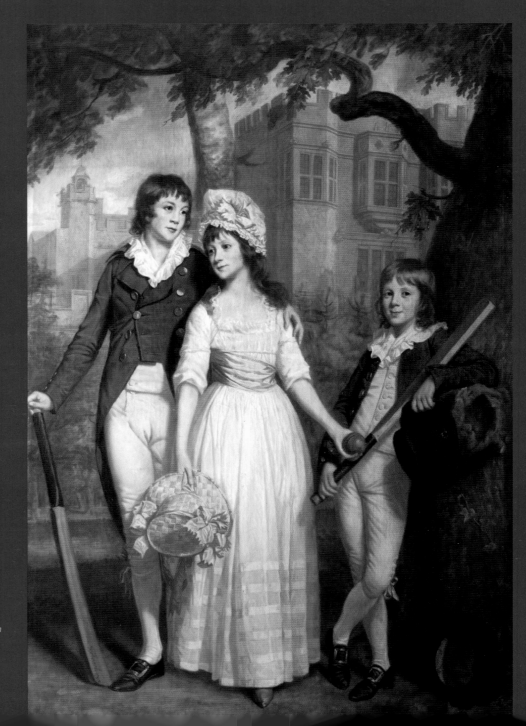

249. *Portrait of William, Mary Ann, and John De la Pole at Old Shute* by Thomas Beach, 1793. The painting is more noticeable for its depiction of a cricket ball and bats but the background indicated the status of the three children.

Old Shute

1793

A portion of Old Shute remains, a victim of a change of fashion in architecture.

Shute was cut in half shortly after this portrait was painted. New Shute was then being built and the most direct way from the gatehouse to it led through what then became known as Old Shute. Half of it was demolished and the stone reused to build up the sides of the new drive. The owner's mother, Elizabeth Mills, had brought wealth from several slave plantations in the West Indies[159] and presumably this helped pay to build New Shute. The following generation was compensated with £5,296 for the loss of its slaves in the 1830s.[160]

New Shute was built upon a hill in an agricultural field to take advantage of the views to the sea. Not only could the family look out upon miles of the countryside, but all those living there saw this new prominent house. In contrast, the family's ancient home lay obscured in a fold of the landscape.

Certain parts of the old landscape were kept, such as the retained gatehouse which established the lineage of the family to visitors and locals, but by the 1840s, when Shute was mapped for tithes, it appears that the great fruit tree planting by the seventeenth-century member of the Pole family had disappeared.

Sir John William de la Pole, who built New Shute, died a few years afterwards in 1799. The building of the house, and the early death of Sir John at the age of 42, led to the invention of a curse.

> In a field of standing corn he built
> In a field of straight green corn.
> His eldest son shall never be heir
> Nay, never his eldest born.[161]

The village notion of a curse is one of two associated with an ornamental landscape in Devon. Lady de la Pole stands confidently in her portrait in the midst of this new garden (see Introduction), unaware of the whisperings that would later follow her family. Old Shute was renamed as Shute Barton by the National Trust. The gatehouse is managed by the Landmark Trust.

250. **(Top)** Watercolour by Edward Ashworth entitled *'Gateway to Shute Park. Sir J. de la Pole'*, 13 June 1866.

251. **(Centre)** Circular plaque of blue jasper-dip and a white relief profile bust of the children's mother, Anne, Lady de la Pole, facing right, by Wedgwood, c.1780, in a gilt metal frame.

252. **(Bottom)** Drawing by Edward Ashworth entitled *'Gateway to Shute House, near Colyton'*, 7 July 1866.

Inset: *Vase of Flowers in a Niche*, attributed to Michel Bruno Bellengé, late 1700s.

253. Aquatint by F. Jukes after W. Davey entitled *'View of Rougemont Castle Exeter'*, 1794, with Rougemont House on the left.

Rougemont House

Exeter
1789

Exeter's most unusual garden was created out of the ancient castle ditch.

Francis Jukes' engraving shows a corner of Rougemont House with part of the castle incorporated into the garden. Jukes was one of the first English artists to exploit the newly-discovered method of aquatints but his years of inhaling fumes given off in the printing made him ill and he died at the age of sixty-seven.[162] His view shows the home of an owner who had built alongside what had become fashionable ruins and featured them in his garden.

John Patch, a surgeon at the Royal Devon and Exeter Hospital, built his home in land immediately outside Rougemont Castle in about 1770. His garden included part of the ditch. The house later passed on to Edmund Granger, a wine merchant who believed that a daily half pint of wine was beneficial for health. He altered both the house and gardens and it became a showpiece for Exeter.[163] Robert Southey, the diarist, noted on his visit in 1802 *'I was shown a garden, unique in its kind, which has been made in the old castle ditch. The banks rise sharply on each side; one of the finest poplars in the country grows in the bottom and scarcely overtops the ruined wall'*.[164] The garden attracted a considerable number of visitors partly because of its location in the heart of Exeter and from being the second-largest private garden in the city. Russia's Grand Duchess Helena, for example, visited in 1831.[165]

The Norman tower, in which Joseph Farington drew a gardener with his pots, is the oldest standing fortified gatehouse in the country. It stands in what is now known as Rougemont Gardens, acquired by the City of Exeter a century ago.

254. Engraving by Letitia Byrne after J. Farrington entitled *'Remains of Exeter Castle'*, 1 May 1822. Rougemont House is on the left. Farington made the sketch in October 1810. He wrote of Exeter that *'I do not remember any other English town which so much abounds with subjects of buildings that in form and colour are so well calculated for a painter's purpose. Every day groups of houses, with churches & gates, strike my eye, as I am more and more able to discriminate in the quantity which is before me'*.[166]

Inset: *The White Lily with variegated leaves*, Joseph Constantine Stadler, after Peter Charles Henderson, 1800.

255. Drawing of Bicton entitled *'View taken by C: P Maria Rolle 1795'*.

Bicton

1795

Bicton lay at the heart of one of Devon's great estates and this drawing was made by one of its family members.

Christiana Philippa Maria Rolle, aged about 36 when she made this image, was the daughter of Dennys Rolle of Bicton but appears to have lived at Hudscott House in North Devon where she died in 1831.[167] Bicton was one of her childhood homes along with Stevenstone near Great Torrington.

Her drawing was faithfully copied five years later, in 1800, and shows parkland, complete not merely with ornamental fowl and deer but two sets of strolling people. A carriage approaches the house on the horizon. Bicton has lost its bridge over this serpentine stretch of water.

The house is best known for the changes which occurred in the generation following Miss Rolle's drawing. John Claudius Loudon visited in 1842 and summarised these introductions:

> 'This is an extensive place, celebrated for its improvements, for the collection of rare plants of every kind, for its arboretum on a large scale recently planted, and for its very high keeping. Too much can hardly be said in honour of the late Lord Rolle, through whose munificence the improvements were made, or of the present Lady Rolle, by whose taste and energetic mind His Lordship was stimulated to do so much; and by whom, since His Lordship's death, the improvements have been continued, and the place kept up with a degree of care very rarely to be met with in similar cases.
>
> The surface of the grounds at Bicton would be described as greatly varied in any other English county than Devonshire, but even in that picturesque county they contain many striking beauties. The park is situated within 2½ miles of the sea, of which from various points it affords fine views; and in the interior the landscape is bounded by ranges of hills, some of which are covered with wood, others with cultivated fields, and some are in a wild state. The soil is chiefly sand

256. Copper line engraving entitled 'Bicton, Devonshire' by J. Walker and J. Greig after Miss Rolle, 1800.

257. Detail from C. & J. Greenwood's map showing the position of Bicton and the extent of the grounds, 1827.

Inset: *Blue Passion Flower,* Philip Reinagle, 1800.

and sandy loam. The house, which is well placed on a knoll, is extensive and commodious, containing a suite of magnificent apartments on the principal floor, and very extensive offices, but without any pretensions to architecture. The grounds have been judiciously laid out by Mr Gilpin and a piece of water formed by Mr Glendinning under his direction has an excellent effect. There are two approaches, the one from Exeter, and the other from Sidmouth; the latter passes through an avenue of araucarias, planted in 1842. There are an outer and inner park, and also outer and inner lodges, but none of these lodges has much merit.

In a gardening point of view the most interesting feature about Bicton is the arboretum, which extends from the house, along the boundary of the inner park, till it reaches the flower garden, at the distance of 112 chains, or nearly a mile and a half. The average width is about 3 chains, which will give from 33 to 34 acres, as the whole extent of the ground covered by the trees and shrubs. The planting was commenced in the spring of the year 1839, and continued in the spring of 1840. It would have been better had the extent of ground been greater: but, as it is, it was admirably arranged and planted by Mr Glendinning, while at Bicton; who has, both there, and in various

258. Undated portrait of John, 1st Baron Rolle, by John Doyle.

articles which he has written in the Gardener's Magazine proved himself to be possessed of an excellent taste in landscape-gardening, as well as an enthusiastic love of trees and shrubs. The plants in the arboretum are judiciously disposed according to the space allotted to them, but greater room to the trees would have been an advantage, if it could have been obtained. It was a great step, however, to have formed so new a feature as an arboretum at all; and the merit of having accomplished so desirable an object is, we believe, entirely due to Lady Rolle. We examined a great many of the plants individually, and found many of them with wrong names, the inevitable consequence of the present state of nomenclature in almost all the nurseries; some species were dead, and, with regard to completeness, a number wanting. The care of this arboretum is at present committed to Messrs Veitch and Son, who are taking measures to have all the plants correctly named, and all the blanks and deficiencies supplied. When this shall have been done, the collection, open as it is to the inspection of the horticultural world, will be of inestimable value to the surrounding country. We cannot leave it without noticing the very careful manner in which the plants have been planted on raised hills of prepared soil, and carefully staked and mulched, where staking and mulching were necessary. The boundary of the arboretum on the side next the outer park is a sunk fence, and on the inner side either a strained wire fence or iron hurdles. The arrangement is according to the Natural System, beginning near the house with the Clematideae, and ending at the entrance to the walled flower-garden with the Juniperinae. A green drive leads through the whole. Nothing can be more perfect than the style in which every part of this arboretum is kept; Messrs Veitch and Son having six men constantly employed mowing the grass, and mulching the dug circles round the plants with it, as practised in the Derby Arboretum… destroying weeds as soon as they appear; and removing dead leaves, suckers from grafted plants, insects, decayed blossoms, etc. One great beauty of the Bicton arboretum is, that every tree and shrub which it contains may be seen, and the name on its label read, by a person while sitting in a carriage, and driving through it along the green walk.

There is a drive through a pine wood to a prospect tower, (the latter the best piece of architecture at Bicton,) which deserves notice for its extent and the quantity of evergreens, such as rhododendrons, mahonias, and *Ruscus aculeatus* which have been planted as undergrowth. A great many rare pines, firs, cypresses, and junipers have also been introduced along this drive, so that, by adding more, it will in a short time be interesting as a pinetum. The tower is in the Gothic style, so high as to command a panoramic view of the surrounding country and the sea. It contains several rooms; in one of which, appropriately fitted up, a rich collection of china is tastefully displayed. This tower is understood to have been built by Lady Rolle, entirely unknown to Lord Rolle, and undiscovered by him, as an agreeable surprise for his birthday, October 16 1839, when he completed his 88th year; and, the following birthday Lady Rolle surprised Lord Rolle with the china room.

Connected with the arboretum, so as to form a part of the tour of the place, is a menagerie containing a rich collection of birds, monkeys, kangaroos, and various other foreign animals. Thus, with the arboretum, the drive to the tower, and the flower garden, as means of recreation in the open air; the menagerie and the collection of china, for amusement under cover; and the library and pictures in the house, there is at Bicton every source of enjoyment that can be desired. Nothing is wanting but a collection of shells and minerals, for the sake of those who are fond of these departments of science, and this is about to be formed; a great quantity of shells, and some minerals, having been procured for the purpose, though they are not yet arranged.

The kitchen-garden was judiciously formed and planted by Mr Glendinning. It is supplied with water by several basins lined with stone distributed throughout the garden, and fed by a stream which runs from one to another, thus keeping the water always fresh and clear. The wall trees have been all planted above the surface, and they seem to bear abundant crops. The flower garden contains several acres, and is at a short distance from the house. It is a parallelogram, having the hothouses, &c., which are very extensive, on the north side, with a noble temple in the centre. It is suitably laid out and planted, and kept in the very highest order. The architectural and sculptural ornaments are vases, stone baskets, statues, busts, and a candelabrum fountain with a jet from the upper part, which rises to a considerable height, and has a splendid effect from every part of the garden, but more especially from an upper terrace walk, and when brought in a line with an obelisk in the park which forms the termination to a vista. There is water enough, we

259. Watercolour of the Bicton Mausoleum, mid to late nineteenth century. Augustus Welby Pugin was hired by Lady Louisa Rolle in 1850 to convert the redundant church at Bicton into a mausoleum for her recently deceased husband. This creation marked the end of the period of great change in the gardens which was undertaken by Lady Maria Rolle's brother John, 1st Baron Rolle.[168]

understand, to form a cascade over stone steps in the ancient style, which would be a magnificent substitute for the green terrace slopes which form the commencement of the vista.

The whole of the gardens at Bicton are under the direction of Mr James Barnes, and we must say that we do not think we ever before saw culture, order, and neatness carried to such a high degree of perfection, in so many departments, and on so large a scale, and all by the care and superintendence of one man. From the commonest kitchen crop in the open garden, and the mushrooms in the sheds, up to the pineapples, the heaths, and the Orchidaceae, every thing seemed to be alike healthy and vigorous. We could not help noticing the evenness of the crops of cabbages, cauliflowers, savoys, &c. in the kitchen-garden; and the extraordinary vigour and beauty of the pines, heaths, hothouse plants, chrysanthemums, &c., in the houses; and nothing could exceed the neatness of the lawn, the walks, and the flower-beds.'[169]

Bicton is now home to Bicton College.

260. Watercolour entitled *'In the quarry at Peamore JWA October 1796'*, by John White Abbott, 1796.

Peamore Park

near Shillingford St George
1796

The increasing appreciation of the natural beauty found in woodland in shown in these late Georgian watercolours.

261. Watercolour by Francis Towne, c.1786, entitled 'In Peamore Park in the County of Devon the seat of Rich. Hippis. Coxe Esquire drawn on the spot by Francis Towne'.

Both John White Abbot and Francis Towne painted the wooded scenery of this mansion situated near Exeter. Swete and Polwhele each described the grounds as undulating and both also praised its woodland. At this time Peamore was the home of Henry Hippisley Coxe who had inherited from his brother Richard in 1786. In 1822 it passed to the Kekewich family who were one of the few in Devon to own slaves abroad. In 1833 the government compensated Samuel Trehawke Kekewich, an Exeter M.P., £3,013 7d for his financial loss in freeing his 113 slaves in Grenada.[170]

Both Towne and Abbot might have known of the most illustrious tree in the parkland: a specimen of the London plane, one of the earliest in the country, was planted by the end of the eighteenth century.[171] The house is divided into multiple ownership.

262. Detail of map of Peamore Park, 1792

Inset: A park scene, Thomas Rowlandson, late eighteenth century.

263. Portrait of Francis Towne by John Downman, 1795.

178

Arlington Court

1797

Arlington Court was home to the Chichesters, a family which, like the Fortescues, once stretched across North Devon in a number of the county's great houses.

This is one of the four views by Maria Pixell which are at Arlington. Pixell was *'extravagantly lauded'* for her artistry during her lifetime and died in 1805, a few years after this painting was made.[172] The mansion house was subsequently rebuilt on a nearby site. The two towers for the bridge seen in the accompanying drawing still stand but the bridge itself was never completed.

The census records that the gardeners at Arlington changed regularly in the nineteenth century: Richard George Lewis, an Irishman, was employed in 1851 and then Charles Somerville of nearby Shirwell was there in 1861. He was followed by John Bowen, who was born in Arlington, in 1871 and then after another decade two other men, both from North Devon, were the gardeners.[173]

The last of the family to live at Arlington was Rosalie Chichester, a woman who is chiefly remembered for her aversion to hunting. The house is now owned by the National Trust.

264. (Left) Oil painting entitled *'St James Church and Old Arlington Court'* by Maria Pixell, 1797.

265. Drawing by William Dredge of intended suspension bridge, 26 March 1849.

Inset: *Passion Flower,* Sydenham Teak Edwards, 1799.

266. Untitled watercolour on six sheets by John White Abbott, 1804. The original mount is inscribed *'Canonteign Devon, given to Elizabeth Abbott March 1832'* and *'JWA Augt. 27 1804'*.

267. Watercolour on six sheets entitled *' View near Canonteign, Devon'* by John White Abbott, 1803.

268. View entitled *'Canonteign Augt. 20, 1808'* by John White Abbott.

Canonteign

Christow
1804

John White Abbott's four views of Canonteign show off his skills as an artist as well as express a growing interest amongst the public for the English landscape.

Inset: *Poppies and Tradascanthus,* formerly attributed to Jacques-Laurent Agasse, c.1800.

269. View entitled *'Canonteign'*, signed by John White Abbott, and dated 21 September 1801.

Canonteign House was later rebuilt for Admiral Edward Pellew, later the second Viscount Exmouth, in 1828 on a new site above Canonteign Barton. It took advantage of the view which the older building, a mile or so to the east in the valley, did not have. The pleasure grounds of the new mansion included the waterfall[174] which Reverend Swete visited a decade earlier than the first of Abbott's four views. Not surprisingly Swete found the cascade, as he termed it, highly picturesque although he had great difficulty in ascending its heights due to the amorous nature of the brambles which clung to him as he climbed.[175] A generation later, in 1832, another writer noted *'the present mansion is a plain and neat structure, standing amidst very picturesque grounds in which… is a lofty cascade, flowing from a wooded height, over bold ledges of craggy rocks'.*[176]

270. Watercolour with pen and ink by Francis Towne entitled *'No 3, Berry Castle in the county of Devon/the outline taken on the spot/Francis Towne'/ 'Finished...1805'*, 1805.

The ruins of
Berry Pomeroy Castle

1805

Berry Pomeroy Castle has been Devon's most popular ruin for several hundred years. Okehampton Castle is its only rival but Berry Pomeroy's position near Totnes in the more populous south made it more popular with visitors because of its accessibility. Francis Towne's watercolour shows the castle in its grand but decaying state.

The de Pomeroy family was here until 1547 when it was purchased by Edward Seymour, Duke of Somerset. Five years later he was executed for felony and this left his ambitious renovations unfinished. Subsequent generations continued to extend the buildings but by the end of the seventeenth century the castle was described as an abandoned ruin.[177] The subsequent arrival of tourists saw the castle become a favourite day visit and site for fashionable picnics.

Reverend Polwhele, one of Devon's Georgian historians, noted that it was *'situated in a deer park, upon a rock, on a rising ground from the east and north, over a pleasant rivulet'* and that *'the ruins of this castle are an object of great curiosity to travellers. The north view seems the most romantic, from the old fragments of the castle breaking through the deep umbrage of the fantastic woods. The stone wall is still traceable round the park of about 500 acres'.*[178] In 1794 William George Maton, a visitor, wrote in his personal journal that the view of the ruins *'afforded us more delight than any thing of a similar nature we had seen in the course of our journey. The approach to the castle is through a thick wood, which extends along the side of a range of hills and which increases the curiosity whilst it awakens the impatience of the travellers, the ruins not being disclosed until he is within a few paces of them'*. Three years later he printed his account and noted that *'the great gate, (with the walls of the south front) the north wing of the court, or quadrangle, some apartments on the west side, and a turret or two, are the principal remains of the building, and these are so finely overhung with the branches of trees and shrubs that grow close to the walls, so beautifully mantled with ivy, and so richly incrusted with moss, that they constitute the most picturesque objects that can be imagined. And when the surrounding scenery is taken into the account — the noble mass of wood fronting the gate, the bold ridges rising in the horizon, and the fertile valley opening to the east — the ruins of Berry Pomeroy Castle must be considered as almost unparalleled in their effect.'*[179] A hundred years later visitors were being admitted every day of the week but Sunday. A small fee was payable to the keeper.[180]

271. Watercolour by William George Maton, 1794, who toured Devon that year.

Inset: *The Picnic*, Thomas Rowlandson, 1798.

272. Watercolour with pen and brown ink after Thomas Girtin, no date, entitled 'Berry Pomeroy Castle Devon/Girtin'.

In 1842 John Claudius Loudon visited and described the recent changes made to the ruins. He wrote:

> 'This is the ruins of what has been a lofty and widely extending castle; but it is now shorn of much of its dignity, by the duke's tenantry having, till within the last twenty years, taken away almost all the master stones of the building, such as the lintels and jambs to the doors, windows, and fireplaces. To prevent the walls of the castle from literally tumbling down, the place of these lintels was supplied some years ago by oak beams, and that of the jambs by common rubble stonework. This gives the whole ruin a mean appearance, and destroys the idea of great age; for no building with wooden lintels can last for centuries. Another circumstance which greatly detracts from its dignity is its being overwhelmed with trees. Such, however, is the height of the walls, and of the well defined portions which

273. Drawing by Thomas Allom, by 1832. It was engraved from John Britton and Edward Wedlake Brayley's *Devonshire Illustrated*. Allom was both an artist and architect.[181]

occur here and there, for example the gatehouse, that, were it not for the want of the master stones, it would not be difficult to render this a grand and impressive ruin; and to restore in it one or two rooms, so as to form a habitation for a person to take care of the whole. The views from the castle must, from its elevation, be very extensive; but it is so shrouded in trees, that we can only see over the precipitous terrace walls to a deep valley, the sides and bottom of which are covered with ancient wood. Immediately within the gatehouse there is an elder tree, the branches of which are covered to their very extremity with Polypodium vulgare, giving it a very singular appearance, which we suppose would be not unlike that of the dank woods of Demerara and other places, where the trees are covered with Orchidacese. In one of the kitchens there is a common maple, which has sprung up out of the floor, and is nearly 50 feet high; and in another kitchen there is a large fireplace, with an oven on one side, and a niche for the turnspit to sit in on the other. Such a tree as this maple might remain, provided the floor were cleared out so far as to show distinctly that it was a floor; but almost all the other trees we would remove, together with as much of the soil and rubbish as would allow us to recognise what the castle had been, the height of the walls in some places, the dimensions of the rooms and their uses in others, and if possible the situation of the staircases; for the stone steps have been generally removed. From these hints may be derived a knowledge of the principle on which ruins in actual scenery are to be treated, viz., that of showing, by what exists, what has been. To show the height of walls, clear away the rubbish, in some places, to their very base; to show lateral extent, uncover or indicate such fragments of foundations as may have belonged to the building when in a perfect state; to show the sizes of the rooms, clear out their floors; and, to show the whole group of ruins at a distance, remove such of the surrounding trees as may be necessary for that purpose.'[182]

The castle is still owned by the Seymour family but administered by English Heritage.

274. Photograph of the ruins, c.1890–1900.

185

275. Copy of a sketch with the caption *'Cockwood House – From a drawing by Louisa H. Drury, about the year 1805'*.

276. Sketch entitled *'The Exe from Cockwood Grounds'* probably by a member of the Merivale family, date unknown.

277. Cockwood House as shown on C. & J. Greenwood's map, 1827.

Cockwood House

near Dawlish
1805

The landscape at Cockwood House received, for some thirty years, great praise for its picturesque nature.

The landscape was designed by Joseph Drury, former headmaster at Harrow. Not long after he died, in 1834, Drury was praised in *The Gentleman's Magazine* for his work at Cockwood *'as a specimen of creative taste in landscape gardening, Cockwood in Devon will be as much visited and celebrated by travellers and poets as The Leasowes (in Shropshire)'.*[183] Unfortunately the house was sold after his death to the Courtenay family who shortly afterwards had it demolished. The railway was then run through the grounds. A grandson remembered:

> *'Very beautiful were the plantations, very comfortable the house, which lay on the verge of the estuary of the Exe. Nothing could be more charming than the rising of the spring tide of a fine morning up to the low boundary wall before our windows. The place has long been sold, the house pulled down, the railroad driven between its site and those tidal waters. The walks in the grounds are almost obliterated, and the seats and arbours which decked it have all utterly perished. The woods have grown and outgrown all proportion, but neither the hand of man nor of nature can destroy the glorious prospect over land and sea and estuary which there are none now to appreciate and enjoy.'*[184]

Drury had studied the work of William Gilpin and Uvedale Price and also consulted Humphry Repton for guidance in designing the landscape at Cockwood.[185]

The situation of the house was near the edge of the Exe Estuary. Drury's granddaughter later recalled that, although judicious planting and design had created a very beautiful garden, the situation was so low that there was a risk of flooding the house. This had happened in November 1824 when the household woke to find *'pots, pipkins, crockery ware, various articles of furniture all dancing an outrageous fandango in all directions with ourselves footed mer-maidens save shoes or stocking endeavouring to save what they could as our house was completely surrounded by the briny element.'*[186]

Inset: *Butterfly hunting,* Thomas Rowlandson, c.1806.

278. Detail from a map which accompanied the sale of Cockwood, 1835.

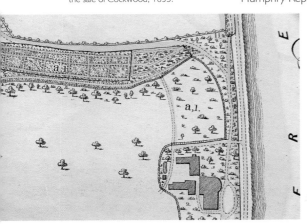

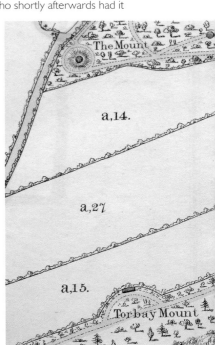
279. Detail from the map which shows two prospect points to the west of the house entitled The Mount and Torbay Mount, 1835.

280. Painting of Ugbrooke by John White
Abbott, 1809.

Ugbrooke

1809

Capability Brown has helped define the appeal of Ugbrooke.

Brown has been associated with the grounds of Ugbrooke through his late eighteenth-century plan of the grounds. Ugbrooke was rebuilt by Robert Adam in the 1760s and has been home to the Clifford family since the sixteenth century. Brown landscaped the grounds in the 1770s and the two stretches of water and undulating parkland are the great feature of the house.

281. Drawing attributed to Mary Sabilla Novello, c.1830.

Inset: *The Gardener's Offering,* Thomas Rowlandson, 1803-1805.

"Addison's Oak", Ugbrook Park. – Coloured on the spot. May 30, 1848.
The tradition says that Addison wrote several papers in the Spectator under this tree. It measures 25 feet in circumference.

282. Drawing of Ugbrooke Oak by Peter Orlando Hutchinson, 1848.

283. Undated watercolour by Reverend John Swete. Swete appended to his drawing a note which claimed 'the grounds however claim most attention – the park being as finely wooded as any in the kingdom, and decorated by an extensive, and in some parts, highly picturesque piece of water. This sketch is taken from the bottom of the lower sheet and exhibits a most rural and pleasing picture'.

284. Pen and ink sketch entitled *'In Ugbrooke Park'* by Thomas Hastings, 1833.

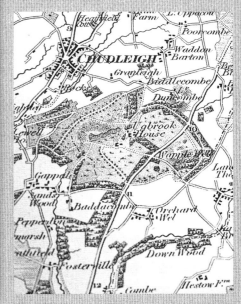

285. Detail of the grounds of Ugbrooke as shown on C. & J. Greenwood's map, 1827.

John Claudius Loudon visited a generation after Abbott painted the grounds and he noted that:

'The park here contains the greatest quantity of fine old wood that we have seen in Devonshire. The trees are not crowded, and many of them, therefore, have attained an immense size, and taken their natural shapes. They are also remarkably well displayed with reference to the inequalities of the surface. Sketches of many of these trees have been taken by Mr (William Andrews) Nesfield. We only measured one or two, a Dutch elm 20 feet round at 4 feet from the ground; and an oak with a trunk 27 feet round, 60 feet high, and with the branches covering a space 120 feet in diameter. What gratified us much was to see a number of young single trees introduced throughout the park in very suitable places. No tree is put down except on the precise spot chosen by Lord Clifford, who, from the remarks he made to us, and the operations going forward, we should conclude to be possessed of good taste in landscape-gardening. The house is a square mass, pierced with equidistant windows all of the same size, without any other merit; it is too meagre to be called elegant, and not lofty enough to be considered grand. A house, however, is within the power of man, but the grounds and the woods of Ugbrooke can only be produced by a fortunate concurrence of natural circumstances many years in operation'.[187]

The trees, so admired by Loudon and by visitors constantly since, continue to have the appeal seen in Abbott's painting.

Shilstone

near Modbury
c.1810

Two families have dominated the landscape at Shilstone: the Hill and then the Savery families have shaped what we see today.

This watercolour shows Shilstone before it was rebuilt sometime around 1810. The view does not show the unusual feature which is largely underground: a seventeenth-century water garden and grotto lie to the left of the painting. It retains a frieze of dancing classical figures which can be seen in part. This area of the garden has been attributed to Thomas Savery, a relation and Surveyor of the Royal Water Works at Hampton Court and who had responsibility for the gardens at Bushey Park. After the date of this watercolour formal gardens were created with five acres of extensive terraces on three sides of the house.[188]

Shilstone is privately owned and home to the Devon Rural Archive.

287. Aerial view of Shilstone, 2011.

Inset: *Gardening*, Thomas Rowlandson, early nineteenth century.

288. Repton's two drawings in his Red Book, 1814, with its moveable flaps. The first is entitled *'General view from the south and east fronts of the cottage at Endsleigh, Devonshire – Dutchess of Bedford.'*.

289. Repton's second engraving is entitled *'General view from the south and east fronts of the cottage at Endsleigh, Devonshire – Dutchess of Bedford'*.

Endsleigh

near Milton Abbot
1814

Endsleigh seems an unlikely home for a duke whose main home was the imposingly grand Woburn Abbey. Even so, it became their seat in Devon for the family's occasional visits. It perches on the border with Cornwall.

Their cottage orné was built in 1810 and four years later Humphry Repton proposed a design for the landscape in one of his now famous Red Books. The Russell family had owned the land since a grant to John, Lord Russell, first Earl of Bedford, at the Dissolution of the Monasteries. They constructed their new retreat on a site which took advantage of the wooded valley. It took the place of a farmhouse, Leigh, and the new building was, appropriately, Endsleigh.

Repton's plans for the house were rejected but his scheme for the grounds received the Russell's approval. He was commissioned when he had reached the age of 62 and was wheelchair-bound due to a carriage accident.

290. Watercolour entitled *'View towards Leigh Wood. View from the Library windows at Endsleigh Cottage – across the Tamar to Warm Wood. View towards Duntarew Wood'* by Repton, 1814.

Inset: *A Bouquet of Flowers with Insects,* Pierre Joseph Redouté, early 1800s.

291. Watercolour entitled *'View from the Window of the Dining Room'* by Repton, 1814.

Repton died only four years later and while planning the grounds in August 1814 he had to be carried *'to places otherwise inaccessible to a cripple'*.[189] Luckily for him Endsleigh's estate manager had ordered the culling of local vipers: 144 were killed that season.[190]

Repton adapted some existing landscaping, possibly by Jeffery Wyatville, the architect. His focus was on Convenience, Comfort and the Picturesque. He discarded the approach of his mentor, Capability Brown, and introduced a variety in the number and character of plantings in and around the house. His two views show that he was not only concerned with the views over the valley but that the existing terraces would be developed to provide

292. Portrait of Humfry Repton, possibly by Henry Richard Cooke, 1820. The title notes him as an *'ingenious artist, who had acquired high celebrity as an architect and landscape gardener'* and that he *'acquitted himself in a manner highly creditable to his talents'*.

other interest closer at hand. The house was intended to be smaller than it appeared but the grounds were those of a rural palace.

Not all of Repton's proposals were acted upon perhaps partly due to his ill health. He may have only visited Endsleigh on this one occasion but an estate account recorded him being given £105 *'on account of journeys to Endsleigh'*.[191] Some details of the garden can be gleaned from the records. For instance, in the spring of 1813 many thousands of trees were sent by Lucombe & Pince, the Exeter nursery. They included 12 variegated hollies and 12 cedars of Lebanon but there were also 2,200 English oaks, birch, Spanish chestnuts and larch each, 875 Scot firs and beech each, and 490 rowans. That same year one Richard Payne and his two horses were hired to transport 'stuff from the woods' to make Rustic Chairs.[192]

Not all visitors appear to have approved of Endsleigh. Miss Sophie Dixon visited in 1830 and commented the thick plantation of ornamental shrubs was:

> *'disposed without taste and barbarously intermingled with rude half-withered furze bushes, briars and nettles, intended perhaps as the evidence of rusticity, but certainly showing an entire want of judgement, and producing a very unpleasing effect, as the contrivance is at once*

293. Untitled watercolour by John Cooke Bourne of the garden front of Endsleigh, c.1845. Bourne had produced a Green Book for Woburn in 1842.

294. Watercolour entitled *'The Swiss Cottage at the Duke of Bedford's Rustic Villa at Endsleigh'* signed Sir Jeffery Wyatville architect. c.1810. The watercolour has the name *'Sir Jeffery Wyatville'* in the bottom left hand corner. He had changed his name from Wyat to Wyatville in 1823 but it has been thought that the cottage was built thirteen years earlier.[193]

295. Watercolour entitled *'The Children's cottage and the Children's Garden'* by Repton, 1814.

perceived to be clumsy; the fact of delicate blossoming shrubs growing from the midst of brambles and furzes, being altogether unnatural and incongruous'.

She was not complimentary about the planting around the Dairy which she thought was well-placed 'if the false taste of its inconsistent decorations be put out of sight'. This was because she felt *'the principal fault is the introduction of an overwhelming number of rhododendrons, which are lavished in clumps and plots without mercy and often where their intrusion entirely spoils the effect which the fine natural disposition of the valley would have produced'*. She was equally scathing of the flower garden (*'tawdry and trifling'*) and the grotto (*'destitute of taste'*). Her most complimentary remarks were when she visited the gardener's lodge where she saw the trellised arbour in the centre and small pond. She felt the flowers mixed in with the fruit trees and vegetables 'exhibit a very gay appearance'.[194]

In contrast, a visitor from Hampshire thought it *'a perfect paradise in its way, tastefully yet plainly fitted up'* and regarded the gardens to have been in keeping with the house.[195]

296. View by Henrietta Matilda Crompton inscribed *'Endsleigh Cottage, Duke of Bedford 7 miles from Tavistock, Swiss Cottage passed by Dartmoor to Devonport Tuesday August 25th'*, 1840.

297. Fordland in Ide, etching by T. H. Williams, 1815. Williams resided in Plymouth but later moved to Exeter.[196]

298

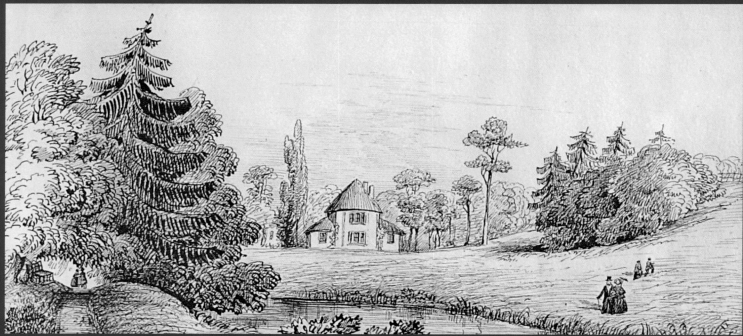

298. – 299. Two drawings by George Townsend, 1800s. Townsend published a number of books of local illustrations including Views of Devon and Cornwall in about 1870. When he died, a bachelor, in 1909 a local journalist noted he was singularly modest and unassuming. Townsend had a particular love for the cathedral and had, it was said, been commissioned by a titled lady whose hobby was the study of bosses. He sketched every boss whilst lying on his back on the scaffolding during the nineteenth-century restoration.[197]

Fordland

near Ide
1815

Fordland was an Exeter Pleasure Garden in the manner that the famous Vauxhall Gardens was that of London.[198] They differed not only in that Fordland was a much more modest affair but also in that it remained respectable.

Inset: *Vauxhall Gardens*, Thomas Rowlandson, 1785.

299.

Thomas Hewitt Williams, an artist who produced several of his own books, engraved a view of Fordland and then described it in 1815 when the garden was at its height. The house stood at the end of a lawn with shrubberies on either side. According to Williams:

'These beautiful Coombs form the place so well known in the county by the name of Fordland, the property of James White Esquire of Exeter, to whose taste it owes its present improved appearance. A Cottage, an occasional residence, is at the end of a sweet little lawn, commanding a view through two vales, rich with water, and luxuriant with oaks. The walks through the various grounds occupy an extent of nearly seven miles; and in various parts, rustic temples, and seats are placed, either for the purpose of rest, or the enjoyment of the prospect… So admirably is the art of improvement concealed, that no expectation can be formed of what is to come; but on passing through

a shrubbery, the senses are surprised and delighted, the effect is quite magical, it is a transportation to Fairy land, the Cottage, the Lawn, the Valleys, the Woods, the Lakes burst on the sight; the impression made is only checked by the desire of exploring the scenes which so suddenly present themselves. It is one of those charming secluded places that give us delight, from the simplicity of its character. The mind is overpowered by places of great extent and diversity, with sumptuous buildings, and extravagant expense, that the fortune of most of its visitors would be unable to support; and by the exclusion of hope, produces a feeling the very opposite to that which constitutes a part of our happiness… In a well-chosen situation, a circular building is placed, and several trees below support at their trunks a variety of seats; a place sufficient for the reception of a large party; from this point the view was taken… The highest interest is excited by a Picture, or Scenery, where there is a full and natural combination of the several parts; with the choice of effect, which arises from, the magic of light and shade; the beauty of a serene morning or evening; or the wildness and agitations of a tempest. But there are many degrees of picturesque pleasure, and places should be valued for what they afford, without the silliness of comparisons. This sweet place is perfect in all the associations which

300. – 302. Three untitled drawings by John Harris, c.1823.

301.

302.

303. Portrait entitled *'Counseller James White of Exeter 1794. Origl. my excellent friend. I drew another for his Nephew Abbott'*, by John Downman, 1794. Councillor White was the owner of Fordland and the uncle of John White Abbott, the artist.

304. A portrait of Benjamin Honeycomb Walker who is representative of the Exonian who visited Fordland.

305.

305. – 306. Two watercolours by John Swete, 1797, entitled *'Fordland Cottage, belonging to James White, Esquire'* and *'Fordland Grounds'*.

306.

wood scenery produces, it has a great variety of surface, and having been formed from a state of rude nature, by the present proprietor, it may, at some future time be further improved; extending the piece of water up the valley, would add greatly to the effect of it'.[199]

Reverend Swete had visited eighteen years earlier, in October 1797, and was given a tour by Councillor White. The house, with a lawn before it, comprised two rooms and within the grounds were the sheet of water and paths leading to a cave, an Alpine bridge and the *'shed'*, the pleasure house which would be called a summerhouse today.[200] It was remembered by a Victorian descendant of John Merivale of Barton Place outside Exeter that White was assisted in the landscaping of Fordland by Merivale.[201]

307. Pickwell in Georgeham, c.1820.
Watercolour entitled *'A View of Picwell House in North Deavon with A distant view of the Isle of Lundy'*, possibly by John Keast, c.1820. When Lord Fortescue purchased Pickwell in 1832 it had thirteen bedrooms. The house itself was some 150 feet across with two parlours and a breakfast room on the ground floor and in addition to the sleeping accommodation there was a library and billiard room. Even so, there was only one *'closet'* to serve the entire house. Another five rooms were in the attic and there was a range of agricultural buildings at the rear.[202] The grounds are largely bereft of any planting except for what may be a shrubbery on one side and the plantation on the other. Pickwell was rebuilt in the early 1900s.

308. View entitled *'Arlinton House John Chichester Esq.'*, possibly by John Keast, c.1820, before the rebuilding of 1820 to 1823 (see page 178).[203]

309. View of Castle Hill in Filleigh entitled *'A View of Phily House the residence of Earl Fortiscue'*, possibly by John Keast, c.1820, which shows it in a different guise to that represented in the eighteenth century (see pages 108–109).

Primitive views of country houses in northeast Devon

Pickwell, Arlington Court, Castle Hill, Manor House (Lynmouth), Tawstock and Watermouth, c.1820

In about 1820 an artist possibly by the name of John Keast toured northeast Devon where he painted six country houses. The recurrent figure in the paintings may be a depiction of the artist.

311. A side view of the house is shown in this view entitled 'View of Lymouth in North Deavon', possibly by John Keast, c.1820.

310. Manor House, Lynmouth, c.1820
Watercolour possibly by John Keast entitled `Lymouth House John Lock Esq.', c.1820.
Lynmouth House, now known as Manor House, was built in the late eighteenth or early nineteenth century. Like the Shell House at Exmouth (see page 264), it appears to have had no planting of any consequence in these early depictions. The design of its landscaping, as with the plan of the seaside aspect of the house with its larger windows, was to take advantage of the outlook. Lynmouth House, which later became known as Manor House, was built in a prominent position for enjoyment of the view of the coastline and Bristol Channel. Lynmouth became a popular resort and in 1834 it was described as being 'at the confluence of the East and West Lyn, is frequented by visitors during the season for the benefit of bathing and the sea air. At the quay small vessels lie in fine weather. The road by which Lynmouth is approached from the south, is formed on the precipitous declivity of the valley, and presents a scene of uncommon richness, the sea giving extent and variety to the prospect, which is terminate by the distant shores of Wales.' [204]
 It would have been unusual to build an ancient house in such an exposed situation. The rise of Napoleon in the last decade of the 1700s gave rise to fears of the invasion of England in the following decade. Lynmouth residents would have been aware before this, in 1797, of the reported sighting of a small French force off the coast at nearby Ilfracombe. Like several other places, it was later claimed that local women paraded in their red petticoats to suggest to the French that the port had a substantial body of soldiers in their military red coats. One such petticoat, long known as being one of these original garments, is housed in the town's museum.[205] The position of Manor House would have made it one of the most exposed buildings in Lynmouth and the lack of any garden plants to obscure it would have increased its vulnerability. The building was until recently a care home.

Inset: *A Thistle,* attributed to John Crome, c.1821.

205

312. Another view by Keast entitled *'View of The Cascades in the River of Lymouth'*, c.1820.

313. Pen and grey ink with watercolour by Thomas Rowlandson entitled *'View from the inn at Lynton'*, c.1811.

314. Watercolour by Nicholas Pococke, 1801, looking from west side of Lynmouth. The perspective is similar to that by Keast and shows the house separated from Lynmouth by the river.

315. *'The View of Taustic House The Residence of Sir Bowcher Wrey Knight & Baronet'*, possibly by John Keast, c.1820.

317. Drawing by Admonition Radcliffe entitled *'Tawstock, Sir Bourchier Wrey's near Barnstaple'*, c.1833.'

318. Lithograph entitled *'Old Tawstock Court, destroyed by fire, November, the 10th 1786. From an ancient painting in the possession of Sir B. L. Wrey, baronet'*, 1840.

316. Tawstock Court, c.1820

Tawstock Court seen from Bishop's Tawton a in *'View of Bishop taughton in Deavon'*, possibly by John Keast, c.1820. The house has a prominence in North Devon because of the view of it from Bishop's Tawton: it lies perched on a hill across the Taw River Valley. This was the seat of the earls of Bath and lay at the centre of a large estate. In the early nineteenth century Tawstock was the home of a descendant, Sir Bourchier Wrey, who had erected a new building after a fire destroyed the ancient house in 1786.

The great geometric gardens which had been a feature in the mid seventeenth century had been removed and a long lawn led down to Tawstock church in the valley below. By this date the ancient woodland around the house was one of the main features of the garden. The building was used as a public school for many years and is now a private residence.

319. Watermouth Castle in Berrynarbor, c.1820

View entitled *'Water Mouth House Joseph Davy Esquire in Devon'* possibly by John Keast, c.1820, which shows the alterations made in 1796.

In 1796 Reverend Swete visited the castle and met Mr Davie, the owner, who was then rebuilding. Swete was told that Lord Clinton of Castle Hill had built the house after he was enthused by a continental visit. He had returned to Devon determined to erect classical buildings. In 1796 the grounds consisted of a few open fields, and like Manor House in Lynmouth, the house was built to take advantage of the spectacular countryside.

Miss Sophie Dixon visited in 1830 and her description shows the development in the ten years since this drawing was made. She noted it was *'built in an elegant castellated style, and a very extensive plan, but remains at present in so unfinished a state as to convey but little idea of the effect, were it completed. The entrance is by a fine Gothic archway, to which form the windows correspond, and a terrace is raised round the building, enclosed by a low parapet wall. The plantations comprehend a large part of the two declivities of the valley, but cannot be termed flourishing, as the sea blasts have proved very inimical to the young trees, especially at the mouth of the dell, where it opens upon the cliffs and tide'.*[206] The house was said to be dilapidated in 1845 and was shortly afterwards rebuilt.[207] It is now a Family Attraction.

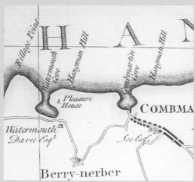

320. Watermouth as shown by Benjamin Donn in his map of 1765.

321. Watercolour by Reverend John Swete entitled *'Watermouth seat of – Davie Esquire'*, 1796.

322. A distant glimpse of Watermouth is seen in 'View of A Cavern in the North of Devon', possibly by John Keast, c.1820.

323. Lithograph entitled *'Watermouth, North Devon, the seat of J. D. Bassett Esquire'*, c.1837.

324. View of the Exeter Workhouse, c.1820s, by an unknown artist. Photograph by Mary Hare, c.1912. It was presumably destroyed during the Blitz in May 1942.

Exeter Workhouse

c.1820s

The Workhouse was one of the grandest buildings erected in the late seventeenth century in Exeter and like the Custom House it was built outside the ancient city walls.

The city of Exeter built one workhouse to serve the entire population and it erected a magnificent building. On first sight it could be mistaken for a palatial residence. The foreground is deceptive in giving an illusion of elegance: the shrubbery, along with the line of trees, helps give an impression of luxury. One writer described how the tall elm trees spread their green foliage as one approached the doors. Closer inspection of the painting shows the individuals depicted are inmates. The institution gained an unsavoury reputation by the early 1800s and the use of garden plants in this painting disguises a building which few would then have willingly entered.[208] The workhouse was later converted to use as the city's hospital but was destroyed during the bombing in May 1942. The site of the building is now occupied by the Exeter Police Station.

Another painting of a city hospital, that of the Wonford Home for the Insane, is also misleading. The building was erected in 1870 and this painting of a tea party on the lawn could easily be mistaken for one in the grounds of a country house. This was its intent: it was proudly asserted that *'the grounds are without confining walls, and the general appearance of the House and Grounds, about twenty acres in extent, is that of a nobleman's residence. The one aim of all entrusted with the responsibility of erecting this mansion was, that it should partake of the character of a Home and not of an Asylum.'*[209] The building remains but the extensive grounds have been encroached upon by the building of the Royal Devon & Exeter Hospital.

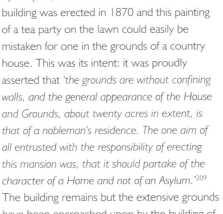

326. Oil painting entitled *'Tea on the lawn of Wonford'* by an unknown artist, no date given.

325. Vignette of the workhouse by John Rocque, 1744.

Inset: *Hollyhocks*, attributed to John Constable, c.1826.

Axminster carpet
1822

Flowers inspired the designs in Devon's earliest carpets.

328. Original scale drawing belonging to the Axminster carpet for the Royal Pavilion Saloon at Brighton, 1822.

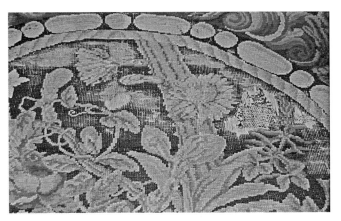

327. (Left) An Axminster carpet after a design by Robert Adam formerly at Harewood House, 1791.

Inset: *Marsh-tits and Crab Apple Flowers,* Teisai Hokuba, c.1820.

329. Detail of the Axminster carpet at Dumfries Castle, late 1750s.

The Axminster firm originated in 1755 when one Thomas Whitty began copying Turkish carpets in the East Devon town. The production at Axminster was a considerable success and in 1789 the factory was visited by King George III. One visitor noted in 1791 that *'the most elegant designs are traced out by the fingers of old women and children'*. William Gilpin, the father of the Picturesque Movement, also visited the carpet factory. He wrote that it was worth visiting and commented that some of the carpets *'display a very rich combination of colours but in general they are so gay that furniture must be glaring to be in harmony with them. Of course they are too gay to be beautiful'*. In his opinion British carpets had too much meaning. Gilpin felt *'it often represents fruits and flowers and baskets and other things which are generally ill represented or awkwardly larger than life or at least improperly placed under our feet.'*[210] He would have had a strong opinion of the Axminster carpet at Brighton. In the Royal Pavilion a carpet was purchased with a design in which flowers feature in a manner which he would also have criticised.

The factory was destroyed by a fire and production moved to Wilton in the 1830s. Carpet-making returned to Axminster nearly a century later.

330. An Axminster carpet from Lansdowne House, London, after 1777.

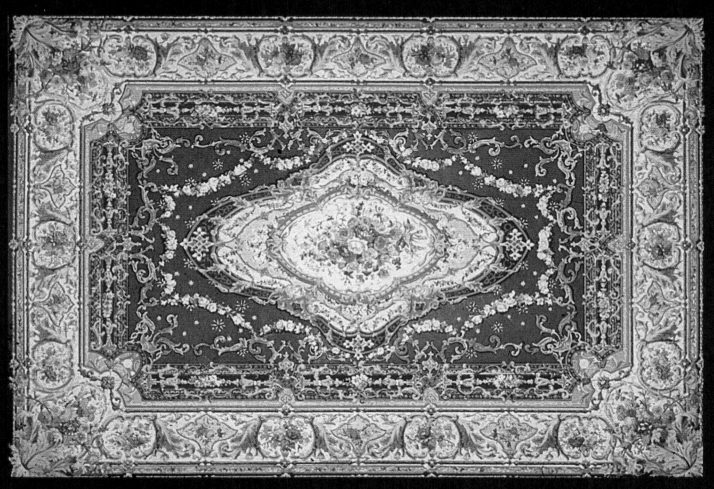

331. Design for an Axminster carpet, 1852, during the interval when they were not produced at Axminster.

332. Watercolour by John Baverstock Knight of Sidmouth, c.1823. Knight was a land surveyor and artist. He produced tithe maps of Dorset parishes in the 1830s and 1840s but was better known for his skill as an artist. Knight was called *'a magnificent specimen of the country squire'*.[211]

Knowle and Sidmouth's other cottages orné

1826

The first few years of the nineteenth century saw Sidmouth evolve from being a fishing village and select resort to also becoming a domicile for wealthy people from other parts of the country.

333. Lithograph by and after G. Rowe entitled *'From the drawing room window of Knowle Cottage Sidmouth (T. L. Fish Esquire)'*, 1826.

Visitors began their stay by renting rooms and cottages for several months but gradually new cottages were erected as principal homes. Their preferred style of architecture was the cottage orné. The gardens matched the style of their new homes. The cottage orné, or decorated cottage, originated with the Picturesque Movement and comprised rustic buildings with an abundance of timber. They were often thatched. At this time, in 1841, the census shows that Sidmouth had more than 30 men who were employed full time as gardeners. A few owners of the new cottages orné had their own live-in gardeners but the majority appear to have worked more casually.[212]

The most illustrious cottage orné in Devon was Knowle. It had been built for Lord de Despenser in 1810 and then purchased by Thomas Fish a few years later. A veranda, some three hundred feet long, ran along the eastern side of the house and was covered with climbing plants. The house was described by one visitor as being *'a complete museum of curiosities and valuable ornaments'*. He *'thought it impossible to do justice to this wonderful place where the most desirous & valuable ornaments are lavished in a manner perfectly incredible to those not eyewitnesses'*. He also approved of the garden.[213]

Knowle was known partly because it was open to the public between the hours of 2 and 4 in the summer months. In 1834 a guide explained the many-faceted wonders of the property. By then it had become a highly popular destination. The unknown writer warned visitors to expect at the entrance gate a:

> *'crash of bonnets, and the destruction of millinery, the screams of the females, and the exclamations of the victors as the iron gate closes behind them with its turmoil and its strife, and passing at once from the purgatory of the squeeze, they enjoy with greater zest the paradise which opens before them'.*

334. Lithograph entitled `Knowle Cottage Sidmouth (T. L. Fish Esquire)' by J. Wallis, 1826.

335. Lithograph entitled `The Dell and Fountain on the Lower Lawn, together with the ocean scenery, as viewed from the drawing room window at Knowle Cottage, Sidmouth, the marine villa orné of Thomas L. Fish Esquire' after C. F. Williams, 1834

Inset: *Bonnet decorated with foliage, 1820s.*

336. Aquatint by T. Sutherland after T. Fidlor entitled 'View from the drawing room of Knowle Cottage', 1823. Ornamental birds are depicted in this print and the next.

337. Aquatint by T. Sutherland after T. Fidlor entitled 'Knowle Cottage, Sidmouth, the residence of T. L. Fish Esquire', 1823.

338. Engraving entitled 'Monstrosities of 1827' by Robert Isaac Cruikshank, 1827, a view of the type of people who crushed the gate at Knowle.

An indicator of the character of Knowle was placed outside the gate: a flower stand stood there which surrounded a pollarded oak. The stand was filled with exotic flowers and surmounted by a globe filled with gold and silver fish. Inside the grounds were similar attractions that led the writer to comment that it was a fairyland.

Knowle had no lack of eye-catching features. The carriage drive had within its turning circle a green mound which was surrounded by three rows of conch and other shells. The mound itself was covered with exotic plants but at its apex stood an orange tree.

There were circular flower stands around the veranda and these had between four and five thousand exotic plants. Balsams were planted in 34 Chinas vases and in the centre of the veranda was a rustic floral seat above which rose a pyramid of rare plants.

The writer's description of the garden is the most detailed of any Devon garden for its time. He noted that in front of this rustic seat was a fountain which rose to a height of 40 feet from out of an oval marble basin filled with fish and surrounded by shells. The marble came from Babbacombe near Torquay. Along the veranda were such plants as *Cactus pentagoni*, orange-leaved myrtles, fir, sycus and fan palms, a dragon plant, *Zamia horrida, Clethra arborea, Yucca aloifolia, Acacia articulata, Dracaena australis* and *Fuchsia globosa gracilis*. The lower lawn was also filled with exotic plants such as variegated gums, a camphor tree (*Laurus camphora*), *Zamia horrida, Yucca aloifolia* and *Yucca uvaria*. A hydrangea was described as gigantic: it had a circumference of nearly 60 feet.

Mr. Fish erected ornamental buildings. There was a Gothic summerhouse and china seats were dispersed throughout the lawn. In a pool stood the Weeping Pillar out of which rose a fountain made of moss, shells, fossils and geological specimens.

The most surprising feature of Knowle lay in its animal life. Silver and gold fish were to be seen throughout the garden and there were two black swans, from Botany Bay, in one pool. Macaws were near the house and other birds included a pelican, two emus, two crown birds, demoiselle birds, gold and silver pheasants, a grey parrot, pair of Peruvian cockatoos, parakeets

339 – 354.

George Rowe's lithographs of Belmont House, Camden Cottage, Cliff Cottage, Coburg Terrace, Cotland House, Cotmaton, Cumberland Cottage, Helens, Levonia Cottage, Myrtle Cottage, North End Cottage, Powys Cottage, Salcombe Hill, Temple Cottage, the vicarage and Woodland Cottage, 1826. Rowe, an *'artist-lithographer'*, was around thirty years old when these were published. He was born and based in Exeter and came to publish his own books. In 1833 Rowe moved to Cheltenham, had a financial setback and tried his luck in the goldmines in Australia. By 1864 he had returned to Exeter where he died.[214]

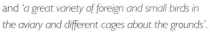

and *'a great variety of foreign and small birds in the aviary and different cages about the grounds'*.

Much more astounding was the variety of other animals which could be found in the ten acres of grounds. Statues stood on pedestals and mixed amongst them were several varieties of deer, a gazelle, two Cape sheep, two small buffaloes and three alpacas. This was not all. Knowle also had seven kangaroos, each of which had been born in the grounds as had one of the alpacas. The kangaroos, or possibly wallabies, were, it was explained, *'the animals which generally excite attention first… they are very docile and even playful when not meddled with but as the tail is the chief means of defence which the animal possesses it can be applied in a manner by no means agreeable to the intruder'*. It was no wonder that there was a crash of bonnets when the doors were first opened in the afternoon.

As to Sidmouth's other houses, in 1813 one visitor commented they were *'highly picturesque and in best picturesque style'*.[215]

355. – 356. Two drawings by George Wightwick of Elfordtown and its summerhouse, c.1826.

355

Elfordtown House

Yelverton

c.1826

George Wightwick's drawing of a home at Yelverton, some nine miles outside Plymouth, illustrates an early suburbanisation of that edge of Dartmoor.

Wightwick moved to Plymouth in 1829 and quickly became one of Devon's most active architects. He was born in 1802 and would have been aged 24 when he made these drawings. Wightwick entered into local society and was a founding member of the Brotherhood of the Blue Friars which was:

'the fancy of these men to form themselves into a small and select literary and convivial club, holding periodical conclaves at the houses of each in succession, there to dine, to crack jokes, to read papers original or selected and to while away the hours in the feast of reason…'.[216]

Elfordtown was advertised in 1782 as a modern-built house but the advert gave no description of an ornamental garden.[217] The house was rented by his step-father William Damant, an architect and surveyor. Damant's daughter Caroline would become Wightwick's wife in 1829 on his 27th birthday.[218] Walter Damant, who was Wightwick's brother-in-law as well as his step-brother, was to become his partner in their architect firm. Wightwick's main view of this three-storey house shows a careful landscape with a veranda covered with climbing plants and shrubberies. His drawing of part of the garden depicts a rustic summerhouse with a covering of thatch and supports formed of branches.

Inset: Flower with three blossoms, unknown, between 1826 and 1866.

357. Watercolour by George Wightwick entitled *'Devon interior'*, 1828. The young woman is Wightwick's fiancée Caroline. The two are sheltering during a storm in a Marystow cottage which belongs to a much less wealthier person than that resident at Elfordtown.

356.

Powderham

Powderham Castle Devon
Lord Courtenays

W. R. 1830

358.

358. –359. Two sketches of Powderham by Admonition Peter Radcliffe of which the first is entitled *'Powderham Castle Devon, Lord Courtenays'*, 1830, no date.

Powderham Castle
1826

In 1830, when Admonition Peter Radcliffe visited, the grounds at Powderham had not been seen for twenty years by their owner, William, 3rd Viscount Courtenay, because he had fled England due to the intolerance he suffered over his sexuality.

Courtenay was born in 1768 and was the only son. He had thirteen sisters. Presumably it befitted his station as the heir to the estate and title to have two christenings. The first was private and the other public.[219] Courtenay was called one of the most beautiful boys in England. He may have inherited his looks from his mother Frances, the daughter of a publican at Wallingford in Berkshire, who was known as a great beauty. Courtenay's mother died in 1782 and his father followed her six years later. An affair by the very young Courtenay with William Beckford was circulated by his uncle to the press in 1784 and caused what became known as the 'Powderham Scandal'. Years later Courtenay may have attempted to circumvent continuing local difficulties by moving; he sought to build a house in Torbay and afterwards near Saltram but his plans did not come to fruition. In 1810 Joseph Farington, the diarist, heard that at Torquay *the people of the place reviled and insulted his servants in terms so opprobrious and this was done with such perseverance that the scheme of finishing the house was given up and it remains a monument of the public opinion against him*.[220] Courtenay fled the country the following year for New York,[221] moved to Paris before the outbreak of war with the United States in 1812, died in that city in May 1835

359.

and was buried at Powderham in June. His body lay in state at the castle which was open to members of the public to pay their respects. It was described as a *'scene of mournful pageantry'*.[222] His second cousin, and namesake, William inherited the title.

Inset: *Still Life: Balsam Apple and Vegetables*, James Peale, 1820s.

225

360. Portrait of William, 3rd Viscount Courtenay, by Richard Cosway.

Before his exile Courtenay, and his father before him, had made great improvements to the grounds. Polwhele noted in 1793 that he had:

'greatly improved and ornamented the house. Among other alterations, he has converted the chapel into a very elegant drawing room. The park and plantations are extensive. Including Warborough in the parish of Kenton, the pleasure grounds belonging to the castle are about ten miles

round. The park itself, two miles round, contains about 400 head of deer. In the plantations are different sorts of firs (all flourishing except the Balm of Gilead) and a variety of beautiful shrubs - planted, for the most part, by the late Lord Courtenay. Not are the forest-trees less vigorous; particularly in the park, where (besides the large clumps of beech, oak, and elm) are several noble chestnut and walnut trees.' [223]

Courtenay was praised by a Regency botanist for having a *'most superb collection'* of plants which included *Mapighia crassifolia*. It had bloomed, allegedly for the first time in England, at Powderham in September 1798. He also had *Hibiscus patersonius*, also known as the Norfolk Island hibiscus, in 1800. That year one visitor noted *'the pleasure grounds are exceedingly fine and extensive, the shrubberies luxuriant and the plantations flourishing'.* [224]

In 1823, whilst in exile, Courtenay sold a considerable portion of the castle's furniture, carpets, curtains and chandeliers and this prompted rumours that the castle itself would be sold. A year later he auctioned the wine from the cellars. In 1830 one visitor thought the *'situation lovely but the house unfurnished and neglected'* and five years later the castle was described as being dilapidated. Even so, the grounds were still being maintained as late as 1831 when a spectacular show of some 500 geraniums was reported in the national press. The castle was also still receiving sightseers albeit Lord Courtenay was no longer in residence: in 1831 it had a visit by Grand Duchess Helena of Russia. [225] In 1808 one visitor noted approval (*'the garden, greenhouses and hot-house are kept in very nice order and there are some fine plants and shrubs in the greenhouse'*) as did the author of *A Botanical Tour through part of the counties of Devon and Cornwall* in 1820 (*'the pleasure grounds are extensive and laid out with considerable taste. The gardens contain a noble collection of exotics; many of the plants had attained a considerable size and luxuriance'*). Samuel and Daniel Lysons were more specific in noting in 1822 that *'the pleasure grounds behind the house are replete with a great variety of flowers and botanical rarities'.* [226]

They also noted that Courtenay lived abroad but that the castle was *'kept up'*. Powderham was possibly being lived in by one or more of his sisters or by his heir, a distant cousin, who was one of Exeter's members of Parliament from 1812 to 1826. Family papers show that the produce from the vegetable garden was being sold throughout his years in exile, perhaps to make up the costs of the garden. [227] A visitor in 1827, sixteen years after Courtenay had fled Powderham, remembered *'in former days when the family*

361. Mezzotint by William Ward after M. Peters with the inscription *'Vice whatever sex or form it may assume leadeth to destruction, - woe to the unruly youth who hath been seduced into its acquaintance, dedication to the... young Nobility of England...'*, 1 June 1802. Courtenay has been thought to be the seated figure on the left and playing cards with him is Thomas Rowlandson. The first printing was on 22 May 1786, two years after Courtenay's public scandal.

were in its glory, tho' to be sure their whole souls seemed wrapped up in their garden, they used to go when breakfast was over in open carriages and stay all day, dining there, a band of music under the trees, dancing on the grass, acting plays'.[228]

It was in the 1840s that the castle had another change in fortune: the railway cut a line along the river and has continually provided a view of the landscape to many thousands of passengers. It was at this time, presumably with income raised by selling the land for the railway, architect Charles Fowler was employed to begin transforming the castle into the building we recognise today. John Claudius Loudon noted with approval in 1842 that Fowler was altering the house but recorded that the magnolias and other exotic plants were neglected: *'the branches are un-pruned, the stems covered with lichens and moss, and the plants choked up in many places with the commonest trees and shrubs'.*[229]

NEPRANI
EPIL CON BEYI

INDOL
CONDITOR
PRESTET
NDI SVBJACET INTVS
hic SITVSES
SAI SITVSES
RDVS
VVS

Mrs Bray and the vicarage garden at Tavistock

1830

The design of the Regency garden at the vicarage in Tavistock was influenced by the appreciation for ancient ruins.

Mrs Anna Bray was one of Devon's earliest novelists and women of letters and her publications brought her some renown in her lifetime and afterwards. She had aspired to be an actress, married at the age of twenty-eight, and then tragically became a widow three years later in May 1821 on the death of her husband, Charles Alfred Stothard, who fell from a ladder in Bere Ferrers whilst drawing ancient glass. Their child was born the following month, died in February 1822 and by the end of that year Mrs Stothard had married Edward Bray, the vicar of Tavistock. She lived there until his death in 1857 when she then moved to London.[230]

Amongst Bray's writing are extensive descriptions of their garden. According to her, it was planned, laid out and planted by her husband with a view to make the garden seem larger and to show the ruins to their best advantage. She also claimed that Humphry Repton, who had presumably been in Tavistock whilst designing the Duke of Bedford's new home at Endsleigh in 1814, did *'so highly… estimate Mr Bray's taste in the art that he more than once consulted him and used good-humouredly to say that if all other trades failed Mr Bray might succeed him in his profession'.* [231]

The character of the garden was dominated by the adjoining remains of the former abbey which had been dissolved at the Reformation and acquired by the Russell family. Mrs Bray described her garden in a series of letters to Robert Southey who was then Poet Laureate. She was particularly enthusiastic of her husband reusing ancient items.

The garden had two sets of antiquities. The first was a pair of sepulchral monuments which date to about the year 600. One she called Cleopatra's Needle. Both are carved of granite, stand at least eight feet high and were brought into the garden by her husband from the locality. Each has a Latin inscription. One notes it was the stone of Nepranus son of Conbevus while the other recorded it as that of Sabinus son of Maccodechetus.

Inset: *A bouquet of flowers with insects, Pierre Joseph Redoute, early nineteenth century.*

363. Engraving entitled *'Still House'* by Adenay, 1879. Mrs Bray wrote in her novel *Fitz of Fitz-ford*
'Within the precincts of the vicarage, at the entrance next the town, stands a gothic arch,
supported on either side by a polygonal tower overgrown with ivy, and decorated with wild flowers; it
presents altogether such a subject as an artist would select for his pencil. This archway was once a
private entrance to the orchard and pleasure-grounds of the abbey. Ascending the dilapidated steps
of one of its towers, you reach the top, whence may be seen a partial view of the town;
Here a busy imagination might find employment in conjuring up the black-hooded monks to people
the now mouldering walls; only that such reveries, from the proximity of this tower to mine host's
stables, stand a chance of being somewhat disturbed by the crack of the post-boy's whip, or a
dialogue between the ostler and his cattle, given in the true accent of broad Devonshire. However,
we have but to descend again the winding stairs, and the imagination need fear no interruption
of her poetic mood, for here will be found food enough for cogitation beneath the vaulted arch,
where lie scattered around, in not unplanned disorder, various fragments of gothic sculpture,
broken pinnacles, mullions of old windows, with several heads of grim and gaping monsters, erst the
ornaments of many a stately column'.[232]

There were also two ancient granite buildings. The Still House is a
small square tower which stands at about twenty feet high. It may have been
part of the Infirmary buildings. The second is still known as Betsy Grimball's
tower. This was, it was suggested in 1830, named after a woman who lived
there after the Reformation. More recently Professor Finberg questioned
whether it may have originally been termed Blessed Grimbald's Tower after
the ninth-century scholar-saint.[233] Each building was used to add interest to the
garden as were the monuments ('*thus you find we have two of these most rare
monuments of antiquity stationed in our garden*').

Mrs Bray also commented on other aspects of the garden. Her
husband planted evergreens (standard and variegated laurel, bay and holly as
well as cedar, juniper and cypress) in order that there was interest outside of
the summer months. All of these, she wrote, grew with a great luxuriance as
did what she described as '*Giant Ivy'*.

There were three particular features in addition to the sepulchral
monuments. The Tea Tree Bower was constructed from a tree which
Reverend Bray had replanted from Abbey House. He had built a framework
from which he overhung the branches. These later rooted and the effect

was to encase the trunk of the tree within a space in which an ancient stone
capital was placed as a seat. The vicarage also had a veranda built in front of
the drawing room windows. This was also a design of the vicar. The frieze
was made of pine and constructed in a zig-zag fashion, apparently to ape
the Norman arches which are occasionally found in local churches such as
Shebbear. Pinecones dangled on wire to act as festoons. Reverend Bray
copied the design from another in the grounds of Mount Edgcumbe. Climbing
plants grew up the trelliswork including honeysuckle, clematis, hydrangea and
the flowering quince. The final feature was the Walking Shed, a *'cool retreat'*
from the summer's heat or shower, which was a thatched building erected
against the boundary wall on the west of their house.[234]

Yet another embellishment was self-consciously learned. The vicar
had three inscriptions placed in the garden. One, suggested by the Book of
Genesis, was on a seat.

> *The man with heavenly wisdom blest,*
> *Seeks in a garden peace and rest,*
> *And there, by worldly evils crossed,*
> *He finds 'a Paradise unlost'.*

Another on the Walking Shed was equally appropriate for the pen of a vicar. It
too had biblical inspiration.

> *'From Storms a shelter, and from heat a shade',*
> *Beneath this shed, my feeble hands have made,*
> *May I with God, like holy Enoch walk,*
> *As friend to friend, like Moses, hear him talk!*
> *And he, who's the true shadow from the heat,*
> *And shelter from the storm, shall guide my feet,*
> *Not only here where first I drew my breath,*
> *But 'whereso'ever I go, through life or death'.*

The third, with a much longer inscription, was placed on an abbey wall. It had
verses to illustrious Tavistock men including Sir Francis Drake.

> *By thee, bold chief! Around th' astonished world,*
> *Brittania's sovereign flag was first unfurl'd.*[235]

In the vicarage ancient monuments and ruins were reused and added
to by other garden ornaments to create a unique Regency garden.

2.8.34

364. Portrait of Mrs Bray, 1834, by William
Brockedon, 1834, using black and red chalk.

SOUTH VIEW OF BYSTOCK HOUSE THE SEAT OF, EDWrd DIVETT ES^{gr}

FRONT VIEW OF BYSTOCK HOUSE THE SEAT OF EDWrd DIVETT ES^{gr}

WEST VIEW OF BYSTOCK HOUSE THE SEAT OF EDWrd DIVETT ES^{gr}

365. Watercolour entitled *'south view of Bystock House the seat of Edward Divett esquire'*, c.1831.

366. Watercolour entitled *'front view of Bystock House the seat of Edward Divett esquire'*, c.1831.

367. Watercolour entitled *'west view of Bystock House the seat of Edward Divett esquire'*, c.1831.

Bystock Court

Exmouth
c.1831

Bystock Court was one of the many genteel homes which lay on the eastern side of the river Exe between Exmouth and Exeter

The mansion house was sold in 1801 and rebuilt by Edward Divett shortly afterwards. His son was elected a member of parliament for the city of Exeter in 1832 and an engraving was published of Bystock the following year. Presumably these drawings were made shortly before he became a member of parliament. They show shrubberies around the entrance to the house along with a particularly well-stocked glasshouse. The west view has flowers beds with an impressive water fountain. Later generations would add to the garden particularly in about 1880 with a very large grotto built by the Veitch firm as well as a series of waterfalls and pond with an island. Bystock was rebuilt in the early 1900s.[236] It is now a care home.

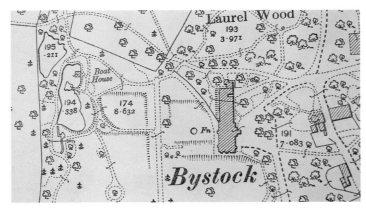

368. Detail of the grounds of Bystock as mapped for the Ordnance Survey in 1905.

369. Steel line engraving by J. Henshall after R. Brown, 1833. It shares the same perspective with illustration 366.

370. Photograph by Camille Silvy of Edward Divett, 7 June 1861. Silvy was a leading portrait photographer in London and retired seven years after taking Divett's photograph.

Inset: *Vase of Flowers*, anonymous after Jean-Baptiste Monnoyer, 1800s.

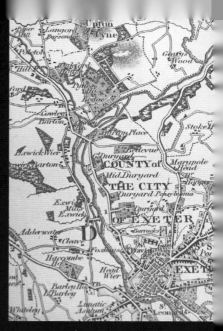

372. Barton Place as depicted on C & J. Greenwood's map of 1827, positioned north of Exeter near Cowley Bridge. Stoke Road was laid out later and Wreford's Lane is shown as the main route to Tiverton.'.

371. Sketch entitled *'Barton Place as it was in the year 1831'*.

Barton Place

outside Exeter
1831

Jane Austen's holidays in Devon from 1802 to 1804 have resulted in one local house being associated with *Sense & Sensibility*.[237]

Barton Place is situated above Cowley Bridge and in what was once called Happy Valley. It was the home of John Merivale and his family when Jane Austen may have found her inspiration to cite it in her writing. The family had been there since it was built in 1797 and members later recalled it was John Merivale who designed the grounds. One descendant wrote *'he took great pleasure in laying out the place having indeed considerable skill in landscape gardening, a talent he had often exercised on behalf of his friends who seem frequently to have asked his advice'*. For some years it was occupied by Admiral Shuldham Peard, the father of Garibaldi's Englishman, but was again inhabited by the Merivales in 1833 following Peard's death.

The grounds reached down to the Exe River but in the early 1830s the city created New North Road which ran through the estate. Merivale complained of the actions of the *'Philistines'* but accepted some £1,500 in compensation. The railway later ran along the same course of the road.[238]

Barton Place is now a care home.

Inset: *Two Roses and Two Small Flowers,* anonymous, 1800s.

375. Drawing with wash entitled 'Barton Place'.

376. Sketch entitled 'Barton Place from a sketch by Alex: Merrivale in 1833'.

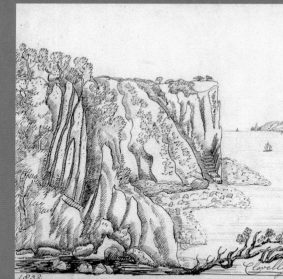

377.– 381. Admonition Peter Radcliffe's sketch of Clovelly Court with four other of her views of Clovelly, 1832.

378.

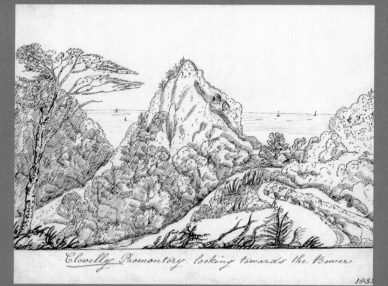

379.

380.

The Hobby Drive
Clovelly Court
1832

The Hobby Drive distinguishes the grounds of Clovelly Court. It takes advantage of the north coast scenery in much the same way as its counterpart did for Lord Revelstoke at Noss Mayo in the South Hams. However, the Hobby Drive was created first and has always been the more illustrious.

Two hundred years ago it was carved out of the woodland overlooking the village of Clovelly and the Bristol Channel. It was laid out by Sir James Hamlyn Williams, second baronet, possibly from an existing footpath and later described as being engineered like an Alpine carriage path.[239] The drive took its name from being a hobby of Williams. In 1828 the gate was locked but visitors were encouraged to seek out the gardener who would allow them to travel the mile and a half drive.[240]

381.

Inset: *Two Roses and Two Small Flowers,*
anonymous, 1800s.

382. Watercolour by 'William Turner of Oxford', undated, entitled 'Clovelly, North Devon'. The Hobby Drive runs along the edge of the cliffs.

384. Wash by Henrietta Matilda Crompton inscribed *'Gallantry Bower, 400 feet high rock in the park of Sir James Hamlyn Williams, Clovelly Court, Barnstaple on Bideford Bay. Bristol Channel'*, 1840. Clovelly Court can be seen in the distance.

383. Portrait of James Hamlyn and his wife Arabella, 1789. Hamlyn was created a baronet in 1795 and was the second generation of the family to live at Clovelly.

385. Pen and ink sketch by Henrietta Matilda Crompton, 1840, on which she wrote *'The picturesque town of Clovelly. Lundy Isle. August 23rd. Sunday. Taken from the Hobby, view from Ilfracombe to Hartland Point'*. She also noted with an 'x' the location of Lady Mary Williams' school. The week that Miss Crompton visited Clovelly she noted that there was already a feel of autumn.[241]

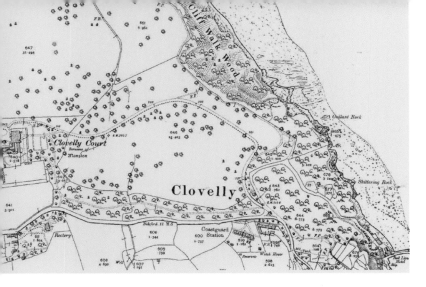

386. Ordnance Survey map of the grounds of Clovelly showing the Hobby Drive, 1891.

387. Photograph entitled *'Clovelly from Hobby Drive'*, c.1890-1900.

The Hobby Drive became a favourite jaunt for visitors to this part of North Devon. One simply called it *'beautiful'*.[242] Another visitor was the Reverend George Tugwell who, in 1863, noted it in his guide to local scenery. He wrote that he strolled:

> *'leisurely down the Hobby road, which winds for ever and for ever along the hill-side, through a charming wilderness of stately timber-trees and luxuriant undergrowth. A profusion of flowers and ferns for the botanist, of cuttings and sections of contorted strata for the geologist, of lovely vistas of wood, and glimpses of the neighbouring sea for the artist render this walk attractive in no common degree, and I leave its well-work track with regret'*.[243]

Forty years earlier a Somerset traveller thought the grounds were romantic and that the gardener was a *'very civil man'*. He wrote *'the summer house called the Cabin is of too grand a scale to attempt description, the rides are very extensive and must be beautifully romantic'*. It was his opinion the drive could not be surpassed in grandeur of scenery. The gardener highlighted a rowan tree which had yellow and orange berries and noted that the nurseryman William Lucombe had acquired specimens from Clovelly.[244]

The most famous incident in the history of the gardens at Clovelly Court took place at a mid-point between today and the creation of the Hobby Drive. In 1909 three suffragettes stole into the grounds during the early hours of a spring morning and decorated the rhododendrons with placards, pamphlets and broadsheets. Prime Minister Herbert Asquith was an overnight guest and woke up to the most curious decorations ever to grace the gardens of Clovelly Court.[245]

388.

Cross Cottage
Bovey Tracey
1836

Cross Cottage is one of the few gardens in this collection to have been drawn by an owner.

Cross Cottage is an early nineteenth-century house in the centre of Bovey Tracey (Moreton Road opposite the hospital). It was named after an ancient cross which was inserted into an outside wall. The modest garden was probably relatively new. The house was home to Dr John G. Croker and his family. Mrs Mary Ann Croker, then forty years old, made the two sketches. The bower, referred to as being Elizabeth's, was presumably that named after her daughter[246] who later founded the Bovey Tracey British School.[247] The Crokers would have been familiar with the nearby garden of the Reverend William Davy who retired to the parish after service in North Bovey. His former garden was said to be curious but in 1826 the second garden at Wilmead Farm in Bovey Tracey was described as even more so and was noted as having walls along the hillside perimeter which gave it the appearance of a castle.[248] His garden, and that depicted by Mrs Croker, show that by the beginning of the Victorian period the affluent members of the middle class were able to have reasonable gardens in which enjoy their leisure time.

388. – 389. Two pen and ink sketches by Annie Croker entitled *'Cross Cottage'* and *'Elizabeth's bower'*, 1836.

389.

Inset: *Flowers in a pitcher,* John Constable, undated.

390. Watercolour by an unknown artist, 1836, showing the front door of Ford's house.

391 – 392. Two photographs of
the garden at Heavitree
House, 1898.

392.

391. Portrait of Richard Ford, after Antonio Chatelain, on canvas, 1840.

393.

394. Detail showing the house.

The Moorish Garden

Heavitree House
1836

What may have been Devon's first garden to have been influenced by Moorish design was created at Heavitree, outside Exeter, in the 1830s. In that garden, in a building covered by myrtle and ivy, was composed one of Exeter's more extraordinary literary achievements.[249]

The village attracted Richard Ford who, while living there, wrote *The Handbook for Travellers in Spain*, an astonishingly popular and influential book. Ford had spent four years travelling in Spain, including a residence at the Alhambra, before he moved to Exeter in 1834. He was delighted with his new city and commented that *'here one has no vices or expenses except eating clotted cream'*. Ford's boast may have been helped by his opinion that Exeter's women were extremely ugly.

In the summer of 1834 he purchased a cob house which was situated near the parish church. Ford renamed it Heavitree House and became obsessed with rebuilding and enlarging his new home. He wrote to one friend *'I have given up the pen for the hoe and spade, all a-delving and digging'*. Ford's enthusiasm continued. He wrote to Lord Addington:

> *'I am content to dig in my garden; like Candide, One must cultivate our own garden – an innocent, refreshing occupation, which gives health to the body, peace to the mind, oblivion for the past, hopes for the future; to do no more harm, if possible, and as much good…'*

The grounds were laid out with terraces and Moorish-patterned flower borders. He embellished the house and garden with architectural curiosities from a variety of sources including the Alhambra.[250] Ford wrote to

Henry 3rd Earl of Carnavon not long after he purchased his new home. He was seeking permission for him and Addington to fish in a stretch of river at Dulverton. In that letter Ford wrote:

> *'this green and beautiful country appears to be a paradise to one coming like myself from the arid sunburnt plains of tawny Saville. I need not say that this new abode is muy ala disposicion de v. s.'.*[251]

An octangular tower was built which was known as *La Torre de Justicia*. The interior decoration included a Moorish ceiling, the walls with ornamental plasterwork and the floor was set with Budleigh Salterton stones *'in an intricate Moorish azulejo or artesonado pattern'*. When the estate was sold a century later the tower was described as *'a Spanish style minaret of two floors'.*[252]

The gardener was John Peter Courpon, aged 23 when the house was built, and he lived with his wife in a nearby cottage in Church Street. Ford's son, Sir Clare, wrote in the 1870s that Courpon had been *'upwards of forty years in the place and to his intelligence, zeal and love of it, is due, in a great measure, the perfect state in which the gardens are kept up and the general character of the place preserved in the spirit my father designed it'.*[253] Courpon was born in Moretonhampstead and was listed as living at Heavitree House in the national censuses from 1841 to 1871. The garden comprised four acres and was planted with pines and cypresses from groves by the Xenil and Guadalquivir rivers.[254]

The garden at Heavitree House was sold in 1938, destroyed for a housing estate in 1949 and within a decade the house was scheduled for demolition and shortly afterwards demolished.[255]

Inset: *A Spanish Garden*, by Martín Rico y Ortega, 1881.

396. Detail showing the house.

395. Lithograph entitled *'Mount Radford for sale by auction by Mr George Robins, at the London Hotel, Exeter, on Saturday, July 1st 1837 at 12 o'clock'* by G. E. Madeley, 1837. The text on the sale catalogue notes *'The ground floor consists of a dining room 20 by 14, a drawing room 20 by 18, and a sitting room to correspond with dining room all occupying the principal front, a back parlor 20 by 16 with store room, closets etc. On the first floor 5 bedrooms & 2 dressing rooms. On the second floor six good bedrooms. The kitchen & other offices occupy the subbasement'.*

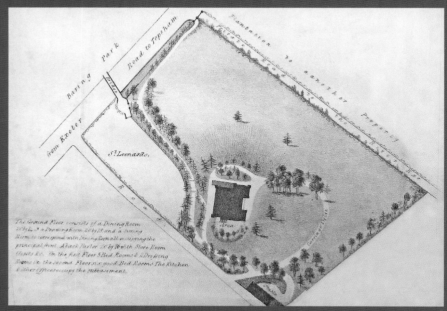

397. The house with the grounds.

Mount Radford

Exeter
1837

Mount Radford may be typical of many medieval houses that were modified or rebuilt by subsequent generations but it is unusual in not only being connected to one of the great financial dynasties in England but also to one which originated in Exeter.

398. Oil painting by William Hogarth entitled *'Portrait of a family'*, c.1735, with figures described similar to those as having been described as strolling the grounds of Mount Radford.

Inset: *Pink roses in a vase*, attributed to Pierre Joseph Redouté, 1838.

John Baring arrived from Germany in 1717, married the daughter of a wealthy grocer ten years later and rose, with his wife's assistance, to become one of the city's wealthiest merchants. Their son John travelled on the continent, returned to Exeter and with his brother initiated the Baring brothers' merchant banking firm. When he retired to Exeter John Baring Senior purchased Mount Radford, a house near to the family home of Larkbeare.[256] A later Exonian recalled the life in the garden: *'The hospitality of the merchant prince made his home the resort of people of the best quality. About the grounds strutted men of fashion, in cocked hats and powdered wigs, in coats of ample skirt, with buckled shoes and gold-headed canes; while gentlewomen of high degree played the parts of youth and beauty, or of comely matron, in costumes differing but little from those rendered familiar by Hogarth. Of their host's personal appearance in his later years we are told that, 'his dress was singular. Coat, waistcoat, breeches, of a light speckled colour - it was called pepper and salt - silk stockings of the same, small steel buckles at his knees, large steel buckles on his shoes. He was a tall, thin man, with powdered hair, and a sharp, penetrating look, who seemed to measure with his gold-headed cane every step as he walked. The people called him Old Turkey Legs - almost everybody had a nickname in those days - but he could smile at the jest, as those legs, with the assistance of the electors, took him to the honourable House.'*[257] Mr Patch, who lived at Rougemont House, is recorded to have said that Baring led *'an almost uninterrupted life of happiness'* until he reached the age of 70 when his children began dying young.[258]

The garden depicted in the illustration was drawn several generations after the earlier description was written. The lightly planted landscape with circular drive and beds were not likely to have been similar to the early eighteenth-century garden described as being of the time of William Hogarth.

399. Watercolour and gouache entitled *'Design for Silverton Park'* from the studio of James Knowles, c.1837.

400. The sale poster, 1892.

SILVERTON PARK,

Within a few minutes' walk of Silverton Station on the main Great Western Railway, 2 Miles from Hele, 4½ Miles from Cullompton, and 6 Miles from the CITY of EXETER.

HIGHLY IMPORTANT SALE
of the VALUABLE CONTENTS of the above MANSION,
COMPRISING THE EQUIPMENT OF ABOUT

60 BED, DRESSING AND RECEPTION ROOMS,
Including a Choice Collection of
Antique Furniture, Curios, Library of about 1,000 Volumes of Books,
&c. &c. belonging to the late EARL OF EGREMONT

THOMPSON, RIPPON & Co.

Are honored with instructions from WILLIAM WYNDHAM Esq. to SELL BY PUBLIC AUCTION on the premises as above, on

TUESDAY, WEDNESDAY & THURSDAY, DEC 6

Silverton Park

1837

Silverton Park was one of the grandest of country houses to be built in Devon but lasted barely two generations. In 1837 George Wyndham, 4th Lord Egremont, inherited the title on his uncle's death but the wealth went to his illegitimate cousins. He spent his seven years as an earl in a great building spree and Silverton Park was his most extravagant endeavour.

401. Painting of Silverton Park, June 1879.

In 1831 Wyndham purchased Combesatchfield, a large country house some eight miles north of Exeter. His architect, James Thomas Knowles, incorporated the old house within his flamboyant design and by 1838 the house had been renamed Silverton Park and the earl, and his countess, began their occasional visits.

Inset: *Seated gardener with a shovel,* William Egley, nineteenth century.

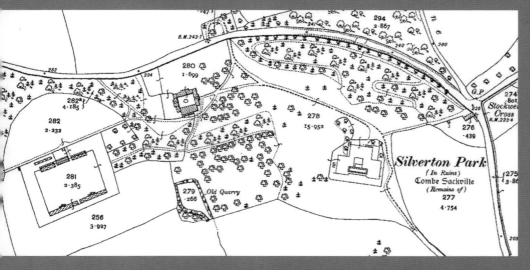

402.– 403. Two photographs of Silverton Park, c.1900.   402.

403.

404. Silverton Park as mapped in 1905

Laetitia Josephine Chalk, the daughter of the Victorian rector of Silverton, later recalled the house:

> 'this property was bought by Lord Egremont who did not bother to pull down the old house but (as at the rectory) built a larger one round it, in the then fashionable Classical style. He sent for workmen from Italy and kept them for many months casting the beautiful frieze which went all round the house and portrayed in base-relief a long procession of people sacrificing bulls. In the centre of the stupendous South Front was a relief of the Nine Gods, with Jupiter and his eagle in the midst'.

She went on to write that:

> 'inside the house were numberless bedrooms no larger than a cabin on a man-of-war, quite big enough for a bachelor said Lord Egremont who had been a sailor. Each contained a bed and a tiny chest of drawers. One room (I remember) had no window but was lighted by a skylight resembling an umbrella. His own bedroom was magnificent and his bath of yellow marble remained for us to wonder at when all else had gone'.[259]

In 1845 the earl died at his new house and his widow only occasionally visited: it was claimed in 1892 that she spent a month there whilst her main home in Somerset was being cleaned.[260] Silverton Park was never completely finished, became a financial burden and the 130 room house was demolished with dynamite in 1901.[261]

The parkland was the dominant garden feature but great sums were spent in enhancing the gardens. The Veitch firm supplied a considerable number of plants on at least one occasion in August 1845.[262] The grounds remain as does the stable block which is now owned by the Landmark Trust.

405. A water colour by Henrietta Matilda
Crompton entitled 'Lynmouth', 1840.

Glen Lyn

Lynmouth
1840

Whereas the garden at Manor House at Lynmouth was minimal and concerned with maximizing the view of the sea, that at nearby Glen Lyn was firmly focused on the heavily wooded and sharp falls of the river Lyn.

In 1834 a correspondent to *Blackwood's Edinburgh Magazine* visited and enthused of the grounds set above Lynmouth:

> *'in the midst of which, as within a theatre, where is particularly delighted to sport and gambol, the little stream was playing in every variety of motion, from humility through grace to dignity. Here it was almost placid, running off into meandering rivulets – here shooting with rapidity over large smooth masses, bearing on its rich transparent bosom white bubbles, like fairy barks in a race - here pouring over the narrow passages of congregated fragments, yet leaving the curious flowers that edged them, and seemed as if with enjoyment looking into the sport and play unhurt – and here in a collected body rushing down, glistening in the power and dignity of a cascade'.*

'The Sketcher' went on to describe how the light was green from the overhanging foliage and that he crossed the stream on bridges made of planks.[263]

In 1859 Charles Kingsley wrote that the grounds were *'a double paradise, the wild Eden of the Past side by side with the cultivated Eden of the Future. How its alternations of Art and Savagery at once startle and relieve the sense, as you pass suddenly out of wildernesses of piled boulders, and torrent-shattered trees, and the roar of a hundred fern-fringed waterfalls into "trim walks, and fragrant alleys green" and the door of a summer-house transports you at a step from Richmond to the Alps. Happy he who "possesses" as the world calls it, and happier still he whose taste could organise, that fairy bower'.* Another Victorian, a visitor from Hampshire, called it *'the most romantic and beautiful walk in the neighbourhood'* and yet in 1830 the housekeeper to the 3rd Countess of Carnavon thought Lynmouth was beautiful but *'the walks are all so hilly, nothing but up and down hills, and the worst I ever saw in my life'.*[264]

406. View by Henrietta Matilda Crompton, 1840, on which she wrote *'Sir W. Herries' cottage, Lynmouth, beautiful'.*

Inset: *A study of ferns, Edward Lear, 1842.*

In 1830 an anonymous lady from Barnstaple was so enchanted with the valley that she featured it in her romantic novel. Her characters visited Glen Lyn.

> *'Mr Mandeville, who was engaged to take tea with them, was also one of the party, and little Willy, who gamboled sportively by their side, seemed as much excited by the view of nature's lonely beauties, as themselves.*
>
> *"Oh look at the water now," said the delighted child, as they paused on approaching the waterfalls, "only see, grandpapa, how it pours down!"*
>
> *"Yes, indeed," said Mr G. "the torrent swollen by the recent rain, presents a most magnificent appearance."*
>
> *"I never saw it so fine," exclaimed Emily, leaning over the bridge; "I would not have missed visiting this charming spot once again for a great deal!"*
>
> *"I think it was on this spot I first had the pleasure of meeting you," observed Mandeville to Emily, as they afterwards proceeded in their walk.*
>
> *"I believe, - yes – I did see you here first," replied Miss Durnford, in a stammering and confused tone, fearing lest he might have overheard any part of her conversation, at the time, with her little charge.'…*

The characters left the grounds with regret while appreciating its rocks, cascades and woodland.[265]

In 1817 Glen Lyn became the home of Sir William Herries and he died there in 1857 whilst the house was being extensively renovated. He had attained the rank of Lieutenant General but lost a leg in the Peninsula War in 1801. Sir William may have chosen North Devon as a place to convalesce. His other home was near Piccadilly.[266]

J. M. W. Turner had sketched the valley six years before Herries' purchase[267] and Lynmouth had already attracted literary visitors such as Coleridge, Shelley and Wordsworth. In about 1838 Herries opened his grounds in the summer to the public. With a hint of disapproval his sister-in-law commented *'good Mr Herries is to let the multitudes of persons of all ranks walk in these grounds'*. In about 1845 one local guide noted *'a greater number of alluring and interesting objects are assembled within a small space, than can be met with in any particular spot about this enviable retreat'*.[268] The following decade another tourist guide advised visitors to see *'Sir William Herries' grounds, close to the Lyndale Hotel. Walk up the hill towards Lynton; at the first gate on the left, ring the bell. This is by far the most beautiful spot in the*

407. Another view by Henrietta Matilda Crompton entitled *'Sir William Herries' grounds 1840'*.

neighbourhood. After passing through the garden and shrubberies, the visitor will be left to his own devices at a gate communicating with a path which winds up the ravine by the side of the waters of the West Lyn.'[269]

Most of the views are by Miss Henrietta Matilda Crompton, the daughter of a wealthy banker. She and her family lived at Micklegate House in York and came to Lynmouth to visit her sister Mary, the wife of Sir William Herries. He referred to Miss Crompton on one occasion as `my dear little Matilda' but when she was in her late twenties she and her sister were described by another woman as *'not very genteel – not elegant enough for me'*. They were also *'all stupidish… vulgarish and occasionally rather provincial'*. Miss Crompton came in for particular criticism for incessant talking: *'tis flip, fancy and nonsense and attempt at wit'*. In turn, Miss Crompton was dismissive of local people at Lynton. In 1840 she commented *'there are no elegant people here at present and I never saw a plainer set of people than there were at church today'*.

She travelled a great deal including on this visit to Lynmouth when she was 46 years old. Painting appears to have been her particular interest and amongst those

408. Detail of a perspective view of Lynmouth by Henrietta Matilda Crompton in which she notes the direction of Barnstaple. Glen Lyn is shown at the bottom.

410. The final view by Henrietta Matilda Crompton entitled *'Waterfall, Lynmouth'*, 1840.

409. A view by Miss Crompton in which she shows the waterfall at Lynmouth, 1840.

who taught her were Copley Fielding and David Cox. Her drawings and paintings first came to light in 1993 when they were discovered amongst the effects of a descendant.[270]

The views of the cascades had popular appeal but another interest brought visitors to Lynmouth and particularly to Glen Lyn. In 1857 Charlotte Chanter, the author of *Ferny Combes*, praised Glen Lyn as being the *'undoubted gem'* of Lynmouth and noted that the ferns there were superb. There was then a mania for ferns and the South West was a leading part of the country to find, and then take home, specimens of different varieties. These could be seen in abundance at Glen Lyn and in the countryside nearby.[271]

Only a short distance separates Manor House and Glen Lyn but the garden attractions of the two have always been greatly different.

411. Steel line engraving entitled *'Waterfalls and bridges in Lady Herries' grounds, Lynton, Devon'*, 1859.

255

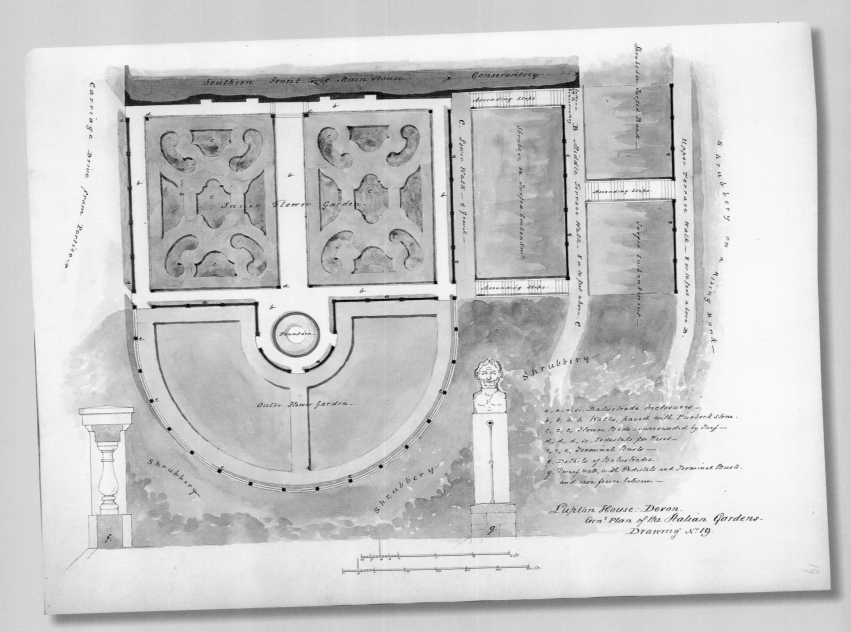

412. Watercolour of plan of the Italian Garden by George Wightwick, c.1840.

The Italian Garden at Lupton Park

near Brixham
c. 1840

The Italian Garden at Lupton survives albeit not as well-maintained as George Wightwick would have wished when it was designed in the first years of the reign of Queen Victoria.

Lupton was acquired by Charles Hayne in the mid eighteenth century and sold to the Buller family towards the end of that century. Sir John Buller-Yarde-Buller, later created Lord Churston, hired George Wightwick to make alterations to the house.[272] He also designed the new garden.

The *'Italian Garden'* came in the waning of interest in the natural, or green, landscape of the eighteenth century. An enthusiasm for ancient gardens led to a reintroduction of elements which can be found in the garden at Lupton. Wightwick's plan was for a garden in two halves. That from the house

414. Mezzotint after Grant of John first Baron Churston, 1850.

413. Photograph of watercolour by William Callow, c.1874. Callow toured the south coast of Devon in 1842, 1877 and in the mid 1880s. He had visited Dartmouth and Torquay in 1842 and Dartmouth, Salcombe and Kingsbridge in 1877. His painting of Lupton might have been derived from these visits but he exhibited paintings of Devon in many other years from 1850 onwards. In 1876 he showed *Two views in South Devon* at the Royal Society of Painters in Watercolours.[273]

Inset: *The Flower Girl*,
Charles Cromwell Ingham, 1846.

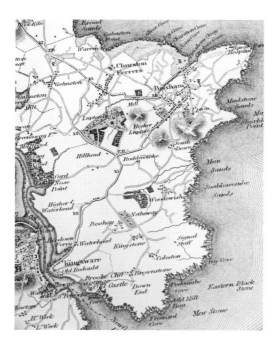

416. Ordnance Survey map of Lupton, 1906, with the Italian Garden clearly seen.

415. Detail from C. & J. Greenwood's map of 1827 showing the position of Lupton and the extent of its grounds.

417. Sketch with the inscription *'Samuel Wills' draught of the front of Lupton, 1750'*. The key to this drawing has not survived.

comprised two sets of inner and outer planting areas dissected by a fountain with walks of Purbeck stone. The inner gardens were planned for parterres filled with flowering plants and set within turf.

A second garden would be seen from the conservatory which had gravel walks, plantings mainly of shrubs or turf. A dwarf wall enclosed the whole scheme. A painting of the garden, made sometime between 1842 and the early 1880s, confirms Wightwick's scheme was followed. The outlines of that design survive today. Lupton is now owned by The Lupton Trust.

418. Watercolour of Lupton by John Swete, nearly half a century before Wightwick's alterations, 1793.

419.

420.

419. – 421. Three watercolours by an unknown
artist of Cliff House, 1842.

421.

Inset: *Basket of Flowers*, Eugène Delacroix
1848–9.

The aloe at Cliff House

Salcombe
1842

These three watercolours capture what was an exciting episode in the garden history of Devon.

In 1842 the blooming in Salcombe of an *Agave americana*, commonly known as the century plant or the American aloe, was heralded as a great event and an admission fee was charged to see the plant. Fifteen years later another specimen bloomed: it stood nine feet high and had a circumference of 46 feet. It was raved about as *'one of the most magnificent specimens of this plant that has ever blossomed'*.[274]

John Claudius Loudon visited in 1842 and wrote *'there is an agave here coming into flower with four stems. Every one of the leaves has been injured at the points, and most of them along the edges; but, whether this was done by accident or by design to throw the plant into flower, we could not ascertain, the gardener not being at home.'*[275] It was also suggested the plant was between 30 and 35 years old but thought not to have been as striking in that the flower stem had branched into seven stalks with the principal ones being ten feet in height.[276]

Cliff House had a reputation for the blooming of agaves: the 1842 flowering was the sixth one recorded for Salcombe. The first was remembered in 1819 as being so noteworthy as to be included in a history of the port. It was recorded that:

> *'in the summer of 1774 a large aloe, the Agave americana, only twenty-eight years old, and which had always stood in the open ground, without covering, flowered here in a garden belonging at that time to the representatives of a Mr Barrabe, the principal custom house officer, then recently deceased, but which at present forms the grass plot before the windows of what has lately received the appellation of Cliff House. It grew to the height of twenty-eight feet, the leaves were six inches thick, and nine feet in length, and the flowers, on forty-two branches, innumerable. In the middle of June it was first observed to have shot forth a flower stem in nearly a horizontal direction. Presently it elevated its head to an angle of forty-five degrees, and in less than a fortnight became perpendicular, making a progress almost visible to the bystander, and increasing in extent about nine inches a day. By the month of August it had reached the height of twenty feet, as the hand bills then distributed expressed, though by the end of September it had risen eight feet more.'*[277]

Aloes were *'never absent'* from Salcombe after 1774 and at Cliff House in particular they continued to bloom. In 1855 *'a splendid one and certainly the finest'* bloomed in the lower garden and three others were then in flower in nearby gardens at the Moult and at Woodville. The latter garden had a plant which flowered in 1820 and was recorded as having had forty flowering branches with an estimated 16,000 blooms. Twelve years later another plant flowered at the Moult and then one again in 1835 at Woodville. The fifth recorded blooming was at the Moult in 1840. By 1861 aloes appear to have become overwhelmingly popular in Salcombe: it was claimed that *'everybody who has the room to spare thinks it necessary to have one or two of these strange productions'*.[278]

Bishopstowe

c.1845

One of Exeter's best-known bishops, and certainly its most infamous, created a house and garden at Torquay and here he lived in pointed exile from Exeter.

Bishopstowe was built in 1841 for Henry Philpotts, Bishop of Exeter, on the eastern side of Torquay. He came to the resort shortly after being consecrated in 1831: the following year he fled his new home at the Bishop's Palace in Exeter because of the cholera outbreak. Nine years later the new mansion was built some 17 miles from his cathedral at Exeter. Interestingly, this was recently after he was compensated with his share of £12,729 4s 4d for the freeing of 665 slaves he owned in the Caribbean.[279] Philpotts received his money in 1835 and then embarked on building his new home. A few years later this was described as:

'Between the hills opening towards this cove (Anstey's Cove), and at a short distance from the sea, stands Bishopstowe, the new palace of the Bishop of Exeter. This beautiful mansion is in the Italian style, and was built in 1841-2, from the design and under the superintendence of Mr Gribble, architect, of Torquay. It is very irregular in its elevations, being composed of several projecting and receding parts, of various heights, forms, and sizes; one of which, at the southern angle, over-tops all the rest, and forms a square tower, with a pointed finial rising from the centre of its roof. The grounds in front rise in three beautiful terraces, connected by flights of steps, and the lower one having a fountain. The house has many handsome apartments, and reflects the highest credit on the skill of the architect; and the views from it and the grounds are varied and pleasing; so much of the sea only being visible as serves to enhance the beauty of the wood and rock in the foreground'.[280]

Shortly after it was built John Claudius Loudon visited and noted:
'We have seldom seen anything so complete: there is one walk which descends through the grounds to a secluded bay on the rocky shore, and another which ascends to a hill or piece of high open table land or downs covered with short turf, where the fresh breeze may be enjoyed, and from which extensive views are obtained. Before the entrance front of the house there is a mass of rock, which might be exposed in such a manner as to form a feature appropriate to the situation; but it has been earthed up and turfed over. Some

422. Coloured lithograph by W. Spreat entitled 'Bishopstowe', c.1845.

423. Watercolour by J. G. Fuller entitled *'Bishop's Stowe near Torquay'*, 1848.

broad margins of turf are wanted along the terrace walls and parapets, to harmonise them with the exterior scenery; but these and other suggestions may easily be carried into effect, if they should be approved of. We found Scilla verna in flower as well as in seed on the downs'[281] In 1859, by which time the gardens would have matured, another visitor noted the garden comprised terraces, statues, lines of cypresses and *'parterres of brilliant colours'*.[282] One particular story was repeated about Philpotts and his pride in Bishopstowe. It was said that *'A lady visitor, thinking to please him, rather gushed over the beauties of the scenery, remarking that it was so like Switzerland. Yes, said the Bishop, drily only there you have mountains and no sea, and here we have sea and no mountains.'*[283]

It was commented in a national journal, twenty years after Philpotts built his Torquay mansion, that the bishop had not lived during those years in his own cathedral city. The *London Review* noted that the palace was shut up and that Philpotts had it exempted from poor rates and local taxes as an empty house. It even claimed *'a lonely donkey grazes in the episcopal garden'* while he lived in his marine villa.[284]

Philpotts died at the age of 92 at Bishopstowe. One Exeter journalist noted the bishop *'for several years past had been little else than a mitred phantom at Bishopstowe'*.[285] He was not well-loved. The *Exeter Flying Post* noted that `few men have spent more money in litigation than the Bishop of Exeter'. The *Times* reported *'As the leaf is beginning to fall, and before he could carry out his proposed resignation, Henry Philpotts drops into his grave carrying with him three generations of work and warfare, several hundred controversies, much that is remembered and much more that is forgotten, and no inconsiderable amount of respect and even affection... The Bishop of Exeter outlived everything that once made him famous and formidable. Length of days brought its gains and losses. He long survived, and, no doubt, learnt to regard with generous kindness the foes he resisted, or provoked, the causes he denounced, the statesmen he defied, the clergy that rebelled against his discipline, the Primate he excommunicated, the writers that lived by abusing him, and the Lords that would not listen to his harangues.'*[286]

424. Steel line engraving entitled *'Bishopstowe'*, 1845. On this copy of the print a note was made *'Bishop of Exeter's country seat, about a mile from Torquay - on the Babbicombe road. He is much hated here'*.

The family sold the mansion, with its ten acres of ground, the following year. Nearly thirty years had passed since it was built and the auction details were able to claim that the mansion, with its vineries, conservatories, hothouses, Italian gardens, lawns and pleasure grounds, kitchen gardens and pasture lands, had *'well matured and finely-shrubbed ornamental grounds; the surrounding views are of the most picturesque and charming character having a richly varied and undulating landscape in the foreground, abutting on the well-known Anstey's Cove, and terminating in extensive and delightful channel prospects.'*[287] In 1929 Bishopstowe became a hotel and then enlarged. It is now known as the Palace Hotel.[288]

425. Undated oil panting entitled *'A view across the artist's garden from his house at Exmouth in Devonshire'* by Francis Danby.

426. Pen and wash by Francis Danby entitled *'Exmouth in 1826'*.

Shell House

Exmouth
c.1846 – 61

This is the only painting in this collection by an internationally known artist who depicted his own garden in Devon.

Francis Danby, the Irish-born landscape painter, came to live at Exmouth in 1846 and remained there until his death fifteen years later.[289] The painting provides the view from his home, Shell House, which stood beyond the Esplanade on The Maer, on what is now the cricket ground. His home was a prominent feature but was largely open to views of the sea. Danby's paintings have been described in terms of their moodiness. A few years after his death a visitor to the Exe Estuary recalled Danby residing at Exmouth and noted that *'doubtless this wild waste of sandy salt-water desert afforded him suitable and effective material for many of his compositions. Such spots, dreary, dismal and desolate though they are, have great attractions for many painters contrasting so sharply with our modern refinement and over-civilisation'.* [290]

Danby led an unconventional life. He had ten children, some with *'a girl who lived in the house as a sort of governess to his children'*, and his wife abandoned them and him for another artist. Danby gave his family a peripatetic lifestyle and he was often penniless. When he died one obituary noted 'a life more sad has been rarely led by a man of undoubted genius'.[291]

Inset: *Still life with flowers and fruit*, Henri Fantin Latour, 1866.

427. Oil painting by an unknown artist of the view from the Maer towards Dawlish Warren.

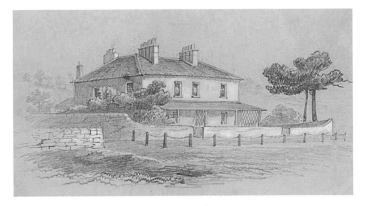

428. Unattributed and undated pencil drawing of the Shell House.

THE RIGHT HON^{BLE} & REV^D LORD VISCOUNT SIDMOUTH'S _ UPOTTERY _ DEVON

429. Painting by Edward Ashworth entitled '*The Right Honble & Revd Lord Sidmouth's, Upottery, Devon / Samuel Greig architect; E. Ashworth Clerk of Works 1846'.*

430. Pencil drawing, probably by Edward Ashworth, entitled 'Lord Sidmouth's house Upottery erecting 1846'.

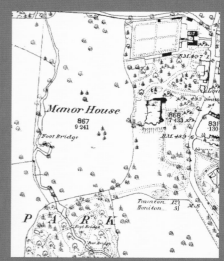

431. Detail from the Ordnance Survey map showing the grounds at Upottery, 1889.

Upottery
1846

Upottery was the home of Reverend William Leonard Addington, 2nd Viscount Sidmouth, whose father had been Prime Minister.

Upon the death of his father, Reverend Addington gave up his rectory at Poole and rebuilt Upottery which then became the family seat. Previous generations of the family had enjoyed various homes and Upottery had never been the principal seat.

This Victorian Tudor house was designed by Samuel Alexis Greig in 1846 (who had just submitted plans for work in St Sidwell parish in Exeter)[292] and stood until it was demolished in 1962. The foundation stone was laid on 25 June 1845, the roof was in place in March 1846 and the building was finally completed the following year.

Edward Ashworth had just returned from the Far East where he had spent several years and Lord Sidmouth employed him as clerk of works to the architect who submitted plans and began building work. The contract was signed on 31 May 1845 and the full cost of the new house was to cost £6,440. Unfortunately Greig died not long afterwards.[293] Upottery may have been Ashworth's first substantial project in Devon but he had just overseen the construction of a house in Hong Kong.[294] He was paid ten pounds and ten shillings per week as clerk.[295]

The kitchen garden lay to the north of the house but towards the southwest was an elaborate network of paths through wooded parkland with a stream and three foot bridges. James Veitch advised on the planting in 1845.[296] The Addington family were the only owners of the house.

432. Oil portrait of Henry Addington, first Viscount Sidmouth, c.1785, by Francis Wheatley. The viscount had a number of homes and is unlikely to have spent a great deal of time at Upottery.

Inset: *Bird's nest with sprays of apple blossom,* William Henry Hunt, c.1847.

The Orangery at Mount Edgcumbe

c.1849

While the south coast of Devon had citrus trees growing relatively unprotected outside, a number of other houses, including Saltram but also notably Mount Edgcumbe, had orangeries.

433. Watercolour by Nicholas Condy, c.1849. This was one of a series of twelve views by Condy of the garden and formed part of the collection of Lord Harmsworth.[297] A few years before Condy painted this view the garden was noted as having a *'central fountain with a caryatidal vase of marble; regular walks diverging therefrom; an orangery of Palladian design opposed by a balustrade terrace and a select party of Heathen family occupying their uniformly arranged pedestals'*.[298]

I n 1789 Reverend Stebbing Shaw visited Mount Edgcumbe and was impressed by the Orangery which had been erected between 1760 and 1785. A watercolour by Nicholas Condy some two generations later shows the exotic character of this part of Mount Edgcumbe. The Orangery was also known as the Italian Garden and was a feature along with two other nationally-minded gardens: it also had French and English Flower Gardens.[299]

434. Untitled watercolour by Thomas Mitchell, late eighteenth century, of a view from Stonehouse looking towards Mount Edgcumbe.

Inset: *Apples, grapes and a cob-nut*, William Henry Hunt, c.1850.

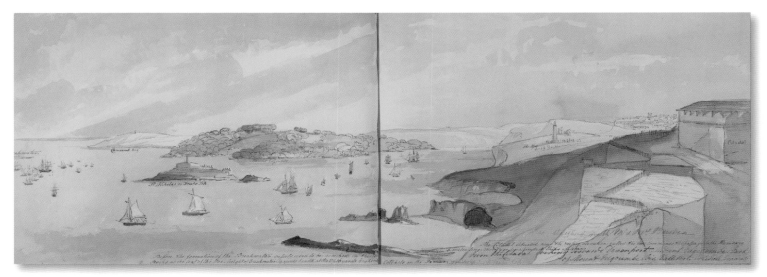

435. View by Henrietta Matilda Crompton of the view from Plymouth to Mount Edgcumbe, 1840.

Shaw, like other visitors, rang the doorbell at the keeper's lodge and was then shown around the grounds. He climbed the lawn to visit the house and afterwards crossed the Green Terrace which had been gravelled. Shaw then passed:

> *'through bowers of various foliage, oaks, chestnuts, limes, plantains, variegated sycamore green and white, etc. to an alcove opposite the gate into the deer park, which affords a similar sweet view. The first object after entering the park is a moss-house, from this we next come to an open bench looking full upon the merchants' harbour of Catwater… From hence we descend through serpentine bowers of bays, myrtles, arbutses, laurestinuses, etc. to Lady Damer's garden (so called) at the end of which is a large stone alcove with a complimentary inscription. Ascending again by similar zig-zags to the terrace.'*

Shaw noted that ten years before a considerable portion of the woodland had been cut down in order to deny French invaders the potential for cover. He noted that Lord Edgcumbe had given his consent but on condition that the Admiralty gave due consideration. He wrote *'If you are convinced, on serious deliberation, that danger may arise from them, down with them. If you are not quite so certain, for heaven's sake let them stand.'* Shaw also visited the Gothic Alcove, *'the White Alcove on the Dry Walks'*, a Doric Alcove,

and the Wilderness in which was a flat stone from which one could see seven towers. Finally he visited the orangery, *'an excellent building, 100 feet by 30, where the fruit ripens in almost equal perfection with that abroad'*.[300]

In 1810 Joseph Farington also crossed the Hamoaze, signed his name in the visitors' book at the lodge and then wrote a note to Lord Edgcumbe asking for permission to walk in the grounds. He spent nearly 5 hours enjoying the views. He had one criticism: the only instance of bad taste, in his opinion, was the form of the ruined tower and its situation.[301] Farington had visited the year before and was made aware of the arrangements for visitors. A *'good-humoured old woman'*, who was the gate-keeper, had informed him every Monday all Plymouth residents, except soldiers and sailors, were allowed to visit on the condition that they were *'decently dressed'*. On one day no less than 905 people had toured the grounds.[302] Three years later it was said that three days in the week (Monday, Wednesday and Friday) were given over to the public to visit. A cottage had been built in the park to provide hot water in order that tea could be made and hampers were brought by the visitors in order that they might have picnics. It gave the park, so it was claimed, the appearance of a fair with groups playing, dancing and singing.[303]

The changing perspectives of Plymouth were one of the attractions of the garden. Mrs Jane Elizabeth Moore visited in about 1786 and commented that *'this situation for variety of extensive views, both of land and water, can surely not be equalled, the eye being directed seven ways'.*[304] A century later, in February 1884, another female visitor, Mrs Florence Glynn, who was staying at Antony, wrote to her husband back on the Isle of Wight *'I believe you have seen Mount Edgcumbe, haven't you? Mrs Pole Carew drove me in a pony carriage with such a charming pair of ponies. We went such a pace up and down such hills. Every now and then close to the sea, bits more like the Gulf of Genoa than anything English - at last we came to the lodge and then we went over the grass and drove to the edge of the Mount. Such a view, my darling, it was lovely. Trees of every description at our feet and then the great open sea and on our left Plymouth – the Dockyards – Stone-House – the great ships, all the creeks etc. Then we drove to the house by a long lonely road still at the edge through trees (quantities of stone pines and cork trees and great ilex, shimmering like olives) hanging over the sea. It was so beautiful. It was very un-English! I did long for you. We found Lord Mount Edgcumbe and one of his daughters at home and went in for a little while and then had a shorter but lovely drive home.'* [305]

Perhaps the most illustrious visit was that of George III and his family in 1789. On alighting the party was met by sixteen female virgins dressed in white who walked ahead of them and carried baskets of flowers. They strewed the path with roses, carnations, jasmine and myrtle with a chorus of *God Save The King*. Rare flowers were then presented to the Royals who proceeded to the walks where the prospects *'surprised and astonished them'.*[306]

John Claudius Loudon was equally enchanted. He wrote in 1842:

> *'High as were our expectations from the published descriptions and the long celebrity of the place, we were not disappointed. We never before looked down on the sea, on shipping, and on a large town, all at our feet, from such a stupendous height. The effect on the mind is sublime in the highest degree, but yet blended with the beautiful. There was something to us quite unearthly in the feeling it created. The separate gardens, as may readily be supposed, are overgrown, and the magnolias and other fine trees greatly injured, by the elms and other common trees and shrubs. One garden, in imitation of an ancient*

Roman burying-ground, which contains a great many altars and urns, is so covered with evergreens, that it is not even mentioned in the guide-book. The only garden worth notice is what is called the Italian garden, though there is nothing Italian in it but the orange trees and a few white painted leaden statues; the former disfigured by the ugly un-architectural tubs, and the latter, with the exception of a few on the parapets of a flight of steps, un-artistically placed. We were sorry to see some alterations going on at the house, the object of which, as it appeared to us, was to change the entrance from the back, where it is at present, to the front, where it will display the finest views from the place before entering the house. Among the plants we noted down were, orange trees in tubs with stems 13 feet high and 12 inches in diameter at the surface of the tub, the heads also being 12 feet in diameter.'* [307]

Condy, born a Cornishman, lived in Plymouth and would have been in his mid fifties when this view was painted. He suffered paralysis not long after he made this painting and died in 1857. Condy was known for favouring garish shades of red and green.[308]

436. *'Mount Edgcumbe, Cornwall'* as depicted by W. B. Stapley, 1860. Stapley appears to have lived at Little Fancy outside Plymouth in 1870 and may have died there.

437. Pen and ink drawing, 1850, by George Townsend of what is now 58 St Leonard's Road, Exeter. The drawing is titled *'Grovelands, Mount Radford'*.

438. Pen and ink drawing by George Townsend entitled *'entrance hall and staircase'*, 1850. The dog is a cut out board.

Grovelands

Exeter
1850

In 1850 Henry Ellis, a wealthy jeweller, moved his household from near the Guildhall in the centre of Exeter to a new house in the select neighbourhood of St Leonard's.

439. Photographic portrait of Henry Ellis towards the end of his life.

The old medieval heart of the city was being left to the working classes whilst men like Ellis preferred to live in homes which were surrounded by greenery and removed from the potential risk of cholera and other infectious diseases. Sanitation and elegance lay at the heart of the aspirational Victorian.

Ellis ran a successful business: he was appointed silversmith to Queen Victoria and the Royal Arms hung over his shop. His prosperity allowed him to move from the increasingly unfashionable city centre.

Ellis planned the back garden where he lamented the behaviour of the builders in disguising a collection of bones, rages, stones, broken bottles and crockery with a thin layer of soil. The plants were his own introduction and he also added the bower and arches of the privet hedge. Ellis' scheme is a new Victorian garden.[309]

Inset: *Flower Study,* Adolphe Braun, c.1854.

440. Pen and ink drawing by George Townsend entitled *'the garden as seen from the parlour'*, 1850.

441. Acland Barton in Landkey, mid to late nineteenth century. Watercolour by Edward Ashworth. The barton was the ancestral home of the Acland family in North Devon. A younger branch settled at Killerton in the early 1600s and their Tudor home became a farmhouse. Ashworth presents a pretty Victorian garden with defined paths and bedding.[310]

442. Acland Barton as shown on Benjamin Donn's map of 1765, positioned near Landkey and to the east of Barnstaple.

443. Brampford Speke Vicarage, mid to late nineteenth century. Watercolour by Edward Ashworth entitled *'Vicarage Brampford Speke'* with notation *'Rectory Brampford Speke'*, mid to late nineteenth century. Ashworth also made two drawings of the church before it was rebuilt in 1853.[311] Brampford Speke's vicarage was at the centre of Devon's greatest ecclesiastical struggles of the nineteenth century. It pitted the would-be vicar against his bishop. In 1847 Bishop Henry Philpotts refused to institute Reverend George Cornelius Gorham as vicar of Brampford Speke. The two men disagreed over the rite of baptism and for three years their dispute was heard in a number of appeals in various courts and committees. Gorham eventually won but Philpotts continued to refuse him. The latter threatened to excommunicate the archbishop of Canterbury if he instituted Gorham but in 1850 he was safely in post in Brampford Speke only to die in the vicarage seven years later.[312] Ashworth's drawing shows only a wooded background to the house and maps of the late nineteenth century give no indication of a developed garden.

Edward Ashworth's architectural views

of Acland Barton, Bramfield Speke Vicarage, Broomfield (Tiverton), Cadhay, The Chantry (Ivybridge), Knightstone (Ottery St Mary), Sand (Sidbury) and Torwood Grange c.1850–70

Victorian architect's collection of drawings of houses provides insights into the variety of Victorian gardens that could be found in Devon.

Edward Ashworth was born near Chulmleigh in 1814 and became one of Devon's most prolific architects. Just before this success he spent several years in the early 1840s living in Hong Kong, New Zealand and Australia. In New Zealand he was employed as a tutor to the children of Governor William Hobson.[313] Ashworth worked as an architect in Hong Kong and there he designed an English house. It was built by local workmen, under the rule of a supervisor who was fond of his opium pipe, but his employer told him they were *'infernal rogues – these Chinamen – confounded rogues, **all** of them'*.[314] Ashworth returned to Devon the following year and found employment with Lord Sidmouth who was rebuilding his mansion at Upottery. One of his surviving drawings shows Devon workmen building the new house but there is no comment in regard to his recent experiences in Hong Kong. Ashworth is remembered for his work in rebuilding Anglican churches in Devon and it is difficult to see how he applied to that work any lessons he learned earlier in the Far East.

Ashworth lived at 17 Dix's Field in Exeter, died in March 1896 and among those attending his funeral were the carver Harry Hems and another leading light in Devon architecture, Reverend Medley Fulford. Ashworth's coffin was embellished with a Gothic floriated brass cross which nearly extended its entire length. One journalist noted Ashworth was a man of marked individuality and an untiring worker. There was no mention of his travels as a young man. One newspaper did note that his *'immense collection of measured drawings of churches and other old buildings is simply priceless'*.[315] It is some of these that are reproduced in the following pages. Part of Ashworth's collection was purchased by Exeter City Library from a member of the family in 1934.

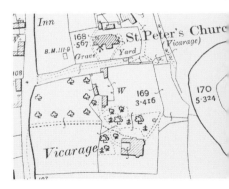

444. Ordnance Survey map of the vicarage at Brampford Speke, 1905.

Inset: *The Gardener – Old Peasant with Cabbage,* Camille Pisarro, post 1883.

445 Broomhill near Tiverton, mid to late nineteenth century.

Watercolour by Edward Ashworth entitled *'Broomhill Tiverton'*, mid to late nineteenth century. Broomhill is an early to mid nineteenth-century building which remains in private ownership. Ashworth shows a lightly planted garden is embellished by the veranda, an eighteenth-century innovation which Reverend Swete commented upon at the Moult two generations earlier but which had become common-place by the early nineteenth century. It must have been built to take advantage of the extensive view.

446. Cadhay near Ottery St Mary, mid to late nineteenth century.

Pen and ink by Edward Ashworth entitled *'Cadhay House'*, mid to late nineteenth century. Cadhay is a sixteenth-century house and one of the architectural gems of Devon. One of its notable features is the chequerwork of sandstone and flint which can be found in the east of the county. Ashworth's drawing shows the main terrace with a planted border. The fishponds lie behind the viewer. A second view by Ashworth shows other planting around the house.[316] Another artist, George Townsend, visited on April 22 1840 and his three sketches also show minimal designed gardens.[317] Cadhay is in private ownership.

447. Ordnance Survey map of Cadhay, 1905, showing the layout of the grounds.

448. Lithograph by R. Ackerman after E. I. J. entitled *'View of Cadhay House, Devon'*, 1820.

449. An earlier view by John Swete entitled *'Cadhay'*, 9 December 1794.

450. The Chantry, Ivybridge, 1858
Watercolour by Edward Ashworth entitled *'Ivybridge Parsonage'*, 1858. The Chantry was Ivybridge's first vicarage and built to the design of Ashworth in 1858.[318] Ivybridge was known nationally as being one of Devon's most picturesque places and was highly visited because it was on the coach road from Plymouth to London. In 1822 one writer gushed Ivybridge was *'beautifully situated in a romantic dell, which, from its foaming stream, dashing over granite rocks, and its thickly-wooded irriguous acclivities, excites the admiration of every traveller. Its name is derived from an antique bridge of one arch, fantastically overhung with ivy; at a short distance below which, a broad sheet of water rushes over a steep rocky bank.'* [319] Ashworth shows the drive which is still in existence but the depicted planting may have been drawn to show off the lines of the vicarage. The Chantry is in private ownership.

451. Second watercolour by Ashworth entitled *'Ivybridge Parsonage'*, 1858.

452. Ordnance Survey map showing Ivybridge's vicarage in 1906.

Knightstone near Ottery St Mary, 1860
A medieval manor house which had become
a farm by the late 1800s. An earlier view by
George Townsend, dated 22 April 1840, the
same date he visited nearby Cadhay, presents
the garden front in a similar way to Ashworth
but does not indicate the formality which he
gives to the approach to the house. In 1874 it
was described as being 'garlanded with ivy and
Virginia creeper'.[320] Knightstone is in private
ownership.

453. Pen and wash signed and dated by
Edward Ashworth entitled *'Knightstone
near Ottery'*, 1860.

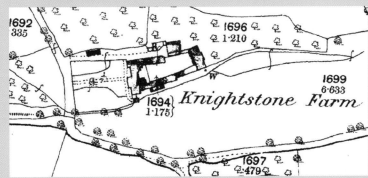

454. Ordnance Survey map showing
Knightstone, 1889.

455. Sand near Sidbury, post 1834

Watercolour by Edward Ashworth entitled *'Sand Sidbury Devon'* with caption *'Built by Rowland Huyshe before 1594 he was one of the sons of James Huyshe of Doniford Somerset. Since the death of James Huyshe in 1724 Sand has been occupied by farmers of the estate. See Gents Mag 1834.'* Sand is a moderately-sized largely Elizabethan manor house. Ashworth's view appears to be a copy of a drawing by Mr G. Holmes which appeared in *The Gentleman's Magazine* in 1834. It was sent to the magazine by Francis Huyshe of Talaton on the 3rd of February of that year. Ashworth replaced the figure of a young woman drawing the house with a couple arriving. Another engraving, very similar in its construction, appeared a few years afterwards.[321] The early Victorian garden which was depicted comprises thick shrubberies. Sand remains in private ownership.

456. Steel line engraving by G. Hollis after G. Holmes, 1834. Holmes appears to have the woman in a bonnet drawing the house.

457. Torwood Grange in Torquay, mid to late 1800s

Pen and wash by Edward Ashworth entitled *'Torwood Grange Torquay'*, mid to late 1800s. It shows the lead cistern which could still be seen in 1878. Torwood Grange, on Torwood Mount, was an outlying farm belonging to Torre Abbey. After the Reformation it was granted to Sir Thomas Dennis in 1541 and then rebuilt by the Ridgeway family eight years later. In 1822 Torwood was described as *'a farmhouse standing on an eminence, and overlooking Torbay'*. It was partly demolished in 1843 and some outbuildings survive including Manor Barn Cottage.[322] Ashworth shows the open courtyard with minimal planting on one side.

460. Watercolour by John Swete entitled *'SE view of Torwood'*, November 1793, with a view of Torbay.

458. Torwood as shown in 1765 on Benjamin Donn's map.

461. Watercolour by John Swete entitled *'Torwood'*, November 1793, with a view of Torbay.

462. Hand-coloured engraving by W. Colebrooke Stockdale entitled *'Woodbine Cottage, Torquay'*, signed and dated 1851. In addition to his skills as an artist, Stockdale also appeared on stage.[323]

Woodbine Cottage

in Torquay
1851

In 1832 Woodbine Cottage, built on Park Hill to the east of the harbour, was defined by one writer as being one of the *'leading ornaments'* of Torquay.[324]

Three years later John Gullet described the garden which was owned by his employer, Anne Johnes. It was published in *The Gardeners' Magazine*. Gullet wrote:

> 'The extent of the grounds of this much admired and most romantic place is about seven acres, on a declivity towards the south-south-west; and, twelve years since, it was what we call in Devonshire a furze break; or it might, perhaps, be more properly called a furze down, with a great part of it a barren rock. In the year 1823, Mrs Johnes took a fancy to build and plant; and the cottage she had erected is certainly the prettiest thing I have ever seen. From the drawing room, at the east end, we enter a pretty conservatory, 40 feet long by 15 feet wife, full of choice creepers, with canted glasses, reflecting the whole three ways. From this we proceed to the flower-garden, in front of the house, which is 60 yards by 30 yards, with a fountain in front of the drawing room window, and laid out in beds of different forms. Here are all the species of magnolia, which do well: rhododendrons, which make no great growth, but flower profusely; myrtles, geraniums, camellias, Pittosporum Tobira, Clethra arborea, Yucca aloifolia, now coming in bloom; and Agave americana; all of which do well in the open air, without protection. Salvias, except S. splendens, are also all found quite hardy perennials; and in some seasons they become quite hardy shrubs, not being injured with the frost. The Cinnamonum Camphora, against the wall, is quite hardy; the Ribes sanguineum, as a dwarf shrub, standing on the grass plot, fruits to great perfection, producing bunches of beautiful blue fruit, 5 inches long. From the flower garden we ascend the grounds by winding walks, almost forming a labyrinth: in one of those walks I have a vinery, which answers also as a green-house, formed in a limestone quarry; which, with the natural rock, and other kinds of rock that I have introduced, completes a rock house, in which are plunged my plants. In this house Psidium cattleianum fruits to near perfection without fire heat; the situation being so favourable that I have had no occasion to light a fire but once for five years, and then only for a few hours, to air the flue. My oranges in this house, I think, are as fine as you ever saw. You may think I boast by saying this; but, should you visit Devonshire at any time, I should be very proud to show them to you. Here I have the cactus tribe in great perfection, suspended from the roof by wife; being of a decided opinion it is much to their advantage, and it also keeps them from those enemies the snail and slug. From this greenhouse we ascend, by winding walks, to a grass terrace, from which we have the most beautiful picturesque views in nature'.

Gullet went on to write 'At the end of this terrace I have a small garden in the French style, the beds of which are edged with sheep's trotters, which gives it a neat appearance.' This may sound very straightforward but what he continued to write is curious for any garden in Devon or elsewhere.

Inset: *Goblets with violets,* Leon Bonvin, 1863.

463. Drawing by Mary Luxmoore entitled *'Woodbine Cottage at Torquay'*, 1830.

'In this place I have a moss house, paved with sheep's trotters in various devices, initials, date of year, etc.; and a table in the middle, covered with fir cones, and edged with the same. Here I have displayed my winter evenings' amusements, all kinds of figures, from the elephant down to the little mouse, made of fir cones, the produce of my own growth and labour. Imagine to yourself a Highland shepherd, with lambs in his bosom, and a shepherdess with her pet lamb, with a flock surrounding them, frightened, as it were, with a fox and hounds in full chase. In another part I have imitated a farm-yard, where the maid is milking her cows, and an old woman feeding her geese; the geese, as well as the old woman, appearing quite frightened: for here the fox is run up, and the huntsman is seen winding his horn.'

He also had a Devon plough, a dove with an olive branch and a flock of canaries. Another terrace, of some 300 yards, had borders of dahlias and other flowers and this led to a grass plot of three quarters of an acre *'with beds for roses, cistus, helianthemums, stocks and various other things'*. A wrought-iron fence, 700 feet long, enclosed the garden.[325]

John Claudius Loudon, who edited the *Gardener's Magazine*, visited a few years later in 1842. He wrote:

'The whole is kept in excellent order by Mr Gullet, who is unquestionably, not only an excellent gardener, but a man of genius as a sculptor and mechanic. To be convinced of this, it is only necessary to see the numerous figures which he has cut out in wood with his knife during the winter evenings, some of which are portraits of well known characters at Torquay; and the manner in which he has brought water from a distant hill, across a valley, and over an intervening hill, by a siphon. In the quarry covered by glass… we found Esperione grapes ripe, and of very superior flavour to the Hamburg. Not only the heat, but the soil, must have some effect in improving the flavour; for, had we not seen the leaves, and the form and close berries of the bunch, we should never have recognised the variety by the taste. A great many Cape, Australian, and Mexican plants flourish in the open air here, without any protection, in winter. The agaves are very large and fine; and Phormium tenax seems a favourite here and in many other places. The Pittosporum tobira stands the winter better than the common laurel. Pelargoniums have stood out five years without any protection. Clianthus puniceus has attained a large size; Phlomis fruticosa has acquired the character of a little tree, and Coronilla glauca and Medicago arborea have become large bushes. In short, there is no greenhouse plant that might not be trusted out here summer and winter. The woods in some places rise from a covering of tutsan, and in others from one of ivy; which is also introduced into dry stonewalls near the bottom, and soon changes these walls into evergreen hedges. The common ash, Mr Gullet finds, will transplant better than any other tree when of large size, and it also stands the sea breeze remarkably well.'

Loudon concluded by noting that *'Miss Johnes is upwards of ninety years of age, and in perfect health.'* [326]

The garden at Woodbine Cottage attracted considerable attention and praise. In 1829 N. T. Carrington wrote in his local guide that:

'Among the groups of gay cottages scattered about the vales and hills, it may be expected that we should specify some. The most distinguished for its command of the bay, the rustic beauty of its structure and extent, stands Mrs Johnes marine villa. The writer recollects when only a few years since, the site was a wild furze-brake; it is now laid out with great taste, planted with rare and luxuriant shrubs, among which, half concealed, are green-houses stored with exotics from America, etc. Supported by a colonnade of pollards, the cottage is inlaid with the several varieties of Devonshire marble. Fountains in the Conservatory and pleasure grounds, diffuse an exquisite freshness in summer: but the fine views spreading out from every point are its most beautiful feature'. [327]

Mrs Johnes died in 1847, aged 97 and was described by one commentator as the Lady Bountiful of Torquay.[328] The property was acquired by Sir John Shelly and ten years later it was auctioned. The *Exeter Flying Post* noted of the garden that :

'immediately in front of the residence is an ornamental fountain, in the centre of the lawn, studded with the most luxuriant shrubs, evergreens, and wild plants… being nestled on the side of a hill, the views are most extensive, the zigzag and serpentine walks of great extent, opening to an ornamental garden, a conservatory, kitchen garden, forcing-pits, etc. The entire estate comprises about six acres, and is completely screened from the town and north-east, being backed by plantation and brushwood; adjoining are about two acres of ornamental ground and garden, with a gardener's lodge, which by a trifling outlay may be converted into a cottage orné; the views are on this side equally commanding'. [329]

Woodbine Cottage was demolished in about 1860.

464. View of Mount Boone, 1852, with the inscription *'To Lady Seale, this plate of the Conservative Festival given in Mount Boone Park, August 23rd 1852, is by permission most respectfully dedicated by her most obliged servant, R. Bufferie'.*

465. Wood engraving entitled *'fete in Mount Boone Park, Dartmouth'*, which appeared in the *Illustrated London News*, 4 September 1852. The long tables can clearly be seen.

Mount Boone

Dartmouth
1852

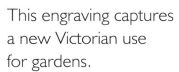

This engraving captures a new Victorian use for gardens.

Dartmouth's premier house, Mount Boone, was located between the town and what is now the Britannia Royal Naval College. In 1852 a grand fete was held in the garden and the *Illustrated London News* reported that 4,000 guests celebrated the re-election of Vice Admiral Sir Thomas Herbert as an M.P. for Dartmouth. Herbert himself was unable to attend. The words *'Herbert'* and *'Church and State'* were spelled out in dahlias at the entrance.[330] It was in the Victorian period that public events were held in large gardens: church fetes, work outings and political rallies became part of the English social year. The gardener employed in the year that this event took place was Richard Midway, a thirty-four year old man from Brixham. He lived in Mount Boone Lodge.[331]

Inset: *Basket of Flowers*, Leon Bonvin, 1863.

466. Pen and wash by Reverend John Swete with inscription *'Dartmouth June 17 1791 from St Petroc's Churchyard'*. Mount Boone can clearly be seen above Dartmouth.

467. Mount Boone as shown by C. & J. Greenwood in their map of 1827.

468. – 470. Three photographs showing Mount Boone, late nineteenth century.

469.

470.

The host was Lady Seale. Her family had owned Mount Boone since the early 1700s. In 1662 the garden was drawn by Willem Schellinks, a travelling Dutch artist, and he shows parterres with what looks like Italian cypresses.[332] A sham castle and hermitage were two features in the Georgian designed landscape. In the 1780s John Seale had set about redesigning the grounds and this included considerable replanting. The family continued to reside in the house until they sold it in 1873. At the end of that century the site was divided into ten building lots.[323]

The depiction of the garden and its fete is impossible to reconcile with the landscape. The only long stretch of open garden lay to the west of the house and from there it would have been impossible to have a view of the river and sea. It is possible that the event was held in one of the fields above the house but the print in the *Illustrated London News* indicates the fete was held next to Mount Boone. It may be that both artists have taken great liberties with depicting the landscape.

471. Watercolour by an unknown artist showing the steps at Cobham leading down to the lawn.

Cobham

in Exeter
1857

Cobham's garden of 1857 is an example of Victorian design.

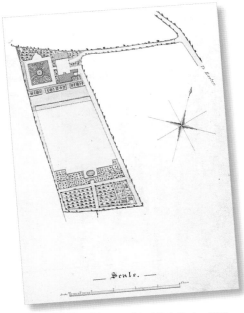

472. Plan of the grounds by J. Pattle Becker, 1857. In 1861 James Pattle Becker, who had been born in Calcutta, lived in Canterbury. He may have been the same man employed to plan the garden at Cobham.[334]

473. Painting of the formal garden, attributed to John Gendall, no date given.

The house had been built on a green field site; it had formerly been known as Whipping Field. The owner, Thomas Shapter, was a prominent former mayor and remembered for his book on Exeter's cholera epidemic of 1832. He later left the city under a cloud: a public scandal enveloped Shapter when it became known that he was the sole beneficiary in the will of a wealthy patient he had treated for mental illness.[335]

The garden takes advantage of the views from the house down to the Exe Estuary. The building has a commanding position and the images show how the land falls below the house to a lawn. Italian cypresses lined the borders. The chief feature was the planting on the west of the house. These are represented as being filled with bright summer bedding plants. In 1881 Shapter employed only two servants, Thomas Chilton, a gardener, and his wife Mary who worked as a cook.[336]

Inset: *A woman seated besides a vase of flowers*, Edgar Degas, 1865.

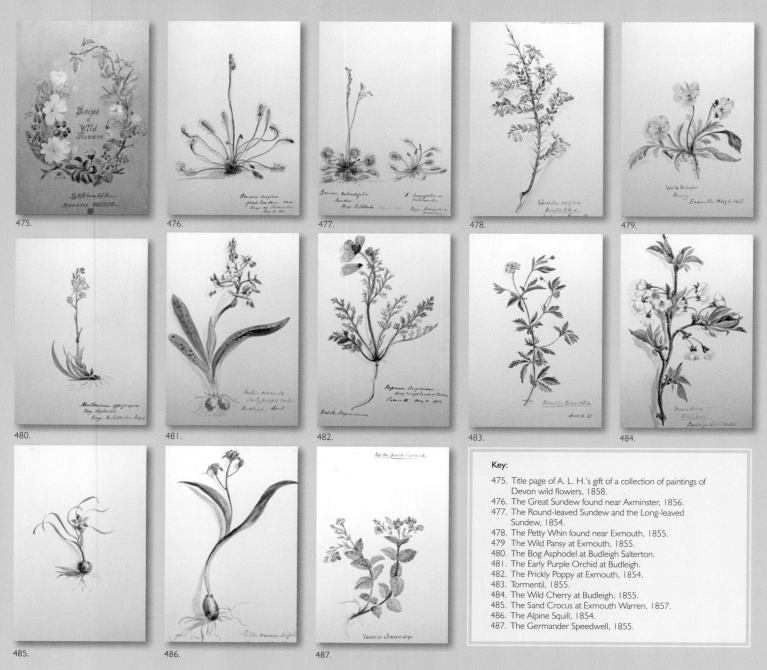

475.   476.   477.   478.   479.

480.   481.   482.   483.   484.

485.   486.   487.

Key:

475. Title page of A. L. H.'s gift of a collection of paintings of Devon wild flowers, 1858.
476. The Great Sundew found near Axminster, 1856.
477. The Round-leaved Sundew and the Long-leaved Sundew, 1854.
478. The Petty Whin found near Exmouth, 1855.
479 The Wild Pansy at Exmouth, 1855.
480. The Bog Asphodel at Budleigh Salterton.
481. The Early Purple Orchid at Budleigh.
482. The Prickly Poppy at Exmouth, 1854.
483. Tormentil, 1855.
484. The Wild Cherry at Budleigh, 1855.
485. The Sand Crocus at Exmouth Warren, 1857.
486. The Alpine Squill, 1854.
487. The Germander Speedwell, 1855.

Wild Flowers
1858

Inspiration for local gardens was increasingly found through the Victorian period in the wild places of the country.

It was during the nineteenth century that wild flowers in Devon were first systematically identified, recorded and catalogued. One collection, of paintings of several dozen plants, survives by an unknown artist for the 1850s. This enthusiast, identified only by his or her initials, travelled throughout Devon, and beyond, to paint wild flowers.[337] Another collection has also been deposited in the local archives. It was painted by Miss A. H. Prideaux in and around 1868.

Inset: *Picking Flowers,*
Auguste Renoir, 1875.

488.

489.

490.

491.

492.

493.

Six watercolours by Miss Prideaux, c.1868, of Devon flowers

488. An Abutilon pictum and sweet pea.
489. Dandelion seed head with a bramble in flower and fruit.
490. Variety of passionflower found at Combe Royal, near Kingsbridge, in October 1868.
491. A plant as yet unidentified, possibly a Japanese Anenome with a poorly drawn leaf or *Abutilon vitifolium 'Alba'*.
492. The Chilean Bellflower noted at Brookfield, November 1868.
493. The top flower is noted as a Banksian rose, 1867, but the tulip with it was unidentified.

494. Pencil drawing by Richard Cresswell entitled *'Compton Castle, Torquay'*, c.1860.

Compton Castle
1860

Compton Castle was the medieval home of the Gilbert family and an exceptional example of a fortified manor house in Devon.

The Gilbert family sold Compton in 1800 and later bought it back only to subsequently give it to the National Trust. In 1878 a tourist guide noted that *'the first remarkable feature which engrosses the attention of the spectator is that of the numerous and highly curious bartizans, or machicolated projections, which hang out over and protect the doors and windows. They are exceedingly interesting, and deserve close examination, intended, as they evidently have been, to enable the inhabitants to hurl ruin on any enemy who might be underneath. The principal entrance in the centre of the front, as well as the postern gate at the end of it, had portcullises; and the walls which protected the building on four sides, and which are for the most part standing, had a square tower at each angle.'*[338]

The later engravings show a gradual development of a garden in front of the house.

Inset: *Grace Rose*, Frederick Sandys, 1866.

495. Watercolour by John Swete entitled *'Compton Castle'*, December 1793.

496. Watercolour by John Swete entitled *'Compton Castle'*, December 1793.

497. Pen and wash by Edward Ashworth entitled *'Compton Castle, Marldon Devon'*, c.1860.

498. Steel line eng

500. Photograph of Compton, 1930s.

501. Photograph of Compton, 1940s.

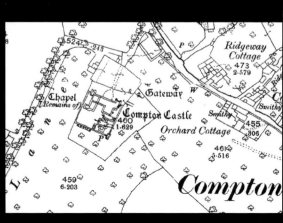

502. Ordnance Survey map of Compton Castle, 1887.

503. Photograph of Creedy Park with the caption 'Old house, West Wing about 1865 before terrace wall was built'.

504. – 508. A collection of Ferguson-Davie family photographs show the family in front of their house, in their conservatory and as the house was before, in about 1865, and after the fire.

505.

506.

507.

508.

Creedy Park

Sandford
1865

Family photographs illustrate the Victorian and Edwardian lives of the Ferguson-Davie family in their mansion outside Crediton. A surviving watercolour is however deceptive in its detail.

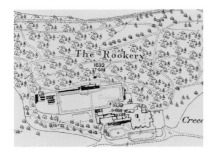

509. Ordnance Survey map of Creedy Park, 1890.

Inset: Peonies, Édouard Manet, 1864-5.

510. Watercolour by an unknown artist of a house which was allegedly Creedy Park, c.1905. It is difficult to see how this could be Creedy Park despite its caption, unless this was an unexecuted plan.

Creedy Park was enlarged and altered in 1846 for the family. In 1915 it was destroyed by fire and a new house was built on the site. Photographs and prints show a more substantial house and if the watercolour was indeed Creedy Park then the artist had a bad eye for accuracy. It is more likely to be a proposal for the new building, if it depicts Creedy Park at all. The Ferguson-Davie family continued to live at Creedy Park after the fire through to the late twentieth century. It is now divided into multi-ownership.

CLOVELLY
NEW INN
NEAT WIN

Spent Sunday at the New Inn at Clovelly

Clovelly

1866

Clovelly is best known for being one of the few privately-owned villages in England but this image shows a garden removed from the public gaze of its famous long street.

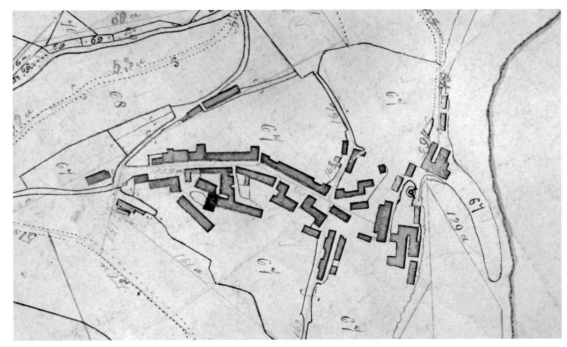

511. Pen, ink and wash by Henrietta Matilda Crompton on which she wrote 'Spent Sunday at the New Inn at Clovelly, steep road of steps to the pier ½ a mile houses on each side all belonging to Sir Hamlyn Williams, August 25', 1840. Her view is of the fronts of the houses which Hemy later painted from the back.

Inset: Flowers in a Vase, Auguste Renoir, 1866.

The flower garden lies at the rear of the line of cottages, possibly at the top of the village. Poppies grow in front of the washing line. It was painted by Charles Napier Hemy when he was a young artist. Hemy visited Clovelly on several occasions and subsequently lived in Cornwall.

He had painted Among the Shingle at Clovelly in 1864 and it was exhibited at the Royal Academy. Although regarded as his youthful masterpiece, the more relevant comparison to Evening Grey is Cottage Gardens – Twilight which he painted

512. Tithe map of Clovelly, 1840, in which at least one site for the location of the painting might be identified.

in 1866.[339] Both are moody if not gloomy and feature gardens at the back of Clovelly's long High Street falling down to the shore. In *Evening Grey* the main figure has been described as having a stillness and melancholy whilst the second painting was noted as having morbid melancholy. In 1900 it was regarded by a writer in *The Magazine of Art* as a *'poetic little work'*.[340] Clovelly's steep valley, which shuts out the morning sun and focuses the sunset through the sea as a prism, accentuates the power of light in these gardens.

Hemy arrived in the village during the summer of 1864 when he was twenty-four years old. He earned a living through painting but the course of his life was marked by his conversion to Roman Catholicism which led him to seek a vocation in the priesthood. Later Hemy entered a continental Dominican Monastery. His strong faith influenced his art as did his fascination with the sea: he had also been apprenticed as a sailor but this too was a failed endeavour. It was claimed in 1881 that *Evening Grey* was painted within a year of Hemy being married.[341]

By 1878 Clovelly's economy was a mixture of farming, seafaring and tourism. It was well known for its herring fishery but visitors were fascinated by its topography, *'a singular and picturesque situation on the side of a steep rock'*. Clovelly remains recognizable from its description at the time: it was noted as *'one of the most romantic places in Devon and the houses being built upon the precipitous side of the sea cliff, one above the other, the main street ascends in flights of steps from the beach and pier'*.[342] It was presumably because of its reputation that Hemy visited in 1866. Within a generation the village was described by its rector as being overrun for six months of the year. He compared it with a fair:

> *'when the visitor arrives in troops and battalions, by land and sea, and with frank simplicity of mind takes all possible pains to destroy the sense of beauty and repose and quiet which he is supposed to value and seek'*.[343]

In 1880 another writer regarded Clovelly as being not just an artists' haunt but as the district's headquarters for them. The entire village was considered worthy of an artist's eye.[344] Charles Dickens described Clovelly in *A Message from the Sea* as having two irregular rows of white houses no two of which were *'alike in chimney, size, shape, door, window, gable, roof-tree, anything'*. The rows were, he wrote, like a crooked ladder and the steps to the top were similar to the rungs.[345] Hemy captured this in the background to his painting and shows the gardens sharing the little space left over from the village buildings.

513. Oil painting by Charles Napier Hemy entitled *'Evening Grey'*, c.1866.

514. Watercolour done for or by William Burges of the south elevation of Knighthayes Court, c.1868.

Knightshayes Court

c. 1868

Knightshayes is known for the colour of its interior decoration rather than for that in its gardens which have a different appeal altogether.

515. Engraving entitled *'Knightshayes N. Devon, the seat of J. H. Amory, Esquire M.P., W. Burges Architect'*, 1870

Inset: *Plums and Mulberries,* William Henry Hunt, c. 1860.

It should also be known for having a direct view to the family's source of wealth, their lace factory. At the time it was being built Charles L. Eastlake, author of *A History of the Gothic Revival*, noted it as a typical example of the Gothic Revival. He described *'massive walls, bold gables, stout mullions nearly half the width of the lights which they divide, large and solid looking chimney shafts, corbelled from the walls or riding on the high pitched roofs, are the principal incidents which give this building dignity and effect. Such gentler graces as are imparted into the design by aid of mouldings or decorative sculpture (as in the central dormer) indicate a French origin. The great feature of the interior is a large hall to be used for the reception of the owner's tenantry. This is fitted up with a gallery and rostrum at one end, and is eminently picturesque both in plan and proportions.'*[346] William Burges designed it for the grandson of John Heathcoat, who had brought his lace machines and workers from Nottingham to Tiverton in 1816. Heathcoat's business partner was Samuel Amory and the marriage of Heathcoat's daughter to Amory's son united the partners' business and their fortunes. It was their son, John Heathcoat Amory, who took the name Heathcoat and later built Knightshayes. Curiously, the previous owner of Knightshayes, Benjamin Dickenson, also took his wife's surname.[347]

Eastlake's borrowed engraving shows slight differences with the garden in Burges' original plan. Burges was not retained to complete the interior and the garden was taken in hand by Edward Kemp who, in addition to retaining the formal gardens and terraces as seen in the watercolour, he also designed the bowling green to the east (now the Pool Garden) and American Garden in the valley to the west of the house. The house was built on the site of a Georgian building, also known as Knightshayes, and it had 3 acres of gardens and lawns as well as parkland. In 1841 there was a shrubbery in the front and the grounds had at least two statues.[348] The house and its estate were purchased for £45,000. Old Knightshayes was itself substantial: it had 3 floors as well as a basement. In 1851 it included a study, morning room, dressing room, lobby, drawing room, library, dining room, closets, 9 bedrooms, 4 dressing rooms and 4 rooms set aside for servants. The contract for the new building was set at £14,080. The first stone was laid in April 1869.[349]

Knighthayes's gardens were not remembered in the early 1900s as exceptional although the gardener, Mr Gregor, won a bronze medal for his Pitmasten Duchess pears at the Gardening and Forestry Exhibition at Earl's Court in 1893.[350] The well-known topiary of the hounds chasing a fox was created for Sir John Amory in the 1920s and reflected the family's longstanding interest in hunting: they had established a pack of *'badger pied'* harriers as well as foxhounds and staghounds. Considerable garden improvements were made in the mid 1900s. Knightshayes has been owned by the National Trust since 1972[351] and the outline of Burges' formal gardens can still be seen.

516. Untitled painting by I. H. Reichel, c.1870, at A La Ronde. A second painting shows the house with a wider perspective.

517. Steel line engraving entitled 'A-La-Ronde near Exmouth', c.1845.

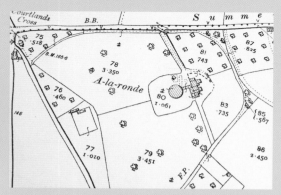

518. Ordnance Survey map showing the grounds at A La Ronde, 1905.

A La Ronde

c.1870

This curious and claustrophobic sixteen-sided building invariably comes first in any alphabetical listing of Devon houses.

This curious and claustrophobic sixteen-sided building invariably comes first in any alphabetical listing of Devon houses. It never attracted the attention of visitors in the manner of other moderately-sized buildings such as Woodbine Cottage or Glyn Lyn but its prominence today lies in its recent purchase by the National Trust.

A La Ronde was built for the Misses Jane and Mary Parminter at the end of the eighteenth century after their long sojourn on the Continent. Filled with tourist souvenirs and knick-knacks, it encapsulates the fussiness of these two non-conformist spinsters from North Devon. In 1880 Reverend Oswald Reichel took residence, the first owner not to be held by Jane Parminter's will that only unmarried kinswomen should inherit. He brought the house some fame, alongside scandal and public derision: a court case revealed a thirteen-year relationship with an unmarried former servant.[352]

The garden is outstanding for its plain character with the most distinguished features being the oaks planted by the Parminters. The ladies stipulated that these would *'remain standing and the hand of man shall not be raised against them till Israel returns and is restored to the Land of Promise'*. Jane Parminter's will, of 1811, gives hope that the garden was once interesting: it had been *'full of bowers, arbours, three obelisks… fountains, glass houses and rare tropical plants, orangeries'*. Thirty-eight years later the will of Mary Parminter recorded the pleasure grounds included not only ornamental trees but *'the new obelisk, fountain, shellery, hothouses, greenhouses and ornamental seats which shall be in or about my gardens, shrubberies, walks and grounds'*.[353] None of this is apparent from Reichel's painting or the later engraving.

Inset: *Hollyhocks*, Ross Sterling Turner, 1876.

519. Detail of watercolour by an unknown artist, 1815, which depicts A La Ronde's position near the river Exe.

520. Broadgate, the former home of the Parminter family, in North Devon, as painted by John Swete, 1789.

521. Tile designed by Morris for Membland, 1876.

Membland tile

1876

The use of floral design in the Arts & Crafts Movement can be seen in this bathroom tile by William Morris of 1876.

522. Photograph entitled *'Membland Hall from the Park'*, 1895.

Morris' tile survives but the house it was placed in, Membland, and along with the garden around it, vanished after a fire of the 1920s. Edward Charles Baring, 1st Baron Revelstoke, commissioned the design from Morris. It was painted in the studio of William de Morgan and is now in the collection of the Victoria & Albert Museum. The tile is composed of 66 individual pieces. Morris is most closely associated with the Arts & Crafts Movement and his tile brings out some of the influences he had on English design: he favoured medieval patterns and this tile owes itself to an appreciation of Gothic geometric shapes. His textiles and wallpapers are better remembered but this tile shows the links in design and the influence of garden plants.

523. Photograph of Membland entitled *'The Hall'* showing considerable greenery, 1895.

524. Photograph of Membland entitled *'The Terrace'*, 1912.

525. Photograph of William Morris by Frederick Hollyer, 1874.

Inset: *Flowers in a Rococo Vase,* Paul Cézanne, c.1876.

526. Watercolour of Combe Royal by Reverend C. E. Dunkinfield showing the view from the drawing room window, no date given. Reverend Dunkinfield married Dorothea, the daughter of John Luscombe. [54]

The Citrusy

at Combe Royal near Kingsbridge
c.1890

527. Wood engraving, untitled, by CB, 1871. The Citrus Walk could easily be mistaken for a viaduct.

The *'Citrusy'* at Combe Royal is one of the great features of Devon's garden history and remained remarkable all through the nineteenth century.

In 1827 the Horticultural Society of London, later the Royal Horticultural Society, awarded the Banksian Medal to its owner for the citrus he exhibited in 1827.[355] Two generations later the garden continued to astonish.

There were a considerable number of citrus trees planted in gardens along the south coast of Devon. Salcombe had an orange tree at Woodville and in 1861 it was described as being *'very many years old'*. In 1819 it had a garden wall *'clothed with a number of orange and lemon trees where fruit as fine*

and fair as if immediately from Portugal is seen in abundance'*. Another garden with citrus in 1861 was the Moult, the occasional home of Lord Courtenay. That same year it had established orange and lime trees growing against the conservatory wall. Cliff House also had citrus trees[356] and in 1834 they could be could be found in at least one other Salcombe garden, at another in Dartmouth and at Kitley and Luscombe near Dawlish.[357] In 1874 it was said that the orange, lemon and citron trees planted against a garden wall at Woodville in Salcombe were thriving. They were protected by temporary frames of reed.[358] Even with all these gardens, the best-recorded citrus garden was that at Combe Royal.

The Luscombe family had been living at Combe Royal since at least the 1770s although in 1809 it was temporarily rented to Bigoe Armstrong of Bath. The arrival of Armstrong's wife, Lady Williams, caused great anticipation and upset in the area. John Luscombe wrote that noses would be put out of joint: *'the idea of her ladyship has already begun to operate upon the minds of somebodys – such swelling of throats, the lord of mercy upon us'*. In the lease Luscombe stipulated that his Orange Walk, as he termed it, would be properly maintained. He noted in the schedule of goods and fixtures that in the garden there was:

> *'a good stone roller with iron frame and handle, deal shutters to orange and lemon tree, complete fire engine with suction, two leather and copper play pipes complete. (NB) summer house now in complete order and repair and to be left in the same state as it now is to all intents and meanings at the expiration of the said term, twelve dozen of flower pots filled with plants of various descriptions'.*[359]

Inset: *Fruit Trees*, Edward Lear, 1863.

528. Pencil sketch of the grounds and entrance of the mansion house at Combe Royal, 1850.

529. Oil painting by Chowkura painted in Shanghai from a photograph, May 1864.

530. Photograph of the Citrus Walk, 1904.

In 1834 readers of the *Gardener's Magazine* were told there were lime, citron, orange and lemon trees planted in a series of walled recesses and that they produced exceptional fruit. Citrons measured between 14 and 18 inches in circumference. The lime tree was given greater protection: it had the benefit of a glass frame whereas the other trees were protected during the winter months only with wooden frames. The lime was a younger tree which may account for it being a less productive fruiter. Eight years later, in 1842, the journal's readers were told the trees were prospering and covered with *'abundance of beautiful fruit'*.[360] Nearly a generation later, in 1871, the wonderfully titled *Journal of Horticulture, Cottage Gardener, Country Gentleman, Beekeeper and Poultry Chronicle* reported citrus growing was a *'peculiarity'* of Combe Royal. The family told the journalist that the grandmother of the owner remembered being told by her grandfather that one Seville Orange tree was 100 years old when he bought the house. The tradition, in 1871,

was that the tree was 250 years old. The name *'Citrusy'* was applied to the row of recesses in which the trees were planted. All were 11 feet high but they varied in width: the lime, shaddock, Seville orange, Mandarin orange, bergamot and orange trees were 12 feet wide but the lemon was 15 feet and the citron 16. It was then still discussed that some years before Queen Victoria had been given a basket of the citrus fruit.[361]

It had been fifteen years earlier, in 1856, that Mr Toward, the Queen's Gardener at Osborne House, visited Combe Royal to see the methods of growing citrus trees. It was just before this that the queen was sent the fruit. It was said that she greatly admired the citrus. In 1904 the trees were still in a thriving condition. The Seville Orange had 200 fruits on it when it was shown by Mr Horsman, the gardener, to J. R. Jackson, a representative of *The Gardeners' Chronicle*.[362] The citrus recesses survive. Combe Royal was formerly held by Devon County Council and is now privately owned.

531. An undated photograph of the nursery in Ilfracombe.

Oxford Park Garden

Ilfracombe
c. 1890

The rise of the seaside resort was accompanied by the development of parks and gardens but also of other gardens to supply the hotels.

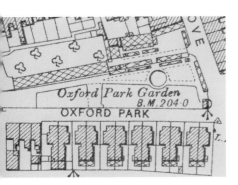

532. Ordnance Survey map of the Oxford Park Garden, 1891.

Inset: *Fruit with Blue-footed Bowl,* Charles Sidney Raleigh, 1893.

533. An undated photograph of the nursery in Ilfracombe.

Amongst the gardens which are often given little consideration are the nurseries which raised plants for sale to the hotels and other tourism businesses. Ilfracombe's Oxford Park Gardens are a fine example of this.[363] The nursery was built in about 1880 and six years later they were described as having seven cool glass houses as well as four hot ones, extensive outdoor bedding, tennis courts, a fishpond, and even 21 beehives. The main glasshouse was 130 feet long.

In 1904 the production comprised not just a variety of ferns but flowers such as orchids, fuchsias, coleus and cineraria as well as grapes (Black Hamburg), melons and cucumbers. Four conservatories were given over to the growing of tomatoes. The two main varieties were Ham Green Favourite and Challenger. Apples, pears and other types of fruit were also being grown. The nursery was in existence for a little more than a single generation. It was sold in 1921 and the land converted to use for parking.[364]

534. Photograph of the summerhouse in the garden at the Moult, c.1895.

The Moult

Salcombe
1895

The Moult is an early example of a second home in Devon.

In 1874 this unusual building, with an equally interesting garden, was described as:

> 'Between the North and South Sands, stands the Moult, the property of the Earl of Devon, but for many years it was the summer residence of the late Lord Justice Sir George Turner. Lady Turner continued to reside there until her death, when her daughters removed from the Moult to another house at Salcombe. The Moult was built in the year 1764, by the late John Hawkins, Esquire, as a mere pleasure box, but he did not live to finish it. He left it to his widow, who in 1780 sold it to the late Henry Whorwood, Esq., of Holton Park, Oxford. The grounds were laid out under his directions, the trees planted, and the house fitted up as a decorated cottage. Since then it has changed hands, until it came into the possession of the respected nobleman who now owns it. The gardens and conservatories contain plants and shrubs rarely to be seen elsewhere.'[365]

In 1808 the Moult had been enlarged and was:

> 'a multiplicity of masonry of different denominations. Here stand ponderous, testudinated gate ways, there mock batteries, while a conspicuous conservatory and cots, cottages and cells, of various shapes and sizes, are scattered over the umbrageous and diversified scene formerly adopted only with shady seats and bosky bowers and the white empurpled shower of mingled blossom'.[366]

It may have been at this time that the summerhouse was erected.

535. Watercolour entitled 'Molt, summer seat of S(amuel) Strode' by John Swete, January 1794. Swete wrote in his accompanying text that he passed through a shrubbery to the house. The 'front of it was singular in its appearance, having about one third from its roof, a projection supported by slender pillars, assuming the form of a piazza, or (as they have frequent in the East Indies) a Veranda: intending to act as a parasol which it effectually does – not admitting the sun to blaze upon the windows except when his beams are too oblique to become obtrusive. The windows both below and above, as well as the upper part of the doorway, which acts as a window are of a Gothic cast, pointed; and the frame-work with the mouldings, cornice and pillars of the Veranda, being painted green, an effect is produced uncommonly light and elegant…'.

Inset: *Chrysanthemums*, Claude Monet, 1882.

536. Aquatint by and after W. Daniell entitled 'Salcombe, Devon', 1825. In his view the Moult is behind the viewer but, like these houses, it is perched along the cliff.

537. Painting of Broadway House, Topsham, c.1900, by either Constance or Hester Froode.

Broadway House

Topsham
c.1900

Broadway House has a representative garden of the upper middle-class Victorian living in a semi-urban situation in Devon.

538.

538. – 540.
Three photographs of the garden at Broadway House from a Froode family album, c.1900.

The house is thought to have been built in the 1770s. It became the home of F. W. L. Ross, a natural history enthusiast and chronicler of Topsham, from the 1830s through to the early 1860s. In 1851 Ross did not have a live-in gardener but he did employ two house servants and a butler.[367] Broadway House was afterwards acquired by one Captain Greatwood and in the 1870s the grounds were described as being beautiful.[368] Three owners, all of whom had surnames beginning with the letter B, followed but in 1898 Dr Froode took possession.[369] Two of his daughters were accomplished artists, Constance and Hester. The latter was better known and painted professionally until her death in 1971. A hint of their upbringing is revealed in the census return of 1911. Their mother, then a widow, wrote across the form *'If I am intelligent enough to fill up this paper, I am intelligent enough to put a cross on a voting paper. No vote, No census.'* Other suffragettes, in Devon as elsewhere in England, used the filling in of census returns to comment upon the refusal of the authorities to give women the right to vote.[370]

The painting and photographs illustrate the edged herbaceous borders and topiary that were popular at the end of the nineteenth century.

539.

540.

Inset: *Roses*, Vincent van Gogh, 1890.

541. Photograph with caption '*Torquay Gardeners about 1910. A Carnival turn-out. In front of Dyer's Cottage, Torbay Road. Mr H. A. Garrett, Borough Surveyor, is seated in front of the wagon. Next but one to him is Steve Young, and next to him is Harry Browning. Mr Dyer, the town gardener, is standing behind'*. Dyer's Cottage was formerly a Victorian tollhouse and was later converted into use as public toilets. It is now being remodelled as a restaurant.

The Torquay public gardens carnival float

c.1910

In the spring of 1891 Torquay Council debated emulating the Riviera by having its own flower festival.

Unlike that in Nice, which was described as a *'battle of flowers'*, the Devon equivalent would be a procession of flowers, possibly with blooms obtained from the Isles of Scilly. The resort, called a generation earlier the Garden of Devon, was discussed as a rival to the French Riviera. The French Battle of Flowers was popular and well-known. In 1883 the Prince of Wales, along with Prime Minister Gladstone, had taken part in festivities on the Promenade des Anglais. For two hours they watched carriages decorated with flowers pass by.[371]

By 1898 Cockington organised its own Battle of Flowers and amongst the decorated carriages were two bicycles covered with flowers which were owned by Miss Westaway and Miss Whitehead. Through the 1890s other parts of the country also had their own Battle of Flowers including such places as Eastbourne, Ventnor and Skegness.[372]

The *Torquay Directory* shows that the resort also held a carnival for three successive years with the first one in 1910.[373] The others were on 21 June 1911 and 26 June 1912. These were not Battles of Flowers but what may be thought more traditional carnivals. In 1911 the carnival had borough representatives in a procession but it is not clear if this float was among them.[374]

The float celebrated one of the most attractive features of the resort. The palm tree symbolised the exotic nature of Torquay. Inexpensive foreign holidays were yet unknown to the general public and a visit to the palm-planted resort gave them a sense of being abroad. The palm also signified Torquay's warmer climate than that which most visitors had at home. The photograph was taken from below the Rock Walk, the popular name for the Royal Terrace Gardens.

542. Postcard entitled *'From Rock Walk, Torquay'*, 1905. The Pavilion was built on the site in 1911.

Inset: *Bouquet in a Chinese vase*, Odilon Redon, c.1912.

543. Postcard entitled *'Terrace Walk & Vane Hill'*, c.1903.

544. Postcard by H. B. Wimbush entitled *'Torquay Rock Walk'*, c.1905.

545. Postcard by Charles E. Flower entitled *'Rock Walk, Torquay'*, 1914.

546. The stained glass window at St Nectan's Church, Welcombe, by William Morris & Company, 1929.

547. Cartoon by Morris of his intended window, 1929.

William Morris' stained glass window

Welcombe
1929

548. Detail of the rural scene in stained glass at St Michael's Church, Axmouth, by Joseph Bell & Son of Bristol, 1890.

549. The complete view of the Axmouth window.

Inset: *Roses,*
Paul de Longpré,
c.1900.

Victorian and later stained glass design often used floral motifs as incidental embellishment but this window in the North Devon parish church at Welcombe uses flowers and ornamental plants as a crucial part of its main decorative scheme.

The fame of the designer, William Morris, was immaterial to the vicar who refused to sanction its insertion in 1929. A local widow had suggested the window be erected as a memorial to her late husband. The vicar wrote to a diocesan figure that the churchwardens and parish council had rejected the design and pleaded that permission be refused for the window. The vicar suggested *'the face is grotesque and the design is artificial and unnatural'*. He was concerned that the window might be forced upon the church. There was some discussion about depicting Jesus in benediction but the design was eventually allowed to be inserted into the church albeit not in the first location suggested by the donor. The unusual colours of the landscape are particularly striking as are those of other windows by other designers at Axmouth and Thurlestone.[375]

550. Detail of the roses depicted in stained glass at All Saints' Church, Thurlestone, by A. J. Davies of the Bromsgrove Guild, 1929.

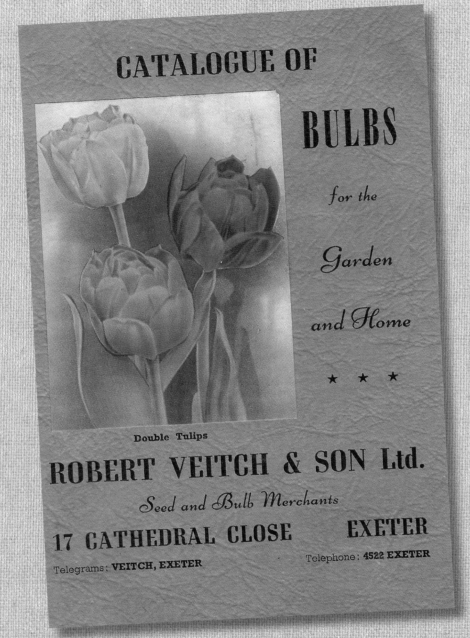

551. Sale catalogue for the Veitch shop, Cathedral Yard, mid nineteenth century..

The Veitch firm
post 1930

Devon's most significant firm in gardening, that which John Veitch began in the late eighteenth century, continued for nearly two centuries but has few records to chronicle its extraordinary history. This sale catalogue gives but a hint of its great contribution to gardening in Devon and across England.

The Veitch firm worked at a number of gardens illustrated in this collection including Shute, Bystock, Nutwell Court and Silverton Park. It was the premier nursery in Devon and one of the most illustrious in the country. This family-run business spanned five generations and rose from a small nursery in Broadclyst to extending itself into Exeter and then to London at Chelsea.[376] Its importance lay in sending plant hunters across the globe and through them the firm introduced more than a thousand plants into English cultivation.

The Acland family were responsible for bringing John Veitch to Devon and by 1808 he was advertising himself as a nurseryman and planter based at Killerton.[377] James Veitch, the second generation, expanded the operations into Exeter and then in 1853 he acquired a site in Chelsea.[378] Other members, notably Sir Harry, became more prominent but even the death of James Veitch was dominated by plants. In 1863 he collected lilies from his garden to place in his wife's coffin and as he leaned over to strew them around her he said '*Oh dear, I never can go through this*', collapsed and died. A few days later husband and wife were buried together in a single grave at Broadclyst.[379] In the late 1800s the Veitch firm opened a shop in Exeter's High Street and then moved this business to 17 Cathedral Yard in 1930. It closed in 1982.

552. Wood engraving attributed to Benjamin Fawcett, nineteenth century, entitled '*Veitch's Lady Slipper*'.

Conclusion

Art is only one tool which can be used to understand garden history.

The very nature of gardens is to change. The consequence is that many illustrations become redundant shortly after they were created. Art preserves these gardens that change or are lost.

The publication of these images brings previously unknown information into the public domain and will invariably stimulate new lines of enquiry. Few historians have investigated garden depictions in wood, plaster and glass but have relied upon traditional formats such as drawing and painting. What this collection shows is that a more open approach raises more questions and hopefully brings substantive rewards.

It also demonstrates that Devon has a great range and variety of gardens. Unusual designs for landscapes have sometimes reflected the place in which they were created and often they are a direct expression of those concerned. The garden at Glen Lyn took advantage of the energetic waterfalls whilst Endsleigh's designed landscape embraced its wooded valley. Other owners introduced new fashions in gardening, such as the formal layouts portrayed by Prideaux in the 1700s or the natural lines of the Picturesque at Oxton several generations later. The changing fashions in garden design have been illustrated in this collection of images and many of the depicted gardens can be visited today to find evidence of their former landscapes.

The art reproduced here also embraces functional rather than only ornamental gardens. The plants themselves are often the focal point whether it be the introduction of foreign plants, such as aloes or citrus, or the planting of old fruit varieties.

For the last twenty-five years the Devon Gardens Trust has endeavoured to investigate and understand the history of local gardens. It was not until the 1970s that much work was done nationally and much of it on Devon has originated from within the Trust. A growing public awareness and appreciation for garden landscapes will further this interest and stimulate the creation of new original depictions of gardens. These will in turn become historic and help future generations understand the interesting gardens that we ourselves live in today.

Art provides us with another individual's interpretation of a garden and forces us to question not merely how accurate a depiction it may be, but what meanings can be found in them. The publication of this collection will hopefully bring forward other art as yet unknown to those interested in the history of Devon's gardens.

553. The outdoor staff at Tracey.

554. An admission ticket to a Devon garden.

Endnotes

1　Debra N. Mancoff's *The Garden in Art* (2011) and Roy Strong's *The Artist & The Garden* (New Haven, 2000) examine the international and national contexts.

2　Ian Maxted, *A history of the book in Devon. 52: Tourism and topographical views (Exeter Working Papers in Book History; 12)*, *http://bookhistory.blogspot* (html) - accessed (4 May 2013).

3　Devon Heritage Centre (hereafter DHC), 1038M/F, 12 March 1792.

4　*A trip to North Devon*, *The Leisure Hour: A Family Journal of Instruction and Recreation*, 1862, (543), 326.

5　Isle of Wight Record Office, OG/CC/1383A-B.

6　For a discussion of these in a national context, see Strong, *The Artist and the Garden*, 17-85, 123.

7　Kate Retford, 'Reynolds's portrait of Mrs Theresa Parker: A case study in context', *The British Art Journal*, Vol. 4, No. 3 (Autumn 2003), 80-6.

8　This portrait is still owned by the hospital.

9　Fred Whishaw, 'In a Devonshire garden', *Longman's Magazine*, 1902, 40 (235), 14-31.

10　Audrey Erskine, 'John Grandison', *Oxford Dictionary of National Biography*.

11　Lillian Randall, *Images on the Margins of Gothic Manuscripts* (1966).

12　Adelaide L. Bennett, 'Additions to the William of Devon Group', *The Art Bulletin*, Vol. 54, No. 1 (March, 1972), 31-40; Elzbieta Temple, 'Further Additions to the William of Devon Group', *Bodleian Library Record*, 2 (1984), 344-48.

13　See Bonnie Young, '*Opus Anglicanum*', *The Metropolitan Museum of Art Bulletin*, NS, Vol. 29, No. 7 (Mar., 1971), 291-8.

14　R. A. S. Macalister, *Ecclesiastical Vestments: their development and history* (1896), 89.

15　*Visitors' guide to Culmstock church* (Culmstock, 2006); *A short history and guide to the parish church of All Saints, Culmstock, Devon* (Culmstock, no date given). 7-8.

16　Cherry & Pevsner, *Devon*, 307.

17　Cherry & Pevsner, *Devon*, 829; J. Chattaway, 'Account of Brixham, Co. Devon', *The Gentleman's Magazine*, August 1830, 115.

18　*A Short Guide Malborough Parish Church* (leaflet on sale in the church).

19　Eds, 'Restoration of ancient chasuble to Barnstaple Church', *Devon & Cornwall Notes & Queries*, 6:4, 1910, 105; Mary Phillips Perry, 'A medieval chasuble at Barnstaple', *Burlington Magazine*, Vol. 18, No. 91, October 1910, 51; Alice Dryden, *The Arts of the Church: Church Embroidery* (Oxford, 1911), 66, 69.

20　*Exeter Flying Post*, 6 May 1847; Todd Gray, *Lost Devon* (Exeter, 2003), 145.

21　H. F. Fulford Williams, 'The vestments of Bishop Grandisson Now In The Azores', *Devonshire Association Transactions*, Vol. 94, 1962, 613-22.

22　William Lawson, *The Country House-Wife's Garden* (1983 edn).

23　Exeter Cathedral Archive, Act Book 2153.

24　DHC, CC6A/143-4, CC5/108, CC24/126, CC5/60, CC.15/37, CC.19B/132-3, CC5/425, CC4/112.

25　DHC, Z19/18/9, page 12.

26　Todd Gray (ed.), *Early-Stuart Mariners and Shipping: the maritime surveys of Devon and Cornwall, 1619-35*, Devon & Cornwall Record Society, NS 33, 1990, 5-6, 24-5, 47-8.

27　Tristram Risdon, *The Chorographical Description or Survey of the County of Devon* (1811 edn), 347.

28　DHC, DD48969-74.

29　DHC, 2160 A/PO 767.

30　DHC, 1142 B/L13/1; 74/9/1/2; 49/26/1/7; Z1/10/35; Z1/17/2/1/1; 136M/T/18; 3799M-0/T/2/9.

31　'Deuchesne's Natural History of Strawberries', *The Monthly Review or Literary Journal*, 1766, Vol. 34, 565; David J. Hawkings, 'John Tradescant and the Plymouth Strawberry', *The Devon Historian*, 1988, Vol. 37, 1988, 28.

32　Mary Edmond, 'Nicholas Hilliard', *Oxford Dictionary of National Biography*.

33　R. W. Parker, *Historic Buildings Survey of the Bishop's Palace Gatehouse, Exeter, Devon* (Exeter, 2013), 10-12.

34　Todd Gray, *Devon's Ancient Bench Ends* (Exeter, 2012).

35　DHC, 235M/E1.

36　Stephen Timmons. 'The Hearth Tax and Finance in the West Country, 1662-92", 52, in Charles Ivar McGrath and Chris Fauske (eds), *Money, Power and Print* (Cradnbury, 2008).

37　Todd Gray (ed.), *Devon Household Accounts, 1627-59*, Devon & Cornwall Record Society, NS Vol. 38, 1995, xxxiii.

38　Jannine Crocker (ed.), *Exeter's Elizabethan Inventories*, Devon & Cornwall Record Society, forthcoming.

39　H. J. Yallop, *The History of the Honiton Lace Industry* (Exeter, 1992).

40　Yallop, *Honiton Lace Industry*, 207-208.

41　Museum of English Rural Life, DEV/3/1/288.

42　Charles Scott-Fox, *Holcombe Court; A Bluett Family Tudor Mansion* (Holcombe Rogus, 2012), 17-19.

43　Gray, *Devon's Ancient Bench Ends*, 47-8.

44　Hugh R. Watkin, *A short description of Torre Abbey, Torquay, Devonshire* (1912), 3.

45　I would like to thank Emeritus Professor Christopher Holdsworth for this translation from the Latin.

46　Ian Tyers, *18 North Street, Exeter, Devon: Dendrochronological analysis of oak panels* (English Heritage Research Department Report Series no. 7-2010).

47　Katharine Gibson, 'Hendrick Danckerts', *Oxford Dictionary of National Biography*.

48　Todd Gray, *The Garden History of Devon* (Exeter, 1995), 156.

49　Hampshire Record Office, 44M69/F10/88/27.

50　John Allan and Stuart Blaylock, *Exeter's Custom House and Quay* (Exeter, 2010), 16.

51　J. Mayne, 'Bradfield, Cullompton, Devon', *The Gardening World*, 27 May 1899, 613.

52　Todd Gray, 'A visit by Edmund Spoure through Devon in 1694', *Devon & Cornwall Notes & Queries*, XXXVII, Part VII, Spring 1995, 217-18.

53　Miles Hadfield, *A History of British Gardening* (1985 edn), 149-50.

54　Robin Bush, *The Book of Exmouth* (1978), 14-15; Gray, *Garden History of Devon*, 151-2.

55　Plymouth & West Devon Record Office (hereafter PWDRO), 69/M/2/243; CRO, RD/1576.

56　CRO, RD/1579.

57　PWDRO, 69/M/6/5.

58　PWDRO, 69/M/2/641; Daniel & Samuel Lysons, *Magna Britannia* (1822), VI, 456.

59　PWDRO, 74/464/8.

60　PWDRO, 74/79/8.

61　*Lysons, Devon*, VI, 521.

62　Metropolitan Museum of Art, painting description.

63　John Harris, 'The Prideaux collection of Topographical Drawings', *Architectural History*, Vol. 7, 1964, 1-109.

64　Michael Trinick, *Dunsland House, Devon* (1969), 16; Gray, *Garden History of Devon*, 92.

65　Gray, *Garden History of Devon*, 106-108; Richard Tyler and Mark Roper, *Forde Abbey* (Thorncombe, no date given), 2-3.

66　John Harris, 'The Prideaux collection of Topographical Drawings', 1.

67　Cherry & Pevsner, *Devon*, 689-90.

68　John Maclean, *A Brief Memoir of the Families o Prideaux of Devon and Cornwall, and of Brune of Hants and Dorset*.

69　Maclean, *A Brief Memoir of the Families o Prideaux of Devon and Cornwall*, 34.

70　Maclean, *A Brief Memoir of the Families o Prideaux of Devon and Cornwall*, 11.

71　Ralph Hyde, 'Samuel Buck', *Oxford Dictionary of National Biography*.

72　See Mary O'Hagan, *A History of Forde House, Newton Abbot, Devon* (Newton Abbot, 1990), for details about the Courtenay family in the house.

73　DHC, 1508M/Devon/Estate/Account Books, volumes 2, 3, 7; Gray, *Garden History of Devon*, 181-3.

74　Gray, *Garden History of Devon*, 183; DHC, 1508M/Devon/Estate/Account Book 5, 47-8. The volume was seen in 1994 and is now unfit for production.

75　DHC, 564M/F11/7.

76　The Conductor, 'Notices of some gardens and country seats in Somersetshire, Devonshire and part of Cornwall', *The Gardener's Magazine*, May 1843, 242-3.

77　Rosemary Lauder, *Vanished Houses of North Devon* (Tiverton, 2005), 49-53.

78　Margaret Reed, *Pilton its Past and its People* (Barnstaple, 1985 edn), 28–31.

79　Robin Fawcett, 'Castle Hill: The Formal and Transitional Garden', in Steven Pugsley (ed.), *Devon Gardens, an historical survey* (Stroud, 1994), 42-58.

80　PWDRO, 407/E1 & F39.

81　There are genealogical details given in John Burke, There are genealogical details given in John Burke, *A Genealogical and Heraldic History of the Commoners of Great Britain and Ireland, Enjoying Territorial Possessions Or High Official Rank* (1835), II, 28. More accurate information is found in the early bishop's transcripts at the Devon Heritage Centre for St Thomas near Exeter. These show the baptisms of Ann Grace on October 1725, Jane on 29 June 1726, Joanna on 11 October 1728, Mary on 19 May 1730, Jasper on 29 December 1731, Walter on 4 August 1733, John on 12 December 1735, William on 12 January 1738, Pollexfen on 24 March 1744. The Tamerton Foliot bishop's transcripts recorded the burial of Jasper on 4 November 1743, the baptism of Copplestone on 25 January 1745 and the burial of Admonition on 12 September 1758.

82   Mrs Bray, *A Description of the Part of Devonshire Bordering on the Tamar and the Tavy: Its Natural History, Manners, Customs, Superstitions, Scenery, Antiquities, Biography of Eminent Persons, &c. &c. in a Series of Letters to Robert Southey, Esq.* (1836), I, 7. Polwhele gave a similar description in 1797: Gray, *Garden History of Devon*, 227-8.

83   J. Britton, *Devonshire & Cornwall illustrated from original drawings by Thomas Allom*, W.H. Bartlett, &c (1832), 94-5.

84   PWDRO, 407/2/4/10.

85   *Royal Cornwall Gazette*, 27 April 1822.

86   Todd Gray (ed.), *Travels In Georgian Devon* (Tiverton, 1998), II, 9.

87   National Archives, E214/532. George Parker's will was proved on 14 June 1743.

88   Gray, *Travels In Georgian Devon*, II, 8-9.

89   Gervase Jackson-Stops, *An English Arcadia, 1600 – 1990* (Washington, 1991), 62.

90   English Heritage, Boringdon List Entry.

91   George Oliver and Pitman Jones, *Genealogy of the family of Courtenay* (no place or date of publication).

92   National Archives, PROB 11/1328/224.

93   Todd Gray (ed.), *Travels in Georgian Devon* (Tiverton, 1997), I, ix.

94   W. G. Plenderleath & T. L. Ormiston (eds), 'The Parish Registers of Powderham, Devon', Devon & Cornwall Record Society Library, ts, 78, 125.

95   Hampshire Record Office, 23M93/103/1/2, page 9.

96   The Conductor, 'Notices of some gardens and country seats in Somersetshire, Devonshire and part of Cornwall', *The Gardener's Magazine*, November 1842, 538-9.

97   John Claudius Loudon, *In Search of English Gardens* (1990 edn), 238.

98   L. Namier & J. Brooke, *The History of Parliament: the House of Commons, 1754-1790* (1964).

99   Gray, *Garden History of Devon*, 165.

100   DHC, 346M/1-450.

101   Ellen G. D'Oench, *The conversation piece: Arthur Devis & his contemporaries* (New Haven, 1980), 20.

102   Ellen G. D'Oench, 'Arthur Devis', *Oxford Dictionary of National Biography*.

103   David Boyd Haycock, 'William Borlase', *Oxford Dictionary of National Biography*.

104   Douglas Pett, *The Parks and Gardens of Cornwall* (Penzance, 1998), 215.

105   Richard Stephens, 'New Material for Francis Towne's Biography', *The Burlington Magazine*, Vol. 138, No 1121, August 1996, 500-505; Timothy Wilcox, 'Francis Towne', *Oxford Dictionary of National Biography*.

106   DHC, 1038M/F, 12 March 1792.

107   'Agricultural Experiment', *The Literary Gazette*, 42, 8 November 1817, 303; Ann B. Shteir, 'Agnes Ibbetson', *Oxford Dictionary of National Biography*.

108   DHC, 1038M/F, 14 February 1792.

109   DHC, 1038M/F, 14 February 1792.

110   Todd Gray, *Remarkable Women of Devon* (Exeter, 2009), 44; Mary Beacock Fryer, *Elizabeth Posthuma Simcoe* (Oxford, 1989), 28.

111   Deborah Graham Vernon, 'William Tomkins', *Oxford Dictionary of National Biography*.

112   English Heritage, Parks & Gardens Register, Listing Saltram No. 1000699.

113   David Japes, 'William Payne', *Oxford Dictionary of National Biography*.

114   Ronald Fletcher, *The Parkers at Saltram, 1769-89* (1970), 176-7.

115   James Greig (ed.), *The Farington Diary* (New York, 1925), V, 285. In 1799 Lady Holland had the same opinion. She wrote that the beauty of the view was dependent upon the tide: The Earl of Ilchester (ed.), *The Journal of Elizabeth Lady Holland 1791-1811* (1908), II, 19.

116   *A diary of the royal tour in June, July, August and September 1789, interspersed with anecdotes, poetry and descriptions, historical, typographical, &c. &c. To which is added, that of their Highness the Prince of Wales, and Duke of York, to York, &c. &c. with characters of The King, Prince of Wales, and the Dukes of York and Clarence; By an observer of the times* (1789), 67.

117   Stebbing Shaw, *A tour to the west of England, in 1788. By the Rev. S. Shaw, M. A. Fellow of Queen's College*, Cambridge (1789), 353.

118   Hilary Young, 'Manufacturing outside the Capital: The British Porcelain Factories, Their Sales Networks and Their Artists, 1745-1795', *Journal of Design History*, Vol. 12, No. 3, Eighteenth-Century Markets and Manufactures in England and France (1999), 262.

119   Mary Jones, *The History of Chudleigh in the County of Devon* (1852), 193-5.

120   Aileen Fox, 'The Retreat, Topsham', *Devon Archaeological Society Proceedings*, no. 49, 1991,131-41.

121   Gray, *Travels in Georgian Devon*, II, 80.

122   Todd Gray, *Devon & the Slave Trade* (Exeter, 2007), 145-7; Aileen Fox, 'The Retreat, Topsham', *Proceedings of the Devon Archaeological Society*, 1991, 131-41.

123   For the North Devon pottery industry see *Alison Grant, North Devon Pottery: The seventeenth century* (Exeter, 1983).

124   Hoskins, *Devon*, 276.

125   Eric Delderfield, *West Country historic houses and their families* (Newton Abbot, 1968), I, 67.

126   Richard Polwhele, *The history of Devonshire* (1793), II, 77– 8.

127   James Dugdale, *The new British traveller or modern panorama of England and Wales* (1819), II, 141-2.

128   Polwhele, *The history of Devonshire*, II, 181-2.

129   *Exeter Flying Post*, 4 June 1898.

130   Gray, *Travels in Georgian Devon*, I, vii-xxii. The introductions to the following three volumes also have biographical information.

131   Hampshire Record Office, 44M69/F10/88/22.

132   J. E. B. Gover, A. Mawer and F. M. Stenton, *The Place Names of Devon* (English Place Names Society, 1932), II, 501.

133   Polwhele, *The history of Devonshire*, II, 155-6.

134   N. R. R. Fisher, 'Robert Balle, merchant of Leghorn and fellow of the Royal Society (ca.1640-ca1734)', *Notes Rec. R. Soc. Lond.* 2001, 55 (3), 351-71; Eveline Cruickshanks, 'Robert Balle', in D. Hayton, E. Cruickshanks & S. Handley, (eds), *The History of Parliament, the House of Commons, 1690-1715* (2002).

135   Polwhele, *The history of Devonshire*, II, 155-6.

136   Gray, *Garden History of Devon*, 146.

137   Britton, *Devonshire & Cornwall illustrated from original drawings*, 64-6.

138   Lysons, *Magna Britannia*, VI, 328.

139   Richard Bradley, *The gentleman and gardeners kalendar, directing what is necessary to be done every month, in the kitchen-garden, fruit-garden, nursery, management of forest-trees, green-house and flower-garden. With directions for the making and ordering hop-grounds. By Richard Bradley, F.R.S. To which is added, The Design of a Green-House (finely Engrav'd) after a New Manner, contriv'd purposely for the good keeping of Exotick Plants, by Seignior Galilei of Florence* (1718), 50.

140   Hadfield, *A History of British Gardening*, 236.

141   Gray, *Garden History of Devon*, 146.

142   Cherry & Pevsner, *Devon*, 557-8.

143   Thomas Moule, *Moule's English counties: Devonshire* (1834), 309-310.

144   R. Fish, 'Mamhead', *The Cottage Gardener and Country Gentleman*, 23 November 1858, 116.

145   The conductor, 'Notices of some gardens and country seats in Somersetshire, Devonshire and part of Cornwall', *The Gardener's Magazine*, October 1842, 493.

146   The Conductor, 'Notices of some gardens and country seats in Somersetshire, Devonshire and part of Cornwall', *The Gardener's Magazine*, October 1842, 494.

147   Polwhele, *Devon*, II, 169-71.

148   William Hyett, *Guide in a tour to the watering places, And their environs, On the south-east coast of Devon* (Exeter, c.1800), 17.

149   Gray, *Travels in Georgian Devon*, II, 154-5.

150   DHC, 1038M/F, 12 March 1792.

151   Also see *The Tour of Doctor Syntax in search of The Picturesque* (1838) which has illustrations by 'Alfred Crowquill'.

152   Todd Gray, *Travels in Georgian Devon* (Tiverton, 1999), III, 111-114.

153   Gray, *Travels in Georgian Devon*, III, 133-4.

154   Gray, *Travels in Georgian Devon*, II, 94-5.

155   Gray, *Travels in Georgian Devon*, II, 77-8.

156   Gray, *Travels in Georgian Devon*, II, 78.

157   Polwhele, *Devon*, II, 361.

158   English Heritage, Listed Building Survey.

159   M. F. Bridie, *The Story of Shute* (Axminster, 1955), 138.

160   University College, London, Legacies of British Slave Ownership Project.

161   Bridie, *The Story of Shute*, 156.

162   Timothy Clayton and Anita McConnell, 'Francis Jukes', *Oxford Dictionary of National Biography*.

163 W. G. Hoskins, *Two Thousand Years in Exeter* (Exeter, 1960), 94; Greig, Farington Diary, VI, 178.

164 Gray, *Garden History of Devon*, 193.

165 *Woolmer's Exeter and Plymouth Gazette*, 20 August 1831.

166 Greig, *Farington Diary*, VI, 160.

167 National Archives, Prob 11/1784/344. She was described as being of Chittlehampton.

168 Todd Gray, *Devon's Fifty Best Churches* (Exeter, 2011), 52-5.

169 The Conductor, 'Notices of some gardens and country seats in Somersetshire, Devonshire and part of Cornwall', *The Gardener's Magazine*, November 1842, 552-4.

170 Gray, *Garden History of Devon*, 176-7; University College London, Legacies of Slave Project, Kekewich of Peamore.

171 P. J. Jarvis, 'North American Plants and Horticultural Innovation in England, 1550-1700', *Geographical Review*, Vol. 63, No. 4 (Oct., 1973), 488; Augustine Henry & Margaret G. Flood, 'The History of the London Plane, Platanus Acerifolia, with Notes on the Genus Platanus', *Proceedings of the Royal Irish Academy. Section B: Biological, Geological, and Chemical Science*, Vol. 35, (1919/1920), 11.

172 Ellen C. Clayton, *English Female Artists* (London, 1876), I, 367.

173 Census, Arlington, 1851-81.

174 Gray, Garden *History of Devon*, 66-7.

175 Gray, *Travels in Georgian Devon*, II, 54-5.

176 Britton, *Devonshire & Cornwall illustrated from original drawings*, 103.

177 Cherry & Pevsner, *Devon*, 166.

178 Richard Polwhele, *The history of Devonshire* (1806), III, 491.

179 DHC, Z19/2/10a-b; W. G. Maton, *Observations relative chiefly to the natural history, picturesque scenery and antiquities of the western counties of England* (1797), 111.

180 R. N. Worth, *Tourist's guide to South Devon: rail, road, river, coast, and moor* (1883), 56.

181 Diana Brooks, 'Thomas Allom', *Oxford Dictionary of National Biography*.

182 The Conductor, 'Notices of some gardens and country seats in Somersetshire, Devonshire and part of Cornwall', *The Gardener's Magazine*, November 1842, 536-7.

183 Yorick, 'The Late Rev. Dr Drury', *The Gentleman's Magazine*, March 1835, 248.

184 Judith Anne Merivale, *Autobiography of Dean Merivale* (1899), 17.

185 S. J. Skedd, 'Joseph Drury', *Oxford Dictionary of National Biography*.

186 DHC, 3237M, unlisted letter of 26 November 1824.

187 The Conductor, 'Notices of some gardens and country seats in Somersetshire, Devonshire and part of Cornwall', *The Gardener's Magazine*, November 1842, 552.

188 Abi Gray, Shilstone, *Archaeological Notes* (Shilstone, 2010).

189 Richard Stone, 'The Creation of Endsleigh: a Regency Picturesque Masterpiece'. in Pugsley, *Devon Gardens*, 76-90.

190 DHC, L1258M/E/A/E/ 29 September 1814.

191 DHC, L1258M/E/A/E17, 14 August 1817.

192 DHC, W1258M/LP4/15 & 51.

193 Richard Stone, 'The Creation of Endsleigh: a Regency Picturesque Masterpiece', in Pugsley, *Devon Gardens*, 89.

194 Miss Dixon, A Journal of Ten Days Excursion on the Western and Northern Borders of Dartmoor (Plymouth, 1830), 5-7.

195 Hampshire Record Office, 23M93/103/1/2, page 6.

196 Ian Maxted, *A history of the book in Devon. 52: Tourism and topographical views* (Exeter Working Papers in Book History; 12), http://bookhistory.blogspot (html) - accessed (4 May 2013).

197 *Exeter Flying Post*, 27 January 1891.

198 Alan Borg and David Coke, *Vauxhall Gardens: a history* (New Haven, 2011).

199 T. H. Williams, *The environs of Exeter* (Exeter, c.1815), no page numbers.

200 Todd Gray (ed.), *Travels in Georgian Devon*, (Tiverton, 2000), IV, 25-8.

201 Anna W. Merivale, *Family Memorials* (Exeter, 1884), 124.

202 DHC, 1262M/E22/96.

203 Bridget Cherry, *Devon*, 129.

204 Thomas Moule, *Moule's English counties: Devonshire*. (1834), 327.

205 Todd Gray, *Remarkable Women of Devon*, 49-52.

206 Dixon, *Journal*, 25-6.

207 Somerset Heritage Centre, DD/SWD/10/11; Todd Gray (ed.), *Travels in Georgian Devon* (Tiverton, 1999), III, 86-9; Cherry & Pevsner, *Devon*, 890-1.

208 Todd Gray, *The Victorian Under Class of Exeter* (Exeter, 2001), 72-96.

209 *Report of the committee of Wonford House* (Exeter, 1876).

210 Todd Gray (ed.), *East Devon the travellers' tales* (Exeter, 2000). xii, 45, 36.

211 Sarah Bendall, 'John Baverstock Knight', *Oxford Dictionary of National Biography*.

212 Census, Sidmouth, 1841.

213 Hampshire Record Office, 23M93/103/1/2, page 11.

214 J. V. Somers-Cocks, Devon *Topographical Prints, 1660–1870* (Exeter, 1977), 6.

215 Anonymous, *Guide to Illustrations and Views of Knowle Cottage, Sidmouth; The elegant Marine Villa Ornee of Thomas Fish, Esquire* (Sidmouth, 1834); Somerset Heritage Centre, DD/SWD/10/1.

216 Keith S. Perkins, 'The inimitable George Wightwick', *The Devon Historian*, Vol. 31, October 1985, 24-8.

217 I am grateful to Peter Hamilton Legget for this reference and for sharing his research into the house.

218 Rosamund Reid, 'The Architectural Work of George Wightwick in Plymouth and the County of Devon', *Transactions of the Devonshire Association*, 128 (1996), 121-5.

219 George Oliver and Pitman Jones, *Genealogy of the Family of Courtenay* (possibly Exeter, no date given).

220 D. S. Neff, 'Bitches, Mollies, and Tommies: Byron, Masculinity, and the History of Sexualities, *Journal of the History of Sexuality*, Vol. 11, No. 3 (Jul., 2002), 414, 423, 428-9; Anita McConnell, 'William Thomas Beckford', *Oxford Dictionary of National Biography*; Bill Bryson, *A short history of private life* (2010), 218-19; Greig, *Farington Diary*, V, 270.

221 Greig, *Farington Diary*, VI, 148, 273.

222 *Woolmer's Exeter & Plymouth Gazette*, 13 June 1835.

223 Polwhele, *Devon*, II, 169-71.

224 Henry Charles Andrews, *The botanist's repository, for new, and rare plants. Containing coloured figures of such plants, as have not hitherto appeared in any similar publication; with all their essential characters, botanically arranged, after the sexual system of the celebrated Linnæus; in English, and Latin. To each description is added, a short history of the plant, as to its time of flowering, culture, native place of growth, when introduced, and by whom. The whole executed by Henry Andrews, author of the coloured engravings of heaths, in folio* (1814) I, plates xlix & iv, plate ccxxxvi. See also Joseph and Nesta Ewan, 'John Lyon, Nurseryman and Plant Hunter, and His Journal, 1799-1814', *Transactions of the American Philosophical Society*, New Series, Vol. 53, No. 2 (1963), 31, 66; William Hyett, *Guide in a tour to the watering places, And their environs, On the south-east coast of Devon* (Exeter, c.1800), 16.

225 *Exeter Flying Post*, 2 October 1823; *The Morning Post*, 25 October 1823; *The Times*, 18 August 1824; Anonymous, *Continuation of Journals in the years 1824, 25, 27, 28, and 29* (1830), 139; *The Observer*, 28 September 1835; *The Standard*, 22 June 1831; *Morning Post*, 25 August 1831.

226 Gray, *Garden History of Devon*, 182-3.

227 Lysons, *Magna Britannia*, VI, lxxxix; DHC, 1508MDevon/Estate/Account Books/ volumes 19 and 40.

228 Gray, *Garden History of Devon*, 182-3.

229 *The Conductor*, 'Notices of some gardens and country seats in Somersetshire, Devonshire and part of Cornwall', *The Gardener's Magazine*, November 1842, 532.

230 Beverly E. Schneller, 'Anna Eliza Bray', *Oxford Dictionary of National Biography*.

231 Mrs Bray, *The Borders of the Tamar and the Tavy* (1879 edn), II, 7, 15-16.

232 *Fitz of Fitz-Ford* (1884 edn) 3.

233 Tom Greeves, *Souvenir Programme - Festival of Dartmoor Literature* (The Dartmoor Society, 2008), 14-15; Bray, *The Borders of the Tamar and the Tavy*, II, 14-18.; H. P. R. Finberg. *Tavistock Abbey* (Newton Abbot, 1969 edn), 287.

234 Bray, *The Borders of the Tamar and the Tavy*, II, 15, 7, 12.

235 Bray, *The Borders of the Tamar and the Tavy*, II, 12-14.

236 Gray, *Garden History of Devon*, 62-3; English Heritage, listed building survey; 'Bystock', *The Gardeners' Chronicle*, 9 April 1881, 474-5.

237 Paul Popiawski, *A Jane Austen Encyclopedia* (1998), 12-13.

238 DHC, 3237M, unlisted collection; Merivale, *Family Memorials*, 124, 190, 194, 306.

239 Frederick Pollock, 'Clovelly', *The English Illustrated Magazine*, 15, December 1884, 160.

240 T. H. Williams, *Devonshire; or directions to the scenery and antiquities* (Exeter, 1828), II, 6.

241 Ashcroft, *Letters & Papers*, 88.

242 Hampshire Record Office, 23M93/103/1/2.

243 Angela Ruthven, *Clovelly and its story* (Clovelly, 1976), 53-4; George Tugwell, *The North-Devon Scenery-Book* (Ilfracombe, 1863), 245.

244 Somerset Heritage Centre, DD/ES/Box 17.

245 Gray, *Remarkable Women of Devon*, 113-115.

246 Census, Bovey Tracey, 1851.

247 Sherryl & Susie Healey, 'Cross Cottage', in Veronica Kennedy (ed.), *The Bovey Book* (Bovey Tracey, 2004), 106.

248 'Rev. William Davy', *The Gentleman's Magazine*, July 1826, 88-9.

249 Richard Ford, *Granada* (Granada, 1955), 174.

250 Rowland E. Prothero (ed.), *The Letters of Richard Ford* (1905), 136, 145-8, 153.

251 Hampshire Record Office, 75M91/B24/36.

252 DHC, 3004A/PZ74.

253 Ian Robertson, *Richard Ford, 1796 – 1858* (Norwich, 2004), 147-9.

254 Ford, *Granada*, 173; *Murray's Handbook for Devon & Cornwall* (1859) (Newton Abbot, 1971 edn), 23; *Exeter Flying Post*, 9 September 1858 & 8 September 1859.

255 Cecily Radford, 'Richard Ford (1796-1858), and his handbook for Travellers in Spain', *Devonshire Association Transactions*, XC, 1958, 165; Robertson, Richard Ford, 323.

256 Hoskins, *Exeter*, 83-4.

257 Robert Dymond, *History of the suburban parish of St. Leonard, Exeter* (Exeter, 1873), 19-21.

258 Greig, *Farington's Diary*, VI, 189.

259 DHC, 2751Z/Z1.

260 *Exeter Flying Post*, 6 September 1838, 4 April 1845, 26 November 1892.

261 *Devon Weekly Times*, 15 November 1901.

262 Somerset Heritage Centre, DD/WY/98.

263 *The Sketcher*, No. VIII, *Blackwood's Edinburgh Magazine* (1834), volume 35, 549-550.

264 Charles Kingsley, *Sir Walter Raleigh and His Time* (1859), 237-8; Hampshire Record Office, 23M93/103/1/2 & 75M91/M12/1.

265 By a Lady, *Mandeville: or, the Lynmouth visitors* (Barnstaple, 1839), 144-6.

266 John Fisher, *Lynmouth Area Character Appraisal* (Exmoor National Park Authority, 2003), 19-20; M. Y. Ashcroft (ed.), *Letters and Papers of Henrietta Matilda Crompton and Her Family* (Northallerton, 1994), viii, 125.

267 Two sketches of the valley form part of the collection at the Tate Gallery.

268 John Slade, *Colloquies: imaginary conversations between a phrenologist and the shade of Dugald Stewart* (1838), 326; Ashcroft, *Letters and Papers*, 88; J. Banfield, *A guide to Ilfracombe and the neighbouring towns* (Ilfracombe c.1845), 51-3.

269 George Tugwell, *The North Devon handbook: being a guide to the topography and archaeology and an introduction to the natural history of the district* (Ilfracombe, 1856), 26.

270 Ashcroft, *Letters and Papers*, vii-x, 88, 84.

271 Charlotte Chanter, *Ferny Combes* (1857), 11.

272 National Trust, Lupton List Entry; Gray, *Garden History of Devon*, 142-3.

273 H. M. Cundall, *William Callow, an autobiography* (1908), 87, 141-2, 144-66.

274 *Royal Cornwall Gazette*, 17 July 1857.

275 The Conductor, 'Notices of some gardens and country seats in Somersetshire, Devonshire and part of Cornwall', *The Gardener's Magazine*, November 1842, 541.

276 S. P. Fox, *Kingsbridge and its Surroundings* (Plymouth, 1874), 152.

277 Gray, *Garden History of Devon*, 5; Abraham Hawkins, *Kingsbridge and Salcombe* (Kingsbridge, 1819), 80-1.

278 Francis Young, *Myrtles and Aloes: or, Our Salcombe sketch Book, with some addenda in the shape of a discursive gossip about Kingsbridge* (1861), 92-3; Fox, Kingsbridge, 148-54.

279 Gray, *Devon and the Slave Trade*, 199-200.

280 William White, *History, gazetteer, and directory of Devonshire* (Sheffield, 1850) 438.

281 The Conductor, 'Notices of some gardens and country seats in Somersetshire, Devonshire and part of Cornwall', *The Gardener's Magazine*, November 1842, 534-5.

282 'Babbicombe to Hope's Nose', *The Eclectic Review*, 1, June 1859, 613.

283 *The Bradford Observer*, 6 August 1869; John Lloyd Warden Page, *The coasts of Devon and Lundy Island* (1895), 372.

284 'Men of Mark Number LIV, the bishop of Exeter', *The London Review*, 30 August 1862, 192.

285 *Exeter Flying Post*, 13 October 1869.

286 *Exeter Flying Post*, 22 September 1869.

287 *Exeter Flying Post*, 26 January 1870.

288 Gray, *Garden History of Devon*, 49.

289 Francis Greenacre, 'Francis Danby', *Oxford Dictionary of National Biography*; Smiles and Pidgley, *Perfection of England*, 50-1.

290 James John Hissey, *On the Box Seat from London to Land's End* (1886), 174.

291 Francis Greenacre, 'Francis Danby', *Oxford Dictionary of National Biography*.

292 DHC, St Sidwell parish, 3429A-2/PB 12.

293 Gray, *Lost Devon*, 62-5; DHC, 152M/Box68/Estate 1. The contract was with John Ware, Exeter builder.

294 Edward Ashworth, 'How Chinese Workmen Built a Chinese House', *The Builder*, 1 November 1851, 686-8.

295 DHC, 152M/Box65/Estate 5/letter of 26 August 1846.

296 DHC, 152M/Box65/Estate 5/letter of 24 November 1845.

297 These paintings are, at the time of going to press, in the process of being auctioned; Brown, *Images of Mount Edgcumbe*, 2.

298 *Nettleton's Guide to Plymouth, Stonehouse and Devonport and to the adjoining country* (Plymouth, 1836), 113.

299 Anonymous, *The Picture of Plymouth* (1812), 147.

300 Cynthia Gaskell Brown, *Images of Mount Edgcumbe Cornwall* (Mount Edgcumbe, 2000), 29; Stebbing Shaw, *A tour to the west of England, in 1788. By the Rev. S. Shaw, M. A. Fellow of Queen's College, Cambridge* (1789), 353-66.

301 James Greig (ed), *The Farington Diary* (New York, 1926), VI, 110-111.

302 Greig, *Farington Diary*, V, 288.

303 'Art. 26. Observations and Remarks during four Excursions made to various Parts of Great Britain, in the Years 1810 and 1811', *Monthly Review* (February 1813), 218.

304 Jane Elizabeth Moore, *Genuine memoirs of Jane Elizabeth Moore. Late of Bermondsey, in the county of Surrey. Written by herself: containing the singular adventures of herself and family. Her Sentimental Journey through Great Britain: specifying the various Manufactures carried on at each Town. A comprehensive Treatise on the Trade, Manufactures, Navigation, Laws and Police of this Kingdom, and the necessity of a Country Hospital* (c.1786), II.

305 Isle of Wight Record Office, OG/CC/1382A.

306 An Observer of the Times, *A diary of the royal tour in June, July, August and September, 1789* (1789), 81.

307 The Conductor, 'Notices of some gardens and country seats in Somersetshire, Devonshire and part of Cornwall', *The Gardener's Magazine*, November 1842, 547-8.

308 G. C. Boase, rev. Mark Pottle, 'Nicholas Condy', *Oxford Dictionary of National Biography*.

309 Clive N. Ponsford, *Time in Exeter* (Exeter, 1978), 126-48; DHC, 76/20/1-8.

310 Cherry & Pevsner, *Devon*, 125-6.

311 DHC, P&D40117-8.

312 John Wolffe, 'John Cornelius Gorham', *Oxford Dictionary of National Biography*.

313 Janet Paul, 'Artists of the Hobson Album', *Turnbull Library Record* (Vol. 18, no. 1, May 1985), 22-32; Elizabeth Stewart Marsden, 'An Edition of the journal of Edward Ashworth' (MA thesis, University of Wellington, 1992).

314 Edward Ashworth, 'How Chinese Workmen Built a Chinese House', *The Builder*, 1 November 1851, 686-8.

315 *The Devon Weekly Times*, 13 March 1896; Exeter Flying Post, 14 & 21 March 1896.

316 DHC, P&D05458.

317 DHC, P&D06610-12.

318 PWDRO, 733/box 3350, memo book of payments by Lady Sophia Rogers including to building of the parsonage at Ivybridge, 1858. I am grateful to Judith Farmer for this reference.

319 Britton, *Devonshire & Cornwall illustrated from original drawings*, 102.

320 DHC, P&D06613; M. G. Watkins, 'On Ottery East Hill', *Fraser's Magazine*, Vol. 10, August 1874, 210.

321 *The Gentleman's Magazine*, March 1834, 265-6; DHC, SC2467.

322 English Heritage, Pastscape, Torwood Manor House; Lysons, Devon, VI, 524-5; George Oliver & John Pike Jones, *Ecclesiastical Antiquities of Devon* (Exeter, 1828), 80; John Fisher, *Warberries Conservation Area Character Appraisal* (Torbay District Council, 2006), with revisions by Hal Bishop, 2.17.

323 *Morning Post*, 13 June 1860.

324 Octavian Blewitt, *The Panorama of Torquay* (1832), 93.

325 John Gullet, 'Description of Woodbine Cottage, Torquay, the Residence of Mrs Johnes', *The Gardener's Magazine*, NS, Vol. II, 1836, 26-8.

326 John Sales and Priscilla Boniface, *In Search of English Gardens* (1988), 237; The Conductor, 'Notices of some gardens and country seats in Somersetshire, Devonshire and part of Cornwall', *The Gardener's Magazine*, November 1842, 535-6.

327 N. T. Carrington, Th*e Teignmouth, Dawlish, and Torquay Guide* (Teignmouth, 1829), 94-5.

328 R. Dymond & J. T. White, *A chronological record of events relating to Torquay and neighbourhood* (Torquay, n.d.), 32.

329 Leslie Retallick, *Torre Abbey Historic House and Gallery, Catalogue of the Art Collections* (Torquay, 2004), 13; Exeter Flying Post, 5 February 1857.

330 *Illustrated London News*, 4 September 1852

331 Census, Townstall, 1851.

332 Gray, *Lost Devon*, 94.

333 Percy Russell, *Dartmouth* (1950), 148-50, 154-5; Josephine Brown, 'Mr Seale's Woods: The Eighteenth Century Landscape of Mount Boone, Dartmouth', *The Devon Garden Trust Journal* (3, 2013), 15.

334 Census, 1861.

335 Robert Newton, *Victorian Exeter* (Leicester, 1968), 175

336 Census, St Sidwell's Parish, 1881.

337 Todd Gray, *Victorian Wild Flowers of Devon* (Exeter, 2001).

338 Hoskins, *Devon*, 432; *Cockrem's tourists' guide to Torquay and its neighbourhood* (Torquay, 1878) 111-112.

339 It was sold at Christies on 20 May 2004, Sale 9850, Lot 557.

340 Smiles and Pidgley, *The Perfection of England*, 65-6; Arthur Fish, 'The Work of C. Napier Hemy, A.R.A.', *The Magazine of Art*, January 1900, 3.

341 Peter McGann, Days of My Youth (Victoria, 2006), 77; 'Charles Napier Hemy', *The Art Journal*, August 1881, 226.

342 *History, Gazetteer and Directory of the County of Devon* (Sheffield, 1878-9), 227-8.

343 William Harrison, 'Clovelly by the Rector of Clovelly', *The Art Journal*, November 1896, 321.

344 W. W. Fenn, 'Favourite Sketching Grounds: Clovelly', *The Magazine of Art*, January 1880, 87.

345 Rosalind Northcote, *Devon, its moorland, streams and coasts* (1930), 214-215.

346 Charles L. Eastlake, *A History of the Gothic Revival* (1872), 356-7.

347 *Exeter Flying Post*, 1 May 1845.

348 Jackson-Stops, *An English Arcadia*, 138; Jo Moore, *Knightshayes* (Swindon, 2013), 14-15; DHC, 1926B/D/E/1/1; *The Cornwall Royal Gazette*, 12 February 1841.

349 DHC, 1926B/W/E/20/1-3 & 1926B/W/F2/7; 'Mansion at Knightshayes', *The Architect*, Vol. IV, 2 July 1870.

350 *Exeter Flying Post*, 7 October 1893.

351 *The Times*, 31 October 1911, page 15; Jo Moore, Knightshayes (Swindon, 2013), 14-15; Edward Hyam, 'In an English Garden', *Illustrated London News*, 20 February 1965, page 20; Richard Bisgrove, *The National Trust Book of the English Garden* (1990), 248-9, 254.

352 'The A La Ronde Story', National Trust, 2011, 14-15.

353 Lynne Walker, 'The Entry of Women into the Architectural Profession in Britain', *Woman's Art Journal*, Vol. 7, No. 1, Spring-Summer 1986, 13-14; English Heritage, List Entry, A La Ronde.

354 *Exeter Flying Post*, 27 May 1868.

355 John Luscombe, 'Description of the lime, citron, orange and lemon trees at Coombe Royal', *The Gardener's Magazine*, Vol. 1, 1834, 36.

356 Francis Young, *Myrtles and Aloes: or, Our Salcombe sketch Book, with some addenda in the shape of a discursive gossip about Kingsbridge* (1861), 10, 88; Hawkins, *Kingsbridge and Salcombe*, 86.

357 John Claudius Loudon, *Arboretum et fruticetum britannicum*, Vol. 1, 396.

358 Fox, *Kingsbridge*, 153.

359 Museum of English Rural Life, DEV/EG31.

360 *The Gardener's Magazine*, Vol. 1, 1834, 36 & Vol. 8, 1842, 539-40.

361 'Combe Royal', *Journal of Horticulture, Cottage Gardener, Country Gentleman, Beekeeper and Poultry Chronicle*, NS Vol. 21, 31 August 1871, 162-4.

362 Museum of English Rural Life, DEV 3c 1/7-9; J. R. Jackson, 'Combe Royal', *The Gardeners' Chronicle*, 3rs Series, Vol. 35, 2 January 1904, 1-3.

363 See NDRO, 2458A/C.166.

364 *Ilfracombe Chronicle*, 8 May 1886, 6 August 1904 & 20 August 1921.

365 Fox, *Kingsbridge*, 171-2.

366 Hawkins, *Kingsbridge*, 99-101.

367 *Exeter Flying Post*, 28 May 1846, 14 November 1860, 29 April 1863; Census, Topsham, 1851.

368 *Exeter Flying Post*, 17 & 24 July 1878 & 18 May 1881.

369 *Exeter Flying Post*, 6 April 1889, 27 December 1890, 5 March 1898, 27 August 1898.

370 Gray, *Remarkable Women of Devon*, 108-109.

371 *Exeter Flying Post*, 7 March 1891 & 20 September 1871; *The Graphic*, 17 February 1883.

372 *Exeter Flying Post*, 11 June 1898; *Birmingham Daily Post*, 27 January 1895; *The Morning Post*, 5 April 1894; *The Bristol Mercury and Daily Post*, 23 May 1899.

373 *Torquay Directory*, 13 July 1910.

374 I am grateful to Mark Pool for these details.

375 DHC, Welcombe Faculty Petitions, 7.

376 DHC, 346M/E386; S. Heriz-Smith, 'The Veitch nurseries of Killerton and Exeter, c.1780 to 1863, Part 1', *Garden History*, Vol. 16, No. 1, Spring 1988, 41-57.

377 *Exeter Flying Post*, 21 July 1808; Audrey Le Lievre, 'To the Nobility and gentry about to plant; nurseries and nurserymen', in Pugsley (ed.), *Devon Gardens*, 93-4.

378 Elizabeth Baigen, 'Veitch Family', *Oxford Dictionary of National Biography*; Toby Musgrove, Chris Gardener & Will Musgrove, *The Plant Hunters* (1999), 131-54.

379 *Exeter Flying Post*, May 1863.

Index

Picture Credits

The inside jacket illustrations also appear on pages 160 & 180.
The illustrations in the introduction and in the main series are in
bold. All images remain the copyright of the owners and have been
reproduced with the kind permission of:

Bearnes Littlewood & Hampton Ltd, 55. Sale 29
January 2013 Stuart Blaylock, 19. & 20.
Bodleian Library, 49. Ashmole 1461, f.15r
The British Library Board, 15-16. Royal Ms 1 d.i,
fo.5r; 216. K Top Vol 11, no. 117.
The British Museum, 1 12. 2010.7081.4114;
m 13. 1868.0822.2097; n 14.1868.0808.6114;
37. 1874.0509.87; 52. 1863.0725.682; 150.
Heal, Portraits.124; 220. 1944,1014.13;
222. 1998,0314.11; 253. 1908,0218.10;
255. 1956,0714.56; 258. 1882,1209.73;
260. 2012,7037.1; 263. 1936,1116.31.3;
273. 1944,1014.6; 292. Heal,
Portraits.170; 303. 1967, 1014.186; 314.
1870.1210.233; 360. 1902.1011.3538; 361.
1868,0612.950; 414. 2010.7081.4320;
536. 1872,1012.3122AN966978; 434.
1882,1014.28
Castle Hill Estates 157. (author's photographs)
Christies, 170. Lot 52 Sale 8750, 16 October
1997
Cliff House Trust, 419-21. (author's
photographs)
Cornwall Record Office, 50. ANT/FX/23
(author's photograph)
Dartmouth Museum, 464. DO201; 465. A0701;
468-9. A07091-2, A07121
Denver Art Museum, 160. Berger Collection,
TL-17968
Devon & Exeter Institution, 28-9. D20; 30.
EDAS Scrapbook 3; 147. SC2389; 158.
SC1112; 162. SC2743; 259. D57; 390. D66
(author's photographs)
Devon Heritage Centre, a. 5242/box 19/7*;
g. 2028A/PO/1/9/3*; o-p. no reference; q.
3237M, unlisted collection*; 9. W1258M/
D84/15; 10. W1258M/D82/18*; 11-12.
W1258M/Vol II/A1/6*; 13. ECA, Charter 36*;
14. ECA, Charter 40*; 32. SC1401; 34. 152M/
C1815/OH49-52*; 53. 235M/E3; 74. SC3333;
76. 564M/F4/96*; 77. 564M/F4/94*; 78.
564M/F4/84*; 79. 564M/F4/88*; 93-4. 404M/
B1*; 109. 6107/M/E1*; 111. Wembury tithe
map*; 112-114. Z18/82*; 148. SC2390; 161.
Z19/2/21*; 168. Tithe map, Plympton St Mary*;
171-2. 90M/E1*; 176. 346M/F196-487*;
177-82. 564M/F16/69, 72, 76, 80, 84, 94*;
183. P&D08418; 188-9. Z19/16/1*; 193.
SC0028a; 208. 564M/F6/1/19; 210. 564M/
F6/161*; 211. 564M/F6/159*; 217. Z19/2/21;
221. 3341/Z/1*; 223. DHC, 3341/Z/1*; 224.
3341/Z/1*; 225. 3341/Z/1*; 226. 3341/Z/1*;
227. 3341/Z/1*; 228. 3341/Z/10*; 229.
SDev/1787/OGL; 236. s750.924/OGL; 237.
P&D40049; 238. SC2409; 240. Z19/2/12*;
241. Z19/2/21*; 242. 564M/F11/181*; 243.
564M/F7/7*; 244. 564M/F6/131*; 245.
564M/F6/143*; 246-7. 3321 add 3*; 250.
P&D05553; 252. P&D05467; 254. SC776;
256. SC176; 271. DHC, Z19/2/10a-b; 275-6.
3237M, unlisted collection; 278-9. Z18/58;
281.1486Z/Z1; 282. Z19/2/8D/117; 283.
Z19/2/12; 297. SC1189; 298-9. 76/20/5/218*;
300-302. Z19/2/4*; 304. Z19/2/4*; 305.
564M/F13/107*; 306. 564M/F13/119*;
307-312. 315-16, 319. 322. sxDEV/1820/
LAN*; 317. P&D02713; 318. SC2807;
321. 564M/F10/167*; 323. SC0104*; 324.
P&D59047; 331. P&D45841; 357. P&D09454;
358-9. P&D02206-7; 365. EXM00251; 366.
EXM00252; 367. EXM00253; 369. SC3462;

371, 373-6. 3237M, unlisted collection*; 377.
P&D00720; 378. P&D0075; 379. P&D00707;
380. P&D00708; 381. P&D00704; 388-9.
2160Aadd/7PZ3-4*; 395-7. SC1036*; 401.
P&D05557; 402-3. 2751Z/Z1*); 411. SC1577;
417. DD69252*; 418. 564M/F4/14*; 423.
P&D08750; 424. SC3103; 426. EXM10317;
427. EXM10265; 428. EXM00106; 429.
P&D05585; 430. P&D05584; 437-8, 440.
76/20/8*; 439. 76/20/7, frontispiece; 441.
P&D44709; 443. P&D40120; 445. P&D05573;
446. P&D05457; 448. SC1853; 449. 564M/
F7/5; 450. P&D05536; 451. P&D05537; 453.
P&D44353; 455. P&D05468; 457. P&D05476;
459. 564M/F4/14*; 460. 564M/F4/22*;
461. 564M/F4/18*; 471. P&D08405; 472.
P&D08410; 473. P&D08406; 474. P&D07580;
475-87. Z19/50/3*; 488-93. Z19/50/3*; 494.
P&D03618; 495. 564M/F4/120*; 496. 564M/
F4/124*; 497. P&D05541; 498. SC1714;
499. SC1713A; 503. 2346M/F115*; 504-8.
2346M/F125*, F140-1*, E47* & F126*; 510.
P&D02407; 512. Tithe map of Clovelly; 517.
SC1096; 520. Z19/2/170*; 522. 3641Z/Z1;
523. 3641Z/Z1; 524. 547B/877; 535. 564M/
F4/184*; 547. Welcome Faculty Petitions, 7
(author's photographs noted by asterix)*
Devonshire Association, 394. Transactions
of the Devonshire Association, XC, 1958,
between pages 154 & 155 (author's
photograph)
Devon Partnership NHS Trust, 326.
Devon Rural Archive, 286-7.
Dumfries Castle, 328.
English Heritage, 413. B/76337
Earle Vandekar of Knightsbridge, 214-215.
Exeter Cathedral Library & Archives (all Exeter
Dean & Chapter Mss) 1. 3502; 2. 3625; 3.
3506; 4. 3508; 5. 3506; 6. 3505b; 7. 3505b;
8. 3504; 38. D&C 3530; 40. no reference
number (author's photographs)
David Fenwick 35.
The Fitzwilliam Museum, Cambridge 54.
Sampler T.201928
S. Franses Ltd. 330.
Howard Furnivall, 192.; page 328
Hampshire Record Office, pages 5 & 6,
115M88/D3; page 7, 115M88/D1/26; 159.
115M88/D3, no. 537; 554. 44m69/E13/12/84
(author's photographs)
Hartland Abbey, 102-106.
Ilfracombe Museum, 531. Ilfcm 8310; 533.
Ilfcm17294d
Kent History and Library Centre, 97. U269/
O173 (author's photograph)
Library of the United States Congress, 175.
LOT 13415, no. 296; 275. LOT 13415, no.
297; 387. LOT 13415, no. 215; 542. Lot
13415, no. 923
The Metropolitan Museum of Modern Art,
110. 25.110.1; 270. 2013.73; 280. 2007.38;
329. 1970.141
Museum of English Rural Life, 60. DEV/3/1/288;
261. 2009.342; 526. FR DEV3C/7/8; 528. DEV
3C/7/6; 529. DEV 3C/7/7; 534. DEV3a/8/59
(author's photographs)
National Gallery of Art (Washington), main
cover illustration, Paul Mellon Collection
1983.1.40; i 9. Rosenwald Collection
1943.3.836; 88. 1945.5.1039; 184. Paul
Mellon Collection 1983.1.40; 187. Paul Mellon

Collection 1964.2.4; 313. 1995.52.157
National Portrait Gallery, 364. 2515(71); 370.
Ax54208; 391.1888
National Trust, k 11. CMS PCF 352356; 115.
CMS PCF 35554; 195. 872240; 205. CMS PCF
872251; 206. CMS PCF 872252; 264. 46896;
265. 578076; 514. 93944; 516. 14335
North Devon Athenaeum, 154-5.
North Devon Record Office, d-e. B1041/1
(author's photographs)
Ordnance Survey Maps (Crown Copyright):
194, 235, 368, 386, 416, 431, 444, 447,
452, 454, 502, 509, 518, 532. (author's
photographs)
Padstow, 85-7, 117-40, 152-3. (author's
photographs)
Plymouth Museum and Art Gallery, 108.
PLYM.zo.202
Lord Rennell, 95-6, 98-101, 190. (copies at
Cornwall Record Office, F.S. 3/93/3, 120,
130a, 12-1)
Royal Institute of British Architects, 164.
RIBA12660; 231. RIBA3982; 232. RIBA21867;
294. RIBA12660; 355. RIBA22016; 356.
RIBA22228; 412. RIBA82255
Royal Pavilion & Museums (Brighton) 327.
Tate 165. D09211; 218. T08553; 219.
T01155; 233. T10351; 513. N04921
Somerset Heritage Centre, 248. DD/WY/Box
98; 262. DD/HI/C/521/1; 400. WY/Box 98
(author's photographs)
Topsham Museum, 537-41.
Torquay Museum, 422. PR5407; 462. PR8283;
541. PR4950
Victoria & Albert Museum, 17. W.39-1914; 18.
W.25-1959; 31. T.766-1995; 36. P163-1910;
57. T.86 to B-1973; 58. 319-1878; 59. 785-
1864; 145. T.148-1911; 169. T.260&A-1969;
200. 414:707/1, 2-1885; 201. 414:689-1885;
202. 414:684-1885; 203. 414:687/A-1885;
204. 414:693-1885; 205. 414:687-1885;
213. C.140-1977; 251. 414:1257-1885; 267.
P56-1924; 383. E.11-2002; 521. C.36-1972;
525. 7714-1938
Western Morning News, 433.
Nigel Wiggins, 61-73. (author's photographs)
His Grace the Duke of Bedford and the Trustees
of the Bedford Estates, 290, 291, 293, 295.
Yale Center for British Art, inside front
jacket B1977.14.38 & B1988.6; Page 1,
B1975.4.1164; pages 2-3, B1986.29.569;
b-c 2-3, B2001.2.246; f 6.
B1976.1.30; h 8. B2001.2.246; 75. B1977.14;
84. B1976.7.105; 116. B1978.43.13; 149.
B1977.14.12236; 173. B1986.29.409; 174.
Folio A 2010 22; 186. B1977.14.51; 191.
B1977.14.4284; 196. B1977.14.1490(8);
239. NC825.D48 L89 1830; 266. B2002.9.1;
268. B1977.14.5637; 269. B1977.14.5192;
272. B1975.3.1189; 284. B1977.14; 296.
Folio A 2010 22; 332. B1975.4.1553; 338.
B1977.14.9708; 382. B1977.14.6302; 384.
Folio A 2010 22; 385. Folio A 2010 22; 398.
B1977.14.58; 399. B1975.2.370; 405-410.
Folio A 2010 22; 425. B2001.2.245; 432.
B1977.14.116; 436. DA670.D9 S73; 463.
NC825.D48 L89 1830; 466. B1977.14.3846;
511. Folio A 2010 22; 519. B1977.14 (some
author's photographs)
Illustrations photographed by the author, some
from private collections: 21, 22, 24-7, 41-8, 80-
3, 90-92, 107, 142-4, 248; 288-9. (Humphry
Repton, *Fragments on the theory and practice
of landscape gardening… to establish fixed
principles in the respective arts,* 1816); 156, 167,
185, 320, 442, 458 (Benjamin Donn, *A map of
the county of Devon, with the city and county of
Exeter,* 1755); 163, 257, 277, 285, 372, 415,
467 (C. & J. Greenwood, *Map of the county of
Devon from an actual survey made in the years
1825 & 1826, 1827*); 325; 333-7; 339-55.

(George Rowe, *Forty-Eight Views of Cottages and
Scenery at Sidmouth, Devon,* Sidmouth, 1826);
362. (*The Gentleman's Magazine,* March, 1830);
363. (Mrs Bray, *The Borders of the Tamar and
the Tavy,* 1879 edn); 456. (*The Gentleman's
Magazine,* 1834, 265); 527. (*Journal of
Horticulture and Cottage Gardener,* 31 August
1871); 515. (*The Architect,* 2 July 1870); 530.
(*The Gardeners' Chronicle,* 3rd Series, Vol. 35, 2
January 1904); 546, 548-50.
Private collections, 33, 51, 56, 249, 500-501,
543-5, 551, 552.

Signifiers:
The Los Angeles County Museum of Art, 10.
M.2003.108.7; 20. M.82.5; 88. M.81.250

The Metropolitan Museum of Art, 1.
17.190.8339.6; 2. 09.137.30; 3. 64.101.1291;
4. 16.32.323; 9. 71.5; 11. 1970.705; 13.
81.1.652; 16. 2013.147; 17. 11.134.1; 18.
71.6; 21. 59.23.53; 27. 35.10.11; 28. 2004.85;
29. 61.557.3; 30. 41.190.119; 31. 07.225.470;
34. 64.101.519; 36. 41.25.4; 38. 07.225.504;
40. 2007.426; 41. 65.692.9; 42. 48.187.737;
44. 2009.379; 45. 07.225.461; 49. 2009.221;
59. JP2363 60; 60. 2008.303; 62. 39.52; 64.
27.70.1; 65. 28.55.3; 68. 81.1.666; 72. 02.7.1;
73. 67.187.60; 75. 1980.3; 78. 1987.1161; 82.
29.100.128; 85. 1976.201.16; 91. 1973.323.3;
92. 29.100.106; 93. 1993.400.5; 94. 64.266;
95. 64.235.2

The National Gallery of Art (Washington), 5.
1948.11.240; 6. 1948.11.241; 7. 2006.11.41;
14. 1992.51.5; 18. 1949.5.367; 19. 1977.7.1;
22. 1980.45.502; 33. 1980.62.20; 55.
1988.12.1; 56. 1945.5.205; 63. 988.12.1; 69.
2008.38.7; 74. 1995.47.37; 79. 1994.59.6; 83.
1970.17.61; 86. 1983.1.32; 89, 1963.10.10;
96. 1958.10.2

The Walters Art Museum, Baltimore, 15.
37.2623; 23. 37.1674; 80. 37.1656; 81.
37.1508

The Yale Center for British Art, 12.
B1981.25.436; 24. B1981.25.614;
25. B2011.20.10; 26. B1974.3.16; 32.
B1975.4.1968; 35. B1977.14.8882;
37. B2001.2.73; 39. B1970.3.942; 43.
B1975.4.682; 46. B2011.20.7; 47.
B1981.25.516; 48. B1975.3.69; 50.
B1981.25.12; 51. B1975.3.140; 52.
B1975.3.60; 53. B2001.2.1141; 54.
B2001.2.1157; 57. B1981.25.184; 58.
B2001.2.100; 61. B1977.14.1708; 66.
Yale B2001.2.204; 67. B1986.29.344; 70.
B1975.4.1164; 71. B1981.25.416; 76.
B1975.3.965; 77. B1975.3.863; 84. B1993.20;
87. B1977.14.5923; 90. B1975.6.102

The Mint Press
Taddyforde House South, Taddyforde Estate,
New North Road,
Exeter, Devon, UK EX4 4AT

Distribution: Stevensbooks
Telephone: 01392 459760
www.stevensbooks.co.uk

ISBN 978 1 903356 64 7

First published 2013

Book design:
Topics – The Creative Partnership, Exeter.
www.topicsdesign.co.uk

Cover design:
Delphine Jones

Printed in the United Kingdom by
Short Run Press, Exeter